Thoughts
on my
Thoughts
III

Thoughts

on my

Thoughts

III

The <u>TALES</u> That Wagged This Veterinarian

Walter R. Hoge, DVM

Printed in the United States of America

ISBN 979-8-89114-022-6 (sc)
ISBN 979-8-89114-023-3 (hc)
ISBN 979-8-89114-024-0 (e)

Library of Congress Control Number: 2023920830

2023.11.20

MainSpring Books
5901 W. Century Blvd
Suite 750
Los Angeles, CA, US, 90045

www.mainspringbooks.com

Table of Contents

PART II THOUGHTS SHARED WITH FAMILY AND FRIENDS

PREFACE

In August of 2003 my kid's mom passed. I was inspired to write stories about Easter that I had told to my children as they laid on my bed during bed time. For Easter 2004 I sent each of my five children a copy of the stories on 8.5" X 11"

paper. At the time each of them were well on their way to adulthood, living away from home and I'm not sure any of them read the stories.

Some of the negative comments about the book from critics are that there were concepts presented which may be diffucult for children to comprehend. When I told my children stories about Mr. McEaster and his valley I attempted to give enough detail about the events to encourage them to have an appreciation of the Easter Season and the intricute relationship between mankind and nature.

It wasn't until the story was published, after the convincing of my mother in law, that I realized who the book was written for. On the surface it was for my children – underneath it was written to inspire me to continue on, gain a closer understanding of nature and try to be part of the solution and not the problem in my relationships with others.

To me, the basic concepts introduced in Easter: McEaster Valley can be a spring board of encouragment for the reader to learn and share some of the wonders of the world around them. The planet called Earth that provides an environment suitable for living organisms to find a place called home.

Following are some of the interesting discoveries I've found over the years about the world around us directly related to visiting Mr. McEaster and his mystical valley:

more about McEaster Valley and the opportunities there were to contribute of my time and talents towards a good cause. I wonder if there was really only one chance to accept an offer to live there. I would sure like to have some of that musky smelling oil to rub on my sore ankle and back. And, of course I would like to again be able to run like the wind and feel as a youth that all is good and nothing can or will prevent me from being what or whom I wanted to be.

I now have a new young Labrador Retriever by the name of Mani. This one is yellow and a female who has had extensive training to develop her nose. She returns if I whistle two times and she can go and go all day. Just maybe I can find again the spot in the Sierra foothills where I found McEaster Valley. Just maybe Mani could pick up the scent Beau smelled so many years ago. Just maybe my ankle and back could make the climb. Just maybe I'll try again. But just now I'll take a power nap before formalizing my plans.

Easter 2004

PART I

THE WORLD AROUND US AND MC: EASTER VALLEY

1

PARALLEL UNIVERSES AND US

An out-of-body experience (OBE) is a sensation of your consciousness leaving your body. These episodes are often reported by people who've had a near-death experience (NDE). Some might also describe an OBE as a dissociative episode. People typically experience their sense of self inside their physical body. You most likely view the world around you from this vantage point. But during an OBE, you may feel as if you're outside yourself, looking at your body from another perspective. Whether your consciousness can truly leave your physical body hasn't been scientifically proven. For centuries, many people have reported experiencing sensations of their consciousness leaving their body.

What really goes on during an OBE? Does your consciousness actually leave your body? Experts aren't totally sure, but they have a few hunches. According to accounts from people who've experienced them, they generally involve: a feeling of floating outside your body, an altered perception of the world - such as looking down from a height, the feeling that you're looking down at yourself from above, a sense that what's happening is very real.

OBEs typically happen without warning and usually don't last for very long. If you have a neurological condition, such as epilepsy, you may be more likely to and more frequently experience OBEs. But for many people, an OBE will happen very rarely, maybe only once in a lifetime if at all. Some estimates suggest around 5 percent of people have experienced the sensations associated with an OBE, though some suggest this number may be higher.

There's some debate over whether the sensations and perceptions associated with OBEs happen physically or as a sort of hallucinatory experience. A recent 2022 review tried to explore this by evaluating a variety of studies and case reports evaluating consciousness, cognitive awareness, and recall in people who survived cardiac arrest.

They noted that some people report experiencing a separation from their body during resuscitation and some even reported an awareness of events they wouldn't have seen from their actual perspective. In addition, one study included in the review noted that two participants reported having both visual and auditory experiences while in cardiac arrest. Only one was well enough to follow up, but he gave an accurate, detailed description of what took place for about three minutes of his resuscitation from cardiac arrest.

Still, there's no scientific evidence to support the idea that a person's consciousness can actually travel outside the body. Veridical perception is a controversial concept. It refers to the idea that you can leave your body during an OBE, allowing you to witness something that you may not have otherwise. Some anecdotal reports of this phenomena exist, with a few people even providing accurate details about events that have happened during surgical procedures or while clinically dead.

Many people use these stories as evidence to support the existence of life after death. However, the idea of veridical perception is still limited to anecdotal claims and there is no research available to support it.

No one's sure about the exact causes of OBEs, but experts have identified several possible explanations:

A frightening, dangerous, or difficult situation can provoke a fear response, which might cause you to dissociate from the situation and feel as if you're an onlooker. This may make you feel as though you are watching the events from somewhere outside your body.

It is suggested that OBEs could occur as a way to cope with trauma, but more research is needed on this potential link. OBEs during childbirth aren't unusual, epilepsy, migraine, cardiac arrest, brain injuries, drowning, suffocation, strong G-forces (because it causes blood to pool in the lower body, which can lead to loss of conscious), depression, anxiety, Guillain-Barré syndrome. Dissociative disorders, particularly depersonalization-derealization disorder, can involve frequent feelings or episodes where you seem to be observing yourself from outside your body.

Sleep paralysis has also been noted as a possible cause of OBEs. It refers to a temporary state of waking paralysis that occurs during REM sleep and often have hallucinations. In addition, a review of literature from 2020 suggests that sleep-wake disturbances may to dissociative symptoms. This can include a feeling of leaving your body.

Some people report having an OBE while under the influence of anesthesia. Other substances, including cannabis, ketamine, or hallucinogenic drugs such as LSD, can cause this sensation.

OBEs can occur during near-death experiences NDE, often alongside other phenomena like flashbacks of previous memories or seeing a light at the end of a tunnel. Though it's not clear exactly why this happens, it's believed to be caused by disruptions in certain areas of the brain involved with processing sensory information.

Though not backed by research, some people believe that OBEs can occur when your soul or spirit leaves your body. One form is known as "traveling clairvoyance," which some mediums claim allows your soul to visit distant locations in order to gain information. Others believe that certain meditative practices can help you reach a state of consciousness that transcends the body and mind, leading to an OBE. Some people also experiment with astral projection, which is a spiritual practice that involves making an intentional effort to send your consciousness from your body toward a spiritual plane or dimension.[1]

For some of us, the idea of parallel Universes sparks our wildest dreams. If there are other Universes where certain events had different outcomes (where just one crucial decision went a different way) perhaps there could be some way to access them. Perhaps particles, fields, or even people could be transported from one to the other, enabling us to live in a Universe that's better, in some ways, than our own. These ideas have a foothold in theoretical physics as well, from the myriad of possible outcomes from quantum mechanics as well as ideas of the multiverse. But do they have anything to do with observable, measurable reality? Recently, a claim has surfaced asserting that we've found evidence for parallel Universes. There is an article that claimed physicists in Antarctica had found evidence for a parallel universe.

From a physics point of view, parallel Universes are one of those intriguing ideas that's imaginative, compelling, but very difficult to test. They first arose in the context of quantum physics. The thought is that if you take a single electron and shoot it through a double slit, you can only know the probabilities of where it will land; you cannot predict exactly where it will show up.

One remarkable idea (known as the many-worlds interpretation of quantum mechanics) postulates that all the outcomes that can possibly occur actually do happen, but only one outcome can happen in each Universe. It takes an infinite number of parallel Universes to account for all the possibilities, but this interpretation is just as valid as any other. There are no experiments or observations that rule it out.

A second place where parallel Universes arise in physics is from the idea of the multiverse. Our observable Universe began 13.8 billion years ago with the hot Big Bang, but the Big Bang itself wasn't the very beginning. There was a very different phase of the Universe that occurred previously to set up and give rise to the Big Bang: cosmological inflation. When and where inflation ends, a Big Bang occurs.

But inflation doesn't end everywhere at once, and the places where inflation doesn't end continue to inflate, giving rise to more space and more potential Big Bangs. Once inflation begins, in fact, it's virtually impossible to stop inflation from occurring in perpetuity at least somewhere. As time goes on, more Big Bangs (all disconnected from one another) occur, giving rise to an uncountably large number of independent Universes: a multiverse.

May 22, 2020, scientists in Antarctica reported that they had discovered evidence for the existence of parallel Universes. If this were true, it would be absolutely revolutionary. It would prove not only that these other Universes are out there, but matter and energy from them would have the capability to cross over to and interact with matter and energy in our own Universe. Perhaps, if this claim were correct, some of our wildest science fiction dreams would be possible. Perhaps you could travel to a Universe:

Where you chose the job in another country, you stood up to a bully, you kissed the one-who-got-away at the end of the night, or where a life-or-death event that you or your loved one faced at some point in the past had a different outcome?[2]

The theory of multi universes leads me to wonder if we travel to a parallel universe upon death or visit one for a short time during an OBE. They may be out there: to Moses, He declared: "I am the Lord God Almighty, and Endless is my name. ... "And worlds without number have I created; ... and by the Son I created them, which is mine Only Begotten" (Moses 1:3, 33).

Written accounts NDEs date back at least to the Middle Ages, and some researchers say to ancient times. The medical journal Resuscitation published a brief account of the oldest known medical description of an NDE, written by an 18th-century French military doctor. But the modern era of research into NDE is generally said to have begun in 1975. That was the year Raymond A. Moody Jr., a philosopher turned psychiatrist, published Life After Life, a book based on interviews with some 50 experiencers.

Moody's book set off a steady stream of memoirs, TV shows, and articles. Since then, a small community has emerged of psychiatrists, psychologists, cardiologists, and other specialists. They share Moody's belief that consciousness (the mind, the soul, call it what you will) may exist in some nonmaterial form, independent of but closely connected to the brain, and that NDEs may be able to provide evidence of it. The leading members of this coterie have distinguished careers at respectable universities and hospitals.

One book includes an extensive overview of NDEs. The Handbook of Near-Death Experiences: Thirty Years of Investigation, an anthology published in 2009. As The Handbook outlines, by 2005 dozens of studies involving nearly 3,500 subjects who reported having had NDEs became material for some 600 scholarly articles. Many of these articles are in the Journal of Near Death Studies, the IANDS house journal—which, the association proudly notes, is peer-reviewed. International Association of Near-Death Studies was founded in 1981, IANDS is a membership-based, nonprofit 501(c)(3) organization that "promotes research, education, and support around near-death experiences and related experiences. Their mission is to advance a global understanding of these experiences. They envision a future in which all people embrace near-death and related experiences as sources of meaning and inspiration for a better world."

Most of the NDEs have been retrospective, meaning the researchers looked for people who'd had such an experience to come forward and be interviewed. That possesses a couple of problems, scientifically speaking. It means the subjects were self-selecting, so they might not be representative. For instance, people who'd had scary NDEs might have been less eager to tell their stories than people who'd had uplifting ones. (It's notable that, while some studies indeed report only the well-known positive experiences, unpleasant NDEs account for a combined 23 percent of reports across a dozen different studies. They get far less attention, and certainly don't seem to sell nearly as many books.) Most of the interviews took place years after the fact, so memories might have been faulty. And most important, retrospective studies make it pretty much impossible to obtain reliable data on what was actually happening to the subjects' bodies and brains while they felt their souls were elsewhere.

About a dozen prospective studies have been published, several of them in recent years. In these, researchers typically arrange for every consenting patient who survives a specific medical emergency (such as a cardiac arrest) at a hospital to be interviewed as soon as possible thereafter. The patients are asked open-ended questions about what, if anything, they experienced while doctors were trying to revive them. If they report anything unusual, the researchers check their medical records and the accounts of people who treated them, looking for things that might explain the experience or show that their brain was shut down at the relevant time. All told, these studies have collected the near-death experiences of just under 300 people.

The goal for those who believe the mind really does leave the body is to find a verified case of what one prominent researcher has termed "apparently nonphysical veridical perception." In other words, having an experience during which you see or hear things you otherwise couldn't have perceived that are later confirmed to have actually happened. (Veridical means "not illusory.") An out-of-body experience is only one of the 16 possible elements of a near-death experience on the Greyson scale, and the proportion of experiencers who report having had one varies widely from one study to another.[3]

The oldest recorded OBE I can find is about Alma the Younger. He lived in Zarahemla during the end of the reign of the Nephite King Mosiah. It is believed that he was born in 126 BC. As a young man, he, the four sons of Mosiah, and others wanted to destroy the church and actively persecuted its members. After they were visited personally by an angel and rebuked for their actions, Alma fell into an unconscious state, where for three days and three nights he lay unable to move until he felt within that he had been forgiven of his sins.

He later recounted, an angel spoke, "If thou wilt be destroyed of thyself, seek no more to destroy the church of God…I was racked with eternal torment, for my soul was harrowed up to the greatest degree and racked with all my sins…I did remember all my sins for which I was tormented with the pains of hell…I saw that I had rebelled against my God, and that I had not kept his holy commandments…I had murdered many of his children, or rather led them away unto destruction, the very thought of coming into the presence of my God did rack my soul with inexpressible horror…for three days and for three nights was I racked, even with the pains of a damned soul." He had experienced a vision during unconsciousness, in which he renounced his behavior against the church and subsequently received a glimpse of God sitting on his throne (Alma 36:6–22). Alma the Younger subsequently became the first elected chief judge of the Nephites as well as their religious leader.

Paul's conversion experience resulted from an OBE shortly after Christ's death. It is discussed in both the Pauline epistles and in the Acts of the Apostles. According to both sources, Saul/Paul was not a follower of Jesus and did not know him before his crucifixion. Paul's conversion occurred 4-7 years after Jesus's crucifixion in 30 AD. The accounts of Paul's conversion experience describe it as miraculous, supernatural, or otherwise revelatory in nature.

Before his conversion, Paul was known as Saul and was "a Pharisee of Pharisees", who "intensely persecuted" the followers of Jesus. Says Paul in his Epistle to the Galatians: "For you have heard of my previous way of life in Judaism, how intensely I persecuted the church of God and tried to destroy it. I was advancing in Judaism beyond many of my own age among my people and was extremely zealous for the traditions of my fathers." Galatians 1:13–14

Acts of the Apostles discusses Paul's conversion experience at three different points in the text, in far more detail than in the accounts in Paul's letters. The Book of Acts says that Paul was on his way from Jerusalem to Syrian

Damascus with a mandate issued by the High Priest to seek out and arrest followers of Jesus, with the intention of returning them to Jerusalem as prisoners for questioning and possible execution. The journey is interrupted when Paul sees a blinding light, and communicates directly with a divine voice.

Acts 9 states, As he neared Damascus on his journey, suddenly a light from heaven flashed around him. He fell to the ground and heard a voice say to him, "Saul, Saul, why do you persecute me?"

"Who are you, Lord?" Saul asked. "I am Jesus, whom you are persecuting," he replied. "Now get up and go into the city, and you will be told what you must do."

The men traveling with Saul stood there speechless; they heard the sound but did not see anyone. Paul got up from the ground, but when he opened his eyes, he could see nothing. So, they led him by the hand into Damascus. For three days he was blind, and did not eat or drink anything. Acts 9:3–9

The account continues with a description of Ananias of Damascus receiving a divine revelation instructing him to visit Saul at the house of Judas on the Street Called Straight and there lay hands on him to restore his sight (the house of Judas is traditionally believed to have been near the west end of the street). Ananias is initially reluctant, having heard about Saul's persecution, but obeys the divine command: Then Ananias went to the house and entered it. Placing his hands on Saul, he said, "Brother Saul, the Lord—Jesus, who appeared to you on the road as you were coming here—has sent me so that you may see again and be filled with the Holy Spirit." Immediately, something like scales fell from Saul's eyes, and he could see again. He got up and was baptized, and after taking some food, he regained his strength. Acts 9:13–19

Wilford Woodruff Wilford Woodruff and Phoebe Whittemore Carter were married on April 13, 1837, in Kirtland, Ohio. Throughout their life together, they endured many trials, thus growing in their devotion to each other, their children, and the kingdom of God.

One such experience came in the winter of 1838, about five months before Wilford Woodruff's call to the apostleship. As Brother Woodruff led a group of Saints on a journey to gather with other members of the Church, his wife became very ill. He later recounted: "On the 23rd of November my wife, Phoebe, was attacked with a severe headache, which terminated in brain fever. She grew more and more distressed daily as we continued our journey. It was a terrible ordeal for a woman to travel in a wagon over rough roads, afflicted as she was.

At the same time our child was also very sick." In the ensuing days, Sister Woodruff's condition worsened, even though they had been able to pause on their journey and find places to rest. Brother Woodruff recalled: "December 3rd found my wife very low. I spent the day in taking care of her, and the following day I returned to Eaton (a nearby town) to get some things for her. She seemed to be gradually sinking, and in the evening her spirit apparently left her body, and she was dead. "The sisters gathered around her body, weeping, while I stood looking at her in sorrow. The Spirit and power of God began to rest upon me until, for the first time during her sickness, faith filled my soul, although she lay before me as one dead." Strengthened in his faith, Wilford Woodruff gave his wife a priesthood blessing. "I laid my hands upon her," he said, "and in the name of Jesus Christ I rebuked the power of death and the destroyer, and commanded the same to depart from her, and the spirit of life to enter her body. Her spirit returned to her body, and from that hour she was made whole; and we all felt to praise the name of God, and to trust in him and keep his commandments."

"While this operation was going on with me (as my wife related afterwards her spirit left her body (NDE), and she saw her body lying upon the bed, and the sisters weeping. She looked at them and at me, and upon her babe, and, while gazing upon this scene, two personages came into the room. ... One of these messengers informed her that she could have her choice: she might go to rest in the spirit world, or, on one condition she could have the privilege of returning to her tabernacle and continuing her labors upon the earth. The condition was, if she felt that she could stand by her husband, and with him pass through all the cares, trials, tribulations and afflictions of life which he would be called to pass through for the Gospel's sake unto the end. When she looked at the situation of her husband and child she said: 'Yes, I will do it!' At the moment that decision was made the power of faith rested upon me, and when I administered unto her, her spirit entered her tabernacle."

"On the morning of the 6th of Dec., the Spirit said to me: 'Arise, and continue thy journey!' and through the mercy of God my wife was enabled to arise and dress herself and walk to the wagon, and we went on our way rejoicing." Faithful to her promise, Sister Woodruff stood by her husband, even when his duties as an Apostle required him to be away from the family for long periods of time.[4]

In 2006 James R. Doty, MD, a professor in the Department on Neurosurgery at Stanford University relates NDE: Residencies in the mid-1980s were even more grueling than they are now, a kind of medical boot camp – with as much as twenty-four hours at a time spent on shift. We were sleep deprived and under constant scrutiny and pressure. It became normal to blow off some steam now and then - take a break from the mental and physical demands of residency. Some of my colleagues began drinking more than they should – I recognized the signs in them and also in myself. I knew what alcoholism looked like from growing up, but I was trying to balance on the razor's edge between drinking too much on occasion and alcohol abuse. Partying on my rare time off wasn't being out of control, I told myself. I could feel the genetic pull in me at times to seek escape from the pressures and demands of life as a resident, but I wasn't my father. I would never be my father.

One evening four of us decided to go out and celebrate the end of a particularly grueling rotation. We were a close group. We worked together, ate together, guzzled coffee in the cafeteria together. We had bonded the way people do when they go through a traumatic event or a natural disaster together. We were all fighting side by side in the same war – residency.

That night we started drinking around 8 p.m. at a strip club near the hospital. We threw money at the dancers as if we were guys who actually had money to throw away. We moved on to a Spanish restaurant where we drank jug after jug of some kind of Spanish wine. I'm not sure when the cocaine came out, but after pulling antique swords off the wall of the restaurant, and engaging in a life-and-death duel, we were all summarily kicked out.

The four of us piled into the car, which was littered with empty beer cans. We careened through the dark night with the music blaring. I felt myself drift into a happy stupor. Then I heard a voice in my head that said, "Put on your seat belt. Now!" The car started sliding and skidding across the wet asphalt, sideways, into the oncoming lane. Then everything went black.

Walter Reed was only a mile away – just hours before we had been the doctors. Now we were the patients, I was the most injured and the only one wearing a seat belt. As I saw the operating lights shining down on me, it was as if I could feel what every surgery patient in that room had felt. I felt the waves of pain, and fear, and worry and voices that seemed to be all talking at once.

The next voice I heard were doctors discussing my very low blood pressure and high heart rate resulting from internal bleeding. I knew what this meant. I was going to go into cardiac arrest shortly. My brain was going to die. I was going to die.

In the next moment, I felt as if everything shifted and tilted. I was suddenly looking down at myself from the corner of the ceiling. I didn't feel any pain. I could see the rays of light coming off the lightbulbs in zigzag patterns. I could see every droplet of liquid in the IV bags. I could see the top of the chairman's head, and the sweat that dotted his forehead. I looked down and saw myself in the bed. I looked small and vulnerable, and very, very pale. I could see the monitor, their lines and numbers moving up and down erratically, and it seemed as if I could hear the blood in my vessels moving and could sense that there wasn't enough. I could hear my heart-rhythm. I observed all this without emotion. I didn't feel sad, just acutely aware of everything that was happening to me and around me.

The chairman of general surgery was insisting that he couldn't possibly have missed a bleeder in the abdomen, and this could not possibly be the source of my blood loss. I saw the vice chairman put his hand on my leg and say, "You idiot if you don't take him back into surgery, I'm going to. Now!" And then blackness.

My experience after this blackness is something that I would never adequately explain nor ever forget. It is all the more puzzling for being a rather common and yet extraordinary experience. One that has been repeatedly reported over the centuries.

Suddenly I was floating down a narrow river. I was moving slowly at first. Ahead I saw a bright white light, much like the tip of a flame. I began to speed up, and soon I was rushing toward it. All along the sides of the river I saw people I had known, crowding along banks of the river. I thought I saw my father and Ruth. I felt loved and accepted in a way I never had before. Many of the people I saw were still alive. I saw my mom in her bathrobe and my brother laughing with me from our bedroom. I saw the girl Chris who I had a crush on in junior high school. I saw my old orange Sting-Ray bicycle. I saw myself on the bus to Irvine, and I saw myself trying on a white coat for the first time. I saw myself turning my face into the mist on that very same night and I felt the white light getting warmer and closer.

It was getting bigger. I somehow knew that this light was love, and it was the only thing that meant anything in this universe. I just had to reach it, and I knew that when I did, I would be one with all things. This is what I had been searching for. This was the only thing I needed. I wanted to merge with the light. And suddenly I realized that when I merged with that warm, inviting light, I would no longer be part of this world. I would be dead.

"No," I screamed. Or, at least, I thought I screamed. And suddenly I was going backward, away from the light. As if I had stretched a rubber band to its maximum and let go. I was going in reverse so fast that I could barely comprehend it. I felt the presence of all those who had greeted me now falling away.

My eyes were still closed, but I could hear the beep of the monitors. I just had to open my eyes.[5]

If scientists have found parallel universes, we may one day have the opportunity to skip from one time period to another and have experiences only imagined in fiction books and movies about time travel. We might be able to jump from our present universe to another during our pre life, our earlier life or maybe into the future. Maybe during an OBE or NDE we temporarily escape to another universe and then back to the present time. Maybe heaven is found on one of these universes and an OBE is the opportunity to spend a few moments in heaven or pass on to eternity.

It has been said, "There is no such thing as immaterial matter. All spirit is matter, but it is more fine or pure, and can only be discerned by purer eyes; We cannot see it; but when our bodies are purified, we shall see that it is all matter" *Doctrine & Covenants 131:7-8*.

Alma the Younger, the apostle Paul, Phoebe W. Carter and James Doty MD during their OBEs/NDEs may have had their minds (spirits?) somehow become more purified and able to discern with purer eyes.

Somehow, they knew that the light they experienced was love, and it was the only thing that meant anything in this universe. Who knows? A parallel universe whether consisting of material matter or a more fine or pure spiritual matter may reside near our universe. Close enough for us to receive communication of the spirit of light and knowledge from the godhead on high or to spend a few moments during an OBE or forever be immersed through death - to learn that light is love, and that is the only thing that means anything in this universe or other parallel universes.

Have scientists finally found a parallel universe? High-energy neutrinos are minute particles able to pass through virtually everything—including our planet. Some of them are created by exploding stars and gamma ray bursts. The scientists in Antarctica discovered radio pulses that indicated high-energy neutrinos coming upward out of the ground, which led to various different explanations, including that the pulses were: Neutrinos that passed through the Earth's core and then came out of the ground, a "fourth neutrino" known as the sterile neutrino—which would be a completely new discovery, or "dark matter" which is an unknown frontier of particle physics and astrophysics.

The out-there parallel Universe theory came from the absence of a good explanation. That's partly because a check on the ANtarctic Impulsive Transient Antenna (ANITA) results were carried out by the IceCube neutrino detector in Antarctica; it found nothing.

Cue the possibility of a parallel Universe because maybe, just maybe, something "exotic" is going on. Since the high-energy neutrinos were detected coming "up" from the Earth instead of "down" from space they may be traveling back in time and, therefore, could from a parallel Universe. The Big Bang occurred, it formed two Universes; one that flows forward, the other in reverse.

A new paper, published June 11, 2020 in the journal Annals of Glaciology, thinks that the pulses were: Reflections off strange ice formations. Specifically, un-flipped reflections of ultra-high-energy cosmic rays that arrive from space, miss the top layer of ice, then enter the ground to strike deep, or compacted snow. Thus, debunking the theory that scientists found a parallel universe. It was explained that the culprit could be firn under the surface of the ice. Firn is something between snow and glacial ice, it's compacted snow that's not quite dense enough to be ice. Classified as crystalline or granular snow, it's often found on the upper part of a glacier. When cosmic rays, or neutrinos, go through ice at very high energies, they scatter on materials inside the ice, on protons and electrons, and they can make a burst of radio, a big radio signal that scientists can see.

Cosmic rays are high-energy protons and atomic nuclei that move through space at nearly the speed of light. The problem is that these signals have the radio pulse characteristic of a neutrino, but appear to be traversing vastly more than is possible given known physics.

Their idea is that part of the radio pulse from a cosmic ray can get deep into the ice before reflecting, so you can have the reflection without the phase flip. Without flipping the wave, in that case, it really looks like a neutrino. Ordinary neutrinos just don't do that, but cosmic rays at these energies are common.[6]

During my mystical travels in McEaster Valley was I on a parallel universe experiencing an OBE?

"I looked toward the valley. The color of gold had changed to the various colors of vegetation, with a beautiful blue cloudless sky marking the horizon. However, the colors were bright and seemed to glow, more like a painting than the familiar California countryside to which I had become accustomed…as I looked into the valley, I felt warmth and peace that I can only describe as how I felt as a child when I had hurt myself and my mother held me close to her, assuring me that everything would be okay. I was drawn to the valley…my fears and anxieties seemed to melt away…I felt as a young child: everything was good and nothing could or would prevent me from being what or whom I wanted to be…a sense of euphoria…I was invincible. Physically, I had never felt better. My mind was alive, and I could see and hear and smell and taste and touch and feel things better than I ever had before. This was a dream come true. Or was it a dream or heaven? I didn't care. I was treasuring every moment, as every cell of my being was alive and at full alert…[7]

Migraines and epilepsy often go hand in hand. If you have epilepsy, you're more than twice as likely to get migraines as someone who doesn't. The reverse is true, too. People with migraines are more than twice as likely as others to have epilepsy. But few people who have migraines develop epilepsy without another risk factor, like a head injury or stroke.

If you have migraine with aura, you're about twice as likely to have an ischemic stroke in your lifetime, compared to those without migraine. However, the overall risk linked to migraine is still very low, and you're far more likely to have a stroke because of other risk factors like smoking and high blood pressure.

The symptoms associated with the aura are different in each condition as well. In migraine the visual aura usually involves negative symptoms, slow spreading, and is monochromatic. In epilepsy aura is often shorter, more complex and brightly colored.

A migraine aura is typically followed by a headache, light or sound sensitivity, nausea, vomiting and more. An epileptic aura is followed by a seizure. Other symptoms of epileptic auras include: hearing strange sounds or a change in taste, a feeling of déjà vu, sudden surge of emotions and more.

What's the connection? Scientists aren't sure, though they have theories. They do know that migraines and epilepsy have some of the same symptoms and triggers.[8]

I had my first migraine somewhere between 10 and 13 years of age. I clearly remember it occurred near an outdoor clothes line in my back yard. An aura dot formed that spread in a circular manner like a pebble dropped in water. The farther the aura spread out the less vivid it became until it disappeared. I then experienced numbness in my lower lip and mouth followed by a severe head ache that made me feel nauseous for several hours. I thought I was going to die and was afraid to tell my MD dad.

They have continued over the years, become less severe, I do not get headaches, can occur in clusters over a couple of weeks and I continue my normal activities (even performing surgery) during an attack. I know one is coming when I notice letters missing in a word. After a migraine I'm less stressed and anxious for a couple of days. It's like someone letting air out of a tire lowering the pressure inside. Knowing this, when migraines were more severe, I would in a way welcome them. I found out many years later that my father and one of my sisters had migraine headaches.

Epilepsy and migraine headaches are known to include OBEs.[1] When I was inspired to write McEaster Valley shortly after my kid's mom passed, I experienced heightened "spiritual" awareness, and wrote the first draft in a few days. I've had migraine headaches most all my life, they have similar symptoms to epilepsy, and they are associated with OBEs. My "inspired" written comments about my mystical experiences in the valley confirm, at least to me, that my mind was definitely somewhere other than in me. OBE – GOK (God only knows).

He that studies to know duty, and labors in all things to do it, will have two heavens – one of joy, peace and comfort on earth, and the other of glory and happiness beyond the grave.

There is a land where everlasting suns shed everlasting brightness; where the soul drinks from the living streams of love that roll by God's high throne! – myriads of glorious ones bring their accepted offering. Oh! How blest to look from this dark prison to that shrine, to inhale one breath of Paradise divine, and enter into that eternal rest which waits the sons of God! *Sir John Bowring (1792-1872), Eng statesman.*

Bosch, through his painting, seemed to have an understanding of where we will travel during an OBE or death. The bright light, tunnel and presence of living souls being helped on their way, leads one to believe that he was also aware of NDE's. His vivid painting of looking towards the light as the "…blest look from this dark prison to the shrine, to inhale one breath of Paradise divine, and enter into the eternal rest which waits the sons of God!"

1– *What Really Happens During an Out-of-Body Experience? Healthline, Crystal Raypole, Medically reviewed by Nicole Washington (DO, MPH), last reviewed on July 22, 2022.*

2– *Have We Finally Found Evidence for A Parallel Universe? Forbes Daily, Ethan Siegel, May 22, 2020.*

3– *Near Death Experiences, Gideon Lichfield, The Atlantic issue 2015.*

4– *Teachings of Presidents of the Church, Wilford Woodruff, Chapter 16, 160-7, Marriage & Parenthood.*

5– *Into The Magic Shop, James t. Doty, MD, 190-97, 2016.*

6– *Scientists In Antarctica Didn't Find A 'Parallel Universe.' Jamie Carter, Forbes, June 11, 2020.*

7– *Easter: McEaster Valley, Walter R. Hoge, 2010 – 2022 – 2022.*

8– *Migraines and Epilepsy: Is There a Link?, WebMD, Angela Nelson, 08/07/2022.*

WALTER R. HOGE, DVM

Hieronymus Bosch (1450-1516) Netherlands
"Accent of the Blessed to the Heavenly Paradise" around 1490.

2

GOD SENDS ANSWERS
WE CAN UNDERSTAND

Michael McLean's faith crisis all started about 10 years ago when McLean's youngest son told his family that he was gay. He was hoping that if he was good enough, prayed hard enough, served faithfully as a missionary, and kept the commandments that he'd somehow experience a miracle and become straight. However, it's tough enough to be a gay kid in a straight world, but being the son of the songwriting icon of the Mormon Church was impossible for him. The pain was so deep that he'd considered suicide.

To make matters more difficult, McLean and his wife, Lynne, were living in Malibu, California, when Church members in the state were campaigning to pass Proposition 8 - which would only legally recognize marriages between a man and a woman. Mclean would hear from the pulpit that faithful Christians needed to save the family and the future of our country and campaign for votes for this proposition. Meanwhile, his son was planning to marry his partner at McLean's home if the proposition failed.

This would have been tough for any parent, but for the songwriting apologist filmmaker for the Church, this was simply an impossible spot to be in. He felt that he needed answers to save his family and prayed like he had never prayed before. Nothing came. It was like somebody decided to bolt heaven shut. He started to wonder, *what if I've gotten it all wrong? What if I got the church thing wrong? What if I got Heavenly Father wrong?* He kept thinking this would end - that there would be some peace that would come or some answers that would start trickling down. But they didn't. He couldn't believe he was saying it out loud, but he was thinking about an exit strategy. It was so painful.[1]

I purchased Camden Pet Hospital, Inc in 1980, the building I practiced in 1982 and became the treasurer of the Santa Clara Valley Veterinary Medical Association during that year. I served with the secretary, Donald R. Dooley, until his death in 2004. I remember this because he gave me a plaque which reads, "In appreciation for outstanding and dedicated service from 1982 – 1990." The next year I was asked to continue to serve as treasurer for another year and my position as treasurer stretched out until I was finally released on October 21, 2021 when the Wells Fargo checking account we used was closed.

Don's career began as a farmer, then representative of several veterinary drug companies, and finally a veterinary practice manager, public speaker and writer. My file contains copies of *The Dooley Letter* he wrote for the years 1984 to the year he passed in 2004. His monthly letter contained an introduction explaining his reasoning for the subject of that month, a page for the veterinary staff and one to the practice leader. Contained in these letters are many insightful quotes that I will share in another article.

Also, he was a man of faith and when called upon would give Gospel lessons in his home. Just getting back from speaking at a veterinary convention in Australia, he mentioned to me that he was more anxious discussing scriptures to a small group in his home than speaking to several hundred people in a conference hall. Don would often purchase supplies for his dog Alfred from Camden Pet Hospital and would always have an employee take them to him. He did not want anyone to be suspicious that he hadn't paid for the item. He would list the letters ND at the end of his name. It stood for No Degree. However, he was a very learned man and I never heard a colleague speak poorly about him.

A couple of years before Don's death, he mentioned that his wife had signs of dementia first noticed when she would take the laundry out of the washer and place it under the sink instead of into the dryer.

He eventually placed her in a care facility, his wife was often seen with and became attached to a fellow patient. During his evening visits he had dinner with them and tucked each into their separate beds. He understood the situation and was happy that his wife was actively engaged and not depressed spending hours sitting in a chair or lying in bed.

Prior to my kid's mom's death, Don told me that not long after his wife died he had some super experiences about his life that he explained in terms that I interpreted as spiritual. He didn't elaborate on his experiences, but told me to prepare myself for different emotional experiences that I had never believed possible when my wife Sheryl passed.

He was correct and I understand why he could not put into words what he had felt. My moments of loneliness and hollow feelings from the loss of my partner often times made me wonder if it was all worth it or *"what if I've gotten it all wrong? What if I got the church thing wrong? What if I got Heavenly Father wrong?"*

Several months after Sheryl died, August 2003, by mind went into "hyper mode": it exploded with thoughts of love, happiness, vivid memories of family and the wonderful natural world we live in. Just before Easter 2004 I wrote a story, *McEaster Valley*, in a few days and typed copies were sent to each of my five children for Easter. I have concluded that I was unconsciously trying to describe the feelings, Don could not, in the letter I wrote my children.[2]

I suspect Viktor Frankl, the prominent Jewish psychiatrist and neurologist from Vienna must have felt somewhat as Don and I did just after his release from a Nazi concentration camp with the tattoo number of 119104 on his body for the rest of his life.

In 1946 he wrote in nine days *Man's Search for Meaning* about his experiences in the camps. There he was taught by experience what he already felt in his heart: those who are most resilient, who are most likely to survive horrific conditions, are those who have a sense of meaning in their lives. In his words: "A man who becomes conscious of the responsibility he bears toward a human being who affectionately waits for him, or to an unfinished work, will never be able to throw away his life. He knows the 'why' for his existence, and will be able to bear almost any 'how'."[3]

In the midst of his faith crisis, McLean came across a book called *Mother Teresa: Come Be My Light: The Private Writings of the Saint of Calcutta*, which was published years after her death. As he read about her secret 49-year faith crisis, which she confessed through a series of letters to her spiritual advisors and closest confidants, he related to her struggle. She asked, "Why has Heavenly Father abandoned me? Why can't I hear Him or feel His spirit? And I can't tell anybody this is happening."

He understood. What was he going to say? "Hey, all of you who bought my records, just kidding! You are alone. Quit holding on—the light's not coming."

Soon after reading her book, McLean had a dream about Mother Teresa that changed how he approached his crisis. In the dream, the Catholic nun sang about her life while McLean accompanied her on the piano. He recalls, "It was her song about why she hadn't just thrown in the towel, given up on faith, and confessed that believing and following a faith tradition was all too much, too difficult, too foolish." In his dream she sang:

> *I choose to pray to one who doesn't hear me*
> *I choose to wait for love that He conceals*
> *And though God's chosen now not to be near me*
> *I'm keeping promises my heart no longer feels*

McLean says, "So here's a Mormon songwriter having a dream about a dead Catholic nun who sings a song that begs the questions: Am I willing to keep the promises I've made to God even when I feel nothing in response to my deepest yearnings? In the most difficult trial of my faith journey, would I hold on to faith or give in to despair?" Like Mother Teresa, McLean would ultimately choose to hold on—no matter what. He says, "I decided to recommit, I'll wait on the Lord and look for answers that satisfied both my heart and mind. I'd attend church and not escape to the parking lot when I'd hear things that broke my heart or just made me feel like I was not where I truly belonged. I'd show up and shut up and listen and wait."

He would listen and wait for nine years. Then something suddenly changed. "A couple years ago, I was in my little studio office where I write songs when, for a 10-day period, it was like I received a download of songs from heaven," he recalls. "They were coming so fast - songs from the perspectives of people who had different encounters with Jesus, such as the money changer, the guard whose ear got cut off, and the leper."

But it was the perspective of John the Baptist that especially impacted McLean. "John the Baptist had a faith crisis that goes beyond anything I've experienced. While he's locked in prison, about to be executed, he tells some of his disciples to find Jesus and ask Him, 'Are you the one who was to come? Or should we look for another?' He's wondering if, after all he had done, he had gotten it all wrong." McLean continues, "John's disciples find Jesus, and He says, 'Watch me.' He doesn't race to the dungeon to comfort John the Baptist. He starts performing miracles.

Then He tells the disciples to go back and tell John the miracles they saw, in the order they saw them. John realizes that his question is being answered perfectly because 700 years earlier, Isaiah had prophesied that the Messiah would perform these miracles, and they would happen in the order that the disciples saw them. John is getting the perfect answer that is designed perfectly just for him."

McLean realized that God had sent the answers to the questions that had plagued him for nine years in the lyrics to the songs he had just written. "The answers were perfect," he says. "But even more incredible to me than their perfection was that they came to me in a language only I would understand. It was so personal. He sent songs to the songwriter."

He affirms, "You'll know when God answers you because it will be perfect and personal in every way." McLean's experience with a faith crisis has given him deep compassion and a unique perspective that couldn't have been developed any other way. But one of the greatest epiphanies he had, which still impacts him today, came from a memory of his deceased father:

"My father suffered from Alzheimer's, so when he was asked to give a 17-minute talk at an Easter sacrament meeting, I was nervous he would go a little bit off track. In fact, I stood close by so I could come up and rescue him," McLean recalls. "Every scripture, every reference, was about God the Father's greatness, wisdom, and intelligence. And I was getting embarrassed because it was Easter Sunday, and he wasn't talking about Jesus."

But then, with two minutes left, McLean's father surprised him by posing a series of profound questions. My father said, "Isn't it interesting that the Greatest Intelligence in the Universe abandoned His Son at the most pivotal moment in His plan? Could it be that it was at this moment that the Greatest Intelligence of All bore witness to the universe that He had put His faith in Jesus? That He knew Jesus would choose Him no matter what? And could it be that when you think He has abandoned you that He is actually saying, 'I have faith you will choose me even when I'm not there'?" And that is exactly how McLean overcame his faith crisis - by choosing God even when he felt abandoned by Him.

Today, rather than being ashamed of his experience, McLean is using it to share a message of hope with others who might be struggling. "John the Baptist, Joseph Smith, and even Christ himself have felt abandoned by God," he says. "If any of us have ever felt abandoned and wondered where He is, then we're in good company." McLean says songwriters really only write one song, and his is "You're Not Alone." Though the lyrics and melodies are always different, the message remains the same.[1]

God answers our questions in languages we understand. For Michael McLean it was through music, for Viktor Frankel it was his experiences working as a prisoner in the Nazi death camps, for me it was through writing a story that included my family, pets and nature surrounding the Easter holiday, and for Don Dooley I can only imagine because it was special enough that it could only be explained by him in words that I interpreted as spiritual.

1– *Michael McLean Opens Up About His 9-Year Faith Crisis and How He Found His Testimony Again, by Jamie Armstrong, LDS Living Magazine, Saints, Nov/Dec 2016.*

2– *Easter: Easter McEaster Valley, Walter R. Hoge, 2010.*

3– *Anna S. Redsand, Viktor Frankl: A Life Worth Living July 2016, Music & The Spoken Word 02-28-2016.*

3

NUCLEAR RADIATION

During my experiences in the Mystical valley in the Sierra Mountains I observed: "…As the light of the entrance faded behind us, I noticed that all along the tunnel wall, there was a light greenish glow that increased in intensity as the area around us darkened. My first thought was that the glowing light looked like radium which used to be use on the hands of wristwatches to help them glow in the dark. A touch of fear struck me as I thought about radium and the radiation that it emits as it excites phosphorus to produce the light. Marie Curie extracted radium from pitchblende in the early twentieth century and eventually died from the effects of radiation overexposure from the concentrated element."[1]

The radioisotope Radium was first discovered in 1898 by Marie and Pierre Curie, after they extracted a single milligram from ten tons of a uranium ore called pitchblende. It glowed and it didn't take long for entrepreneurs to see the potential value in the luminescent properties of radium.

Just a few years after its discovery zinc sulfide was mixed with it to create paint. The people who worked with it would glow as they walked through the streets at night. It wasn't until 1914 that radium-based luminescent paint started to be produced in the US. By 1921, they weren't just making paints, they were doing the painting, too. Scores of young women, as young as 11-years-old, were hired to paint watch dials with the glow-in-the-dark, radium-based paint. They were also encouraged to put the brush between their lips and twirl it into a point. It was the best way to get truly precise numbers and brush strokes.

It was thought to be super healthy: it was often marketed as a cure-all, and there was a shocking number of products that hit the market just full of radium. People drank radium water and brushed their teeth with radium toothpaste, and radium cosmetics were all the rage. Children played with toys painted with radium, and performers on the New York stage danced and twirled in costumes that glowed. Early experiments using radium to kill cancer cells had been a success. Doctors started experimenting with it as a cure for things like tuberculosis, lupus and for everything from acne and baldness to impotence and insanity.[2]

In 1995, a teenage boy scout in Michigan named David Hahn (more popularly known as the "Radioactive Boy Scout" or the "Nuclear Boy Scout") attracted the attention of local authorities in his Detroit suburb. Hahn caught the law's eye when suspicious materials were found in his car. But further investigation revealed a series of backyard science experiments, including the teen's attempt to build a working nuclear reactor. Utilizing household items and a lead block as a stand-in reactor, Hahn got to work. He collected thorium from lanterns, tritium from gunsights, and lithium from $1,000 worth of batteries he bought himself. He also purchased clocks that scores of young women had been hired to paint the dials with the glow-in-the-dark, radium-based paint. Hahn also employed coffee filters and pickle jars to handle dangerous and potentially deadly chemicals.

Practically a wunderkind, Hahn began studying chemistry at age 10 and had fabricated nitroglycerin by 14. Before attempting to build his reactor, Hahn tarnished his bedroom with his experiments, so his parents moved his work to their basement, before settling on the shed.

Hahn gathered information by contacting the Nuclear Regulatory Commission, hoping to gain insight into the steps of building a breeder reactor. In most cases, Hahn was able to gather the info he needed with the help of aliases and cover stories.

Hahn's interest in creating a breeder reactor was fueled by many things. The teen read about chemical experiments fervently, teaching himself how to manipulate reactions, and was awarded a merit badge for atomic energy in 1991. He supplemented his practical research with long study sessions at his local library

The flames of Hahn's fascination were fanned by two obsessive goals, one being the task of creating a breeder reactor; the other, of collecting each element on the periodic table — regardless of radioactivity.

For Hahn, the creation of a homemade nuclear reactor would have been a more complex task than creating a homemade breeder reactor. Both requiring dangerous materials, breeder reactors utilize the more available chemical isotope Uranium-238 — the chemical element thorium — while nuclear reactors may only use the scarcer Uranium-235. While the uranium used in nuclear reactors are readily fissionable, Uranium-238 and thorium are more available.

During his shed-bound experiments, Hahn persevered through accidental burns on his skin, turning his hair green, and mistakenly causing himself to pass out. When the experiment met its threshold, Hahn had created a crude neutron source. While unable to produce fissionable fuel at the rate of other reactors, the Boy Scout's experiment was already spreading detectable radiation several houses away. As detected by David Hahn's own Geiger counter, his experiment proved radioactive by the time it was disassembled — and left 40,000 town residents potentially at risk.

Police located Hahn's shed after stopping the young teen for unrelated reasons. Finding suspicious materials in his trunk, the scout informed the officers the content was radioactive. From there, it did not take long to uncover the shed and its impact on Hahn's neighborhood.

The local police contacted the federal authorities, leading the Environmental Protection Agency to Hahn's doorstep. Those who entered Hahn's shed lab were warned by a misspelled "Caushon" sign on the wall. Inside, authorities found evidence of Hahn's dangerous hobbies. The remnants of the experiment and materials collected posed numerous health risks, and the EPA declared the property a Superfund hazardous materials cleanup site.

Despite insistence from officials, Hahn refused to be medically evaluated following the long periods he spent around radioactive materials. Since his experiment took place with minimal protection, Hahn's life expectancy was likely shortened after the incident.

Following the lab's dismantling, Hahn achieved his Eagle Scout rank despite efforts to rob him of the honor on account of his dangerous experiment. However, regardless of what progress he made, Hahn had trouble finding direction following the experiment's fallout.

"I was very emotional as a kid, and those experiments gave me a way to get away from that. They gave me some respect," Hahn told Harpers Magazine in 1998.

The collapse of his experiment, turmoil from a failed relationship, and his mother's suicide each contributed to "Nuclear Boy Scout" David Hahn's depression. Attempting to find his place in the world after the disastrous events in his backyard, he tried his hand at college and the military, mostly at the request of his father and step-mother. Hahn served in both the United States Navy and the United States Marine Corps, but only found new complications with mental health as he grew older.[3]

Many environmentalists have opposed nuclear power, citing its dangers and the difficulty of disposing of its radioactive waste. But Richard Rhodes, a Pulitzer Prize-winning author, argues that nuclear is safer than most energy sources and is needed if the world hopes to radically decrease its carbon emissions.

In the late 16th century, when the increasing cost of firewood forced ordinary Londoners to switch reluctantly to coal, Elizabethan preachers railed against a fuel they believed to be, literally, the Devil's excrement. Coal was black, after all, dirty, found in layers underground — down toward Hell at the center of the earth — and smelled strongly of sulfur when it burned. Switching to coal, in houses that usually lacked chimneys, was difficult enough; the clergy's outspoken condemnation, while certainly justified environmentally, further complicated and delayed the timely resolution of an urgent problem in energy supply.

For too many environmentalists concerned with global warming, nuclear energy is today's Devil's excrement. They condemn it for its production and use of radioactive fuels and for the supposed problem of disposing of its waste. In Rhodes' judgment, their condemnation of this efficient, low-carbon source of baseload energy is misplaced. Far from being the Devil's excrement, nuclear power can be, and should be, one major component of our rescue from a hotter, more meteorologically destructive world.

Like all energy sources, nuclear power has advantages and disadvantages. Nuclear power's benefits are:

– First and foremost, since it produces energy via nuclear fission rather than chemical burning, it generates baseload electricity with no output of carbon, the villainous element of global warming.

Switching from coal to natural gas is a step toward decarbonizing, since burning natural gas produces about half the carbon dioxide of burning coal. But switching from coal to nuclear power is radically decarbonizing, since nuclear power plants release greenhouse gases only from the ancillary use of fossil fuels during their construction, mining, fuel processing, maintenance, and decommissioning — about as much as solar power does, which is about 4 to 5 percent as much as a natural gas-fired power plant. Nuclear power also releases less radiation into the environment than any other major energy source.

– Second, nuclear power plants operate at much higher capacity factors than renewable energy sources or fossil fuels. Capacity factor is a measure of what percentage of the time a power plant actually produces energy. It's a problem for all intermittent energy sources. The sun doesn't always shine, nor the wind always blow, nor water always fall through the turbines of a dam.

– Third, nuclear power releases less radiation into the environment than any other major energy source. This statement will seem paradoxical to many, since it's not commonly known that non-nuclear energy sources release any radiation into the environment. They do. The worst offender is coal, a mineral of the earth's crust that contains a substantial volume of the radioactive elements - uranium and thorium. Burning coal gasifies its organic materials, concentrating its mineral components into the remaining waste, called fly ash. So much coal is burned in the world and so much fly ash produced that coal is actually the major source of radioactive releases into the environment.

Nuclear energy downsides mostly are from the public's perception that radiation poses the risk of accidents, and the question of how to dispose of nuclear waste.

There have been three large-scale accidents involving nuclear power reactors since the onset of commercial nuclear power in the mid-1950s: Three-Mile Island in Pennsylvania, Chernobyl in Ukraine, and Fukushima in Japan. Studies indicate even the worst possible accident at a nuclear plant is less destructive than other major industrial accidents.

The partial meltdown of the Three-Mile Island reactor in March 1979, while a disaster for the owners of the Pennsylvania plant, released only a minimal quantity of radiation to the surrounding population.

The explosion and subsequent burnout of a large graphite-moderated, water-cooled reactor at Chernobyl in 1986 was easily the worst nuclear accident in history. Twenty-nine disaster relief workers died of acute radiation exposure in the immediate aftermath of the accident. In the subsequent three decades, studies observed and reported at regular intervals on the health effects of the Chernobyl accident. It has identified no long-term health consequences to populations exposed to Chernobyl fallout except for thyroid cancers in residents of Belarus, Ukraine and western Russia who were children or adolescents at the time of the accident, who drank milk contaminated with 131iodine, and who were not evacuated.

By 2008, studies attributed some 6,500 excess cases of thyroid cancer in the Chernobyl region to the accident, with 15 deaths. The occurrence of these cancers increased dramatically from 1991 to 1995, which researchers attributed mostly to radiation exposure. No increase occurred in adults.

The statistics of Chernobyl irradiations cited here are so low that they must seem intentionally minimized to those who followed the extensive media coverage of the accident and its aftermath. Yet they are the peer-reviewed products of extensive investigation by an international scientific agency of the United Nations. They indicate that even the worst possible accident at a nuclear power plant — the complete meltdown and burnup of its radioactive fuel — was yet far less destructive than other major industrial accidents across the past century.

The accident in Japan at Fukushima Daiichi in March 2011 followed a major earthquake and tsunami. The tsunami flooded out the power supply and cooling systems of three power reactors, causing them to melt down and explode, breaching their confinement. Although 154,000 Japanese citizens were evacuated from a 12-mile exclusion zone around the power station, radiation exposure beyond the station grounds was limited.

According to the report submitted to the International Atomic Energy Agency in June 2011:

"No harmful health effects were found in 195,345 residents living in the vicinity of the plant who were screened by the end of May 2011. All the 1,080 children tested for thyroid gland exposure showed results within safe limits. (There) was no major public exposure, let alone deaths from radiation."

Nuclear waste disposal, although a continuing political problem in the U.S., is not any longer a technological problem. Most U.S. spent fuel, more than 90 percent of which could be recycled to extend nuclear power production by hundreds of years, is stored at present safely in impenetrable concrete-and-steel dry casks on the grounds of operating reactors, its radiation slowly declining.

A final complaint against nuclear power is that it costs too much. Whether or not nuclear power costs too much will ultimately be a matter for markets to decide, but there is no question that a full accounting of the external costs of different energy systems would find nuclear cheaper than coal or natural gas.

Nuclear power is not the only answer to the world-scale threat of global warming. Renewables have their place; so, at least for leveling the flow of electricity when renewables vary, does natural gas. But nuclear deserves better than the anti-nuclear prejudices and fears that have plagued it. It isn't the 21st century's version of the Devil's excrement. It's a valuable, even an irreplaceable, part of the solution to the greatest energy threat in the history of humankind.[4]

Unfortunately, Radium gives off dangerous radiation and many of the young girls who worked in the industry painting glow-in-the-dark paint on watch dials sickened and died. Those sickened became known as the "society of the living dead" and weren't aided by their community. They were shunned. In spite of the fact that these were young mothers, wives, and girls who were dying, the communities they lived in just didn't want to acknowledge what was happening to them. Ottawa, Illinois was known as Death City throughout the 1930s and in 1987, a documentary tried to show just how long-lasting the effects were, in a very graphic way: When one man headed into the Catholic cemetery that is the final resting place of many of the Radium Girls, the Geiger counter he carried went nuts - their remains, six feet down, are still radioactive.

The half-life of Radium is 1600 years. With some of the girl's precautions were taken over concerns of radiation admissions and they were buried in lead-lined coffins. Industrialist and golfer Eben Byers was the poster child for a drink called RadiThor, and drank several bottles of it a day. Holes formed in his skull, his jaw fell off, and his bones began to crumble. He died in 1932, and was so radioactive that he too was buried in a lead-lined coffin.[2]

David Hahn appears to have been a very bright young man growing up under difficult circumstances that if mentored properly may have reached his goal of being "respected" and a contributor to society.

Instead, following his original experiment's disassembly, David Hahn "The Nuclear Boy Scout" once again attracted the police's attention a decade later. Suspected of creating another reactor and storing it in his freezer, Hahn was arrested in 2007 for stealing some detectors. The devices were taken from the apartment complex Hahn was staying in. The theft was significant for the small amounts of radioactive americium found in the smoke detectors. Since americium was found in greater amounts in Hahn's shed in 1995, authorities evacuated residents for five hours — fearing the infamous former Boy Scout was at it again.

At the time of the incident, police had already been tracking Hahn and monitoring the region for radioactivity. Coinciding with his return to the area, authorities took note that Hahn had begun advertising a book written about his experiment.

With their eyes already fixed on Hahn, the police were quick to arrest him on account of his theft. Sixteen smoke detectors across Hahn's building and another in his complex had gone missing. Police found additional empty smoke detectors near Hahn's trash.

Following his arrest, David Hahn pleaded guilty to attempted larceny of a building and was sentenced to 90 days in jail. And about a decade later, Hahn died from a combination of alcohol, diphenhydramine, and fentanyl. The "Nuclear Boy Scout" was just 39 years old.[3]

According to Richard Rhodes, to many scientists, nuclear power is more and more looking like the only answer to the world-scale threat of global warming. Renewables have their place; so, at least for leveling the flow of electricity when renewables vary, does natural gas. But nuclear deserves better than the anti-nuclear prejudices and fears that have plagued it. It isn't the 21st century's version of the Devil's excrement. It's a valuable, even an irreplaceable, part of the solution to the greatest energy threat in the history of humankind.[4]

During my travels going into a mountain tunnel in mystical McEaster Valley, the light greenish glow that increased in intensity as the area around us darkened still intrigues me. My initial thought was Radium. However, the intensity of light leads me to believe that I may well have ended up as the Radium Girls, Mr. Eben Byers or David Hahn if the intense light was from Radium or other nuclear material.

Thoughts about bioluminescence from the fire flies or glow worms causing the greenish glow makes sense. However, I do not recall any insects in the area and I'm still looking for a logical answer.

At least it appears that nuclear is not the Devil's excrement and may turn out be an energy blessing for our energy starved human needs in the future.

1– *Easter: McEaster Valley, Walter R. Hoge, 2010.*
2– *The Radium Girls, Shutterstock, Debra Kelly, 07/14/2020.*
3– *David Hahn, The 'Radioactive Boy Scout' Who Tried To Build A Nuclear Reactor In His Backyard, Andrew Kolba, 11/20/2022.*
4– *Why Nuclear Power Must Be Part of the Energy Solution, Richard Rhodes, Yale School of the Environment, 06/19/2018.*

4

GOOD BETTER BEST

We have to forego some good things in order to choose others that are better or best because they develop faith in the Lord Jesus Christ and strengthen our families. Most of us have more things expected of us than we can possibly do. As breadwinners, as parents, as Church workers and members, we face many choices on what we will do with our time and other resources.

We should begin by recognizing the reality that just because something is good is not a sufficient reason for doing it. The number of good things we can do far exceeds the time available to accomplish them. Some things are better than good, and these are the things that should command priority attention in our lives.

Jesus taught this principle in the home of Martha. While she was "cumbered about much serving" (Luke 10:40), her sister, Mary, "sat at Jesus' feet, and heard his word" (v. 39). When Martha complained that her sister had left her to serve alone, Jesus commended Martha for what she was doing (v. 41) but taught her that "one thing is needful: and Mary hath chosen that good part, which shall not be taken away from her" (v. 42). It was praiseworthy for Martha to be "careful and troubled about many things" (v. 41), but learning the gospel from the Master Teacher was more "needful." The scriptures contain other teachings that some things are more blessed than others (see Acts 20:35; Alma 32:14–15).

A childhood experience introduced me to the idea that some choices are good but others are better. I lived for two years on a farm. We rarely went to town. Our Christmas shopping was done in the Sears, Roebuck catalog. I spent hours poring over its pages. For the rural families of that day, catalog pages were like the shopping mall or the Internet of our time.

Something about some displays of merchandise in the catalog fixed itself in my mind. There were three degrees of quality: good, better, and best. For example, some men's shoes were labeled good ($1.84), some better ($2.98), and some best ($3.45).

As we consider various choices, we should remember that it is not enough that something is good. Other choices are better, and still others are best. Even though a particular choice is more costly, its far greater value may make it the best choice of all.

Consider how we use our time in the choices we make in viewing television, playing video games, surfing the Internet, or reading books or magazines. Of course, it is good to view wholesome entertainment or to obtain interesting information. But not everything of that sort is worth the portion of our life we give to obtain it. Some things are better, and others are best. When the Lord told us to seek learning, He said, "Seek ye out of the best books words of wisdom" (D&C 88:118; emphasis added).[1]

Morgan Pearson interviewed Steve Young on "All In", an LDS Living podcast where the question asked is, "what does it really mean to be all in the gospel of Jesus Christ." Steve is a 2-time NFL MVP, a Super Bowl MVP, a first ballot Hall of Famer, a key member of ESPN's weekly coverage, and holds an undergraduate and law degree from Brigham Young University. He is president and cofounder of HGGC, a private equity firm, and founder of the Forever Young Foundation, a global charity for children, which he co-chairs with his wife, Barb.

Steve's response to the question, "Loving as God loves, seeking another's healing, expecting nothing in return is my definition of the law of love. But your question brings about so much. I've been thinking, drawing on its principles for so long, that it's funny to be introducing them and how it feels. And I want to articulate in a way that people can take it in a really productive way.

And so, if you think about loving as God loves, that's a heck of a statement. But I work off of Scripture. You think about Moses 1:39, and you think about my work and my glory is to bring to pass the immortality and eternal life of men. That's essentially God's mission statement. And in that mission statement, if you kind of think about it in, 'Is there a transaction in there? What does God get?' In his mission statement, usually, if there's a mission, there's something to be achieved, there's something to receive. And, if you think about the scripture, God only receives anything of any glory, through our glory, and through our eternal life and immortality.

And so, if God loves without transaction without seeking anything, I want to love as God loves— seeking others healing, and expecting nothing in return are the key elements of it, because expecting nothing in return are the key elements of it, because expecting nothing in return really is difficult. Because so much of our lives are transactional."[2]

When I think of the Law of Love, I reflect on visits I made with my children to McEaster Valley so many years ago as they laid on my bed and I told them stories about my adventures in this imaginary valley where God's teachings were the center of their existence.

Mr. and Mrs. McEaster were caretakers in this valley and I described them as, "Before we could reach the front porch, the door opened and there appeared a female version of my friend. The only way I can describe her is that she was very much like the perfect wife, the perfect mother, and the perfect grandmother all wrapped up into one. As she greeted us, you could see and feel the love that she had for her husband, and I knew that her concern over my well-being was heartfelt and sincere…While her husband helped bathe and clean me, she immediately began preparing the best smelling (and I might add tasting) meal I could ever remember…After I ate, she reached into the cupboard and opened a vial of what looked like oil and had a musky smell. She placed it into her aged hands, rubbed them together, and placed the material on my sores…Where ever she massaged my skin, it began to heal, and the soreness and tiredness of my body seemed to melt away. It felt so warm and so relaxing. It felt supernatural, maybe even spiritual. The rest of that evening can only be described as warm, friendly, caring, and loving, and my mind and soul were overpowered with peace and joy. I was truly in a state of ecstasy."[3]

We all have times when we feel short bursts of ecstasy that can help "make our day." Our lives can become more filled with such feelings and less consumed by fear of failure if we spend more time rubbing shoulders with the likes of the McEaster family or do as the little bird while receiving help and encouragement from her mamma.

> A little bird needs help to fly mamma pushes her out of the nest and says "Try, try try!"
>
> Even though she is afraid she spreads her wings without looking down oh, oh she hits the ground hard and loud and mamma says "welcome to life, darling"
>
> Oh gee, oh gee, oh gee why is life this way? Ah jay, ah jay, ah jay why is life this way?
>
> Good better best may I never rest until my good is better and my better best.
>
> Even though she is afraid you can feel that she is great when she struggles to come off the ground oh, oh
>
> Fail, follow and try again and again and again. And you don't have to be afraid to fail little girl.
>
> Yet tell me why? Yeah, I will try, try again x4's and I will try again x2's.[4]

Good, better, best may I never rest until
my good is better and my better best.

1– *Good, Better, Best, Dallin H. Oaks, Ensign, 2007.*
2– *An Introduction to the Law of Love, Steve Young, 2022.*
3– *Easter: McEaster Valley, WR Hoge, 2010.*
4– *Y'akoto, Good Better Best, lyrics by Mania.*

5

CARING FOR EACH OTHER

For the first time, researchers have observed ants secreting a milk-like fluid that nourishes others in the colony. Research published in Nature revealed that as pupae (an otherwise inactive developmental stage – ants) produce a nutrient-rich fluid that is consumed by both adults and larvae. Newly hatched larvae depend on this fluid to grow and survive, akin to how mammalian newborns depend on milk. If the ant adults and larvae do not consume the fluid, it builds up and becomes contaminated with fungi, which kill the pupae.

The pupae were considered useless because they are immobile, they spin a cocoon around them in some species, they don't eat, they're just moved around by the ant workers, so they wouldn't contribute anything to ant society.

The discovery was made by observing clonal raider ants (*Ooceraea biroi*) kept in isolation at different stages of their life cycle, to investigate what makes ant colonies so integrated. While observing isolated ant pupae, the researchers were surprised to see droplets of a fluid appearing on their abdominal tips. When this fluid built up, the pupae drowned in it, but they survived when it was removed. By injecting blue food dye into the pupae and tracing where it ended up, the researchers showed that adult ants drink the fluid as it is secreted, and also help their larvae to drink it by carrying them to the pupae. This stops the fluid accumulating. The adults are doing parental care as they're cleaning the pupae, taking the larvae and placing them on the pupae to feed.

The team tested the molecular composition of the fluid and identified 185 proteins that were specific to it, as well as more than 100 metabolites such as amino acids, sugars and vitamins. The compounds identified suggest that the fluid is derived from molting fluids, which are produced when the larvae shed their outer cuticle as they develop into pupae. It's an opportunistic recycling that the ants are doing inside the colony … and a metabolic division of labor.

The researchers also detected pupal 'milk' in species from each of the five biggest ant subfamilies, suggesting that it could play a part in the evolution of ant social structures. It's something that has evolved either shortly after ants became eusocial or maybe even before ants becoming social.

The team now wants to study effects that pupal secretions might have on the adults and larvae in terms of behavior and physiology. Whether larvae develop into queen or worker might be modulated by how much access they have to this fluid. Also, others plan on conducting research investigating whether the secretion of the pupae is also useful in the transfer of intestinal microbial communities that helps ants to digest food.[1]

During my visit to the mystical McEaster Valley in the Sierra Mountains, "…I was told that the large gourd-shaped fruit found there had been developed as a food source for the insects, that produced the main ingredient for the food storage process. Mr. McEaster stated that as they increased the size of the insects…the warmer region in the valley stimulated the gourds and insects to grow rapidly and produce the "milk" as he called it, to add as a preservative to the food products being made. I was told that the insects resembled aphids and the "milk" they secreted from their bodies was a complex carbohydrate (sugar). The sugar is much like the sweet material produced by normal aphids that honeydew ants harvest for their food. The milk was collected during the cleaning process of the pens in which they were kept."[2]

Ants and aphids share a well-documented communal symbiotic relationship, which means they both benefit mutually from their working relationship. Aphids produce a sugary food for the ants, in exchange, ants care for and protect the aphids from predators and parasites.

Aphids are also known as plant lice, they are very small sap-sucking insects that collect the sugar-rich fluids from host plants. Aphids are also the bane of farmers the whole world over. Aphids are known crop destroyers. The aphids must consume large quantities of a plant to gain adequate nutrition. The aphids then excrete equally large quantities of waste, called honeydew, which in turn becomes a sugar-rich meal for ants.

As most people know, where there is sugar, there is bound to be ants. Some ants seek out aphid honeydew and will "milk" the aphids to make them excrete the sugary substance. The ants stroke the aphids with their antennae, stimulating them to release the honeydew. Some aphid species have lost the ability to excrete waste on their own and depend entirely on caretaker ants to milk them.

Aphid-herding ants make sure aphids stay well-fed and safe. When the host plant is depleted of nutrients, the ants carry their aphids to a new food source. If predatory insects or parasites attempt to harm the aphids, the ants will defend them aggressively. Some ants even go so far as to destroy the eggs of known aphid predators like ladybugs.

Some species of ants continue to care for aphids during winter. The ants carry the aphid eggs to their nests for the winter months. They store the precious aphids where temperatures and humidity are optimal, and move them as needed when conditions in the nest change. In spring, when the aphids hatch, the ants carry them to a host plant to feed.

There is a well-documented example of the extraordinary mutualistic symbiotic relationship of a corn root aphid, from the species *Aphis middletonii*, and their caretaker cornfield ants, *Lasius*. Corn root aphids, as their name suggests, live and feed on the roots of corn plants. At the end of the growing season, the aphids deposit eggs in the soil where the corn plants have withered. The cornfield ants collect the aphid eggs and store them for the winter.

Smartweed is a fast-growing weed that can grow in the spring in the cornfields. Cornfield ants carry the newly hatched aphids to the field and deposit them on the temporary host smartweed plants so they can begin feeding. Once the corn plants are growing, the ants move their honeydew-producing partners to the corn plants, their preferred host plant.

While it appears the ants are generous caretakers of aphids, ants are more concerned about maintaining their steady honeydew source than anything else. Aphids are almost always wingless, but certain environmental conditions will trigger them to develop wings. If the aphid population becomes too dense, or food sources decline, aphids can grow wings to fly to a new location. Ants can prevent aphids from dispersing by tearing the wings from aphids before they can become airborne. Also, a recent study has shown that ants can use semiochemicals (which are pheromones or other chemicals that convey signals from one organism to another so as to modify the behavior of the recipient organism) to stop the aphids from developing wings and to impede their ability to walk away.[3]

Communal relationships are those where an individual assumes responsibility for the welfare of his or her partner. In these relationships, when the partner has a specific need, wants support in striving toward a goal, would enjoy being included in an activity, or simply could use the reassurance of care, the other partner strives to be responsive. Importantly, partners do so with no strings attached.

Common examples of communal responsiveness are a mother providing lunch to her child, a person providing encouragement to a friend who is training to run in a marathon, or a person giving his or her romantic partner a compliment. In each case, the benefit enhances or maintains the welfare of the recipient, and the recipient incurs no debt.

Communal relationships vary in strength. In very strong communal relationships, one person assumes a great deal of responsibility for the other person and would do almost anything, unconditionally, to promote his or her welfare. Parents often have very strong communal relationships with their own children, putting their child's welfare above their own welfare and spending years providing emotional and tangible support.

In very weak communal relationships, a person assumes just a small amount of responsibility for another's welfare; yet, within the bounds of that small sense of responsibility, the person is unconditionally responsive to the other person. For instance, most people are willing to tell even a stranger the time or give the stranger directions with no expectation of repayment. Most communal relationships, for instance those with friends, fall somewhere in between these extremes of very high and quite low communal strength.

People have implicit hierarchies of communal relationships ordered according to the degree of communal responsibility they feel for others. A person's entire set of hierarchically arranged communal relationships may be shaped like a triangle with a wide base representing the person's many weak communal relationships and a peak representing the person's few very strong ones.

At the base are the many strangers and passing acquaintances for whom small courtesies may be provided without expecting a specific, precisely equal repayment. Higher in the hierarchy, and fewer in number, are relationships with colleagues and casual friends, higher yet relationships with closer friends and a variety of relatives. For many people, relationships with best friends, immediate family members, and romantic partners are near or at the top. The needs of those higher in the hierarchy take precedence over the needs of those lower in the hierarchy.

Although some communal relationships (e.g., that with one's own infant) may be universal and even dictated by biology or social dictates, others are voluntary. The exact nature of hierarchies will vary from person to person and, certainly, from culture to culture.

Communal relationships can and often are symmetrical, meaning that each person in the relationship feels the same degree of communal responsibility for the other. Friendships, sibling relationships, and romantic relationships often (but not always) exemplify symmetrical communal relationships. Other communal relationships are asymmetrical, with one member assuming more responsibility for the other than vice versa. Perhaps the clearest example of an asymmetrical communal relationship is that which exists between a parent and a newborn infant. The parent typically assumes tremendous communal responsibility for the infant; the infant assumes no communal responsibility for the parent. As the child ages, the asymmetry typically diminishes and, in the parent's old age, may reverse.

Although it might seem that a communal relationship is necessarily an unselfish relationship, the basis for communal relationships can be selfish as well. It is the assumption of some degree of unconditional responsibility for the welfare of another person that is the marker of a communal relationship. However, one can assume such responsibility for unselfish or selfish reasons. For example, one may feel empathy for another when needs arise and assume unconditional responsibility for that person to alleviate their distress. This is a seemingly unselfish reason for communal responsiveness. However, one might assume communal responsibility for rather selfish reasons as well. For instance, one may be communally responsive to a grumpy elderly relative because one fears criticism by others if one does not do so. One may be unconditionally responsive to a peer because one hopes (but cannot require) that the peer will desire a symmetrical communal relationship (friendship) and will be similarly responsive to one's own needs if and when such needs arise. Such reasons are more selfish. It appears likely that there is an evolutionary, as well as a cultural, basis for the existence of communal relationships.

Communal relationships can be very short in duration, such as when one gives a stranger directions with no expectation of repayment, or very long term, as in a typical parent's relationship with his or her child. It is, however, undoubtedly the case that the strength of a communal relationship is positively correlated with the length (and expected length) of that relationship.

Establishing and maintaining strong communal relationships can be difficult. There is evidence that people who are high in self-esteem and high in trust of others are best able to sustain relationships that operate primarily on a communal basis.[4]

Communal relationships at least in the ant and aphid communities can be quite complex: There is a strong maternal caring bond between the egg, larva, pupae and adult ant as well as a communal mutually symbiotic relationship with aphids. The aphids provide for the nutritional needs of the ant and the ant makes sure that the aphids have access to food, freedom from predators and provides them with a safe environment during the winter.

Communal human relationships between individuals and families are much like symbiotic relationships between different animal species. They can and often are symmetrical, meaning that each person (animal) in the relationship has about the same degree of communal responsibility for the other. Other relationships are asymmetrical, with one taking advantage of the other.

Communal human relationships at times require more responsibility for the other and vice versa and the mutual caring for others helps maintain a symbiotic relationship resulting in the best of friendship, unselfishness, nurturing, caring, and loving Christ like relationships. However, the symbiotic communal relationship may be one where one takes advantage of the other and threatens their wellbeing. A communal relationship can become prideful, self-serving, thoughtless, meanness, self-absorbing, sensual, devilish and have little regard for one or all involved in the relationship.

Love is a highly volatile feeling, especially when it's one-sided and not mutual. A mutualistic relationship or marriage involves two-sided love. Mutual love is reciprocated love. It is common and joint love between two people in a relationship or marriage.

Mutuality in love is a fundamental element in any healthy romantic relationship. A secured relationship calls for reciprocity so that two people are working towards a common goal, which is to make their relationship work for the long haul as a couple. Mutual love can surpass anything.

Mutual love helps in making a relationship grow more substantial as both partners feel loved and respected equally. Mutual affection gives rise to a feeling of mutual warmth and fondness for each other. Mutual trust in each other leads to a more honest and transparent relationship. Mutual support for each other in good and in bad times gives a feeling of being there for each other unconditionally. Shared goals are the total sum of everything as both partners make all efforts to reach the same and common destination.[5]

"If I could talk to the animals, learn all their languages, I could take an animal degree. I'd study elephant and eagle, buffalo and beagle, alligator, guinea pig and flea!" *Bobby Darin, Talk To The Animal..."* I would be especially interested in talking to the ant and aphid asking them how their symbiotic relationship has worked so well for them and how it can help little old me.

I suspect it has something to do with the answer Jesus gave when the lawyer asked which of the many commandments from the Old Testament, from the law of Moses, or from the Ten Commandments was the greatest. He summarized all of the commandments in these two verses:

"Thou shalt love the Lord thy God with all thy heart, and with all thy soul, and with all thy mind. This is the first and great commandment. And the second is like unto it, Thou shalt love thy neighbour as thyself." *Matthew 22:37-39*

"As we arise each morning, let us determine to respond with love and kindness to whatever might come our way." *President Thomas S. Monson*

1– *Pupating ants make milk – and scientists only just noticed, Nature, November 2022.*

2– *Easter: Easter McEaster Valley, Walter R. Hoge, 2010.*

3– *How Ants & Aphids Help Each Other, ThoughtCo., Science, Animals & Nature, by Debbie Hadley, 2019.*

4– *Communal Relationships, IRE Search Network, Psychology Research Network, What is Psychology?*

5– *Mutualistic Relationship and Mutually Beneficial Relationship, iSpace, author Raja Surya, 2022.*

6

CHICKEN GENETICS

Poultry is a principal component in the global agricultural economy by serving as one of the primary sources of proteins for humans. Worldwide egg and poultry meat production is close to 73 million tons and 100 million tons respectively. Despite such an increase in the growth of poultry industry, this industry is consistently threatened by various diseases, including those caused by viral, bacterial and parasitic infections. These diseases can lead to substantial economic losses in two ways, firstly there is a reduction in the production of poultry related products, and also the input costs like labor and feed get increased. The impact of these loses in poultry industry impacts the livelihood of poor people in the developing countries where up to 25% of monthly income may be lost due to poultry disease.

Chickens have developed different responses to counter these diseases. These responses include immunological and genetic responses of the poultry. The genetic interaction between the host and the pathogen is a key factor in deciding the disease resistance.[1]

Chicken breasts have recently developed an unpleasant texture known as woody chicken breasts. Woody breast is an ongoing challenge facing the entire poultry industry and it's something all producers have been working to resolve.

While humans have been eating chicken for 2,200 years, woody breasts are relatively new. It first appeared in 2015, affects anywhere between 5-30% of birds, and researchers and geneticists are still attempting to find the exact cause – cure.

According to the National Chicken Council, a woody breast is when chicken breast meat is hard to the touch and often pale in color with poor quality texture. It's commonly confused with white striping, which is when fat replaces muscle tissue. However, a woody chicken breast is characterized by a tougher or more complex consistency. Woody chicken breast meat is coarser with fibers that feel "woody" – hence the name. This woodiness is not found in thighs, wings or other cuts.

Based research, it is believed woody breasts are related to the development of the muscle. If birds are growing really efficiently and fast, they're synthesizing muscle and that adds stress. That stress results in degradation of protein so the composition changes and you get collagen and fat that moves into the muscle. A woody chicken breast may have 2% less protein than a normal breast.

Woody breasts are more common in older and bigger birds. They also tend to be more prevalent in chickens raised for commercial production. Broiler breeds have a long history of genetic modifications to improve their productivity. In 20 years of breeding free range heritage breeds, one seldom encounters the issue. The advice given growers to ensure their chickens don't develop woody breasts is to allow their flocks to maintain natural growth patterns.[2]

During my visit into the mystical McEaster Valley in the Sierra Mountains of California, "My friend mentioned that because of my medical background, he wanted to show me something of interest. We walked into a very clean and neatly kept room. I immediately recognized the smell of chickens. Years ago during my college days in Indiana, a poultry class I was taking visited a chicken farm that smelled about the same. We were learning about the industry- the feeding of the chickens, rearing of young pullets for egg production, care of the eggs produced, and what happens to an old hen, which is called a spent hen...He then led me into a large room where the eggs produced were stored. There was almost every size and color you could imagine. They had even developed many different shapes of speckles that could be produced by the hens. Thoughts of line breeding, cross-breeding, and inbreeding flowed through my mind, and I could only imagine the genetic combinations along with viral components that could produce such an array of eggs."[3]

Chickens have several serious welfare problems that come from bad genetics and can be fixed only with good genetics. The biggest problem in many intensively raised animals is pushing the animal's biology for more and more production.

Bone breakage is a very serious problem in both caged and cage-free hens because laying hens have been over selected for egg production. Commercially bred hens put all their calcium and minerals into forming egg shells, and their own bones become depleted. The bones are so weak that in cage-free systems a hen can break her leg just jumping off her perch. The only way to solve this problem is for the industry to accept the fact that birds with strong bones will produce slightly fewer eggs.

Laying hens develop feather pecking and cannibalism. Feather pecking occurs when one hen pecks at another hen's feathers or pulls a feather out all the way. Severe feather pecking can lead to cannibalism, with the victim hen being wounded and then killed by the hen doing the pecking. It probably occurs from the instinct to forage or explore for food and in the crowded pen targets another bird.

Some modern broiler chickens have genetic problems related to growth. The broiler chicken has been so over selected for rapid growth that its bone physiology is abnormal. In normal bone development, the body first "erects" a scaffolding or frame of cartilage and then fills in the frame with minerals that harden into bone. After the bone has hardened, the cartilage dies off through programmed cell death. In broiler chickens, something may go wrong with the cartilage, so the bones don't have support while they're hardening and end up misshapen. Legs become twisted and the chickens are genetically lame.

Modern broiler chickens have been bred to have large appetites so they'll grow super-fast and reach market weight as soon as possible. The trouble is that the breeder chickens, the parents of the broilers, have the same appetites as their chicks. If you let a broiler breeder chicken eat everything she wants, she will become obese, her fertility will decline, and her life will be shortened. These chickens have to be kept on a strict diet just to maintain normal weight.

There are other genetic problems that no one understands. One of the worst cases was the rapist roosters. The rapist roosters violently attack hens and injure and even kill them. Before the 1990s there weren't any rapist roosters. They just suddenly appeared out of the blue. First it was just one strain of roosters that had become aggressive but within a couple of years almost all strains had developed the same behavior. Nobody knows why. The rapist roosters have two problems: they are hyper-aggressive and they have stopped doing the courtship dance the hen needs to see before she will mate. They've lost the little piece of genetic code that makes them do the dance. When the hens don't see the courtship dance, they don't become sexually receptive, which may make the roosters' aggression worse. An unreceptive hen would be a form of frustration because it is a restraint on the rooster's action.[4]

In the mystical McEaster Valley… "one year, about half the chickens became ill. Their egg production dropped, and the eggs produced were of different sizes and shapes. A lot of these eggs were also speckled…We then arranged to have some specialists brought into the valley to examine our chickens and their eggs…A research doctor whose last name was Jones, from the Center for Disease Control in Atlanta, Georgia, was very helpful. He diagnosed the chickens to have come down with the disease chickenpox."[3]

Although the poultry industry has gained momentum during the last few decades, there are still various impediments like improper infrastructure, unscientific management and above all various deadly infectious diseases which incur huge economic losses on the poultry industry. These diseases include viral diseases like Avian Influenza, Marek's Disease, New Castle disease and bacterial diseases like Colibacillosis, Pasteurellosis and Salmonellosis, etc.

Development of disease resistant poultry has been found a successful practice over the use of drugs or vaccines for disease control. Studies involving genome wide associations to figure out certain candidate genes that are involved in disease resistance have also been carried out. Understanding the genes and biological pathways that confer genetic resistance to various infections will lead towards the development of more resistant commercial poultry flocks or improved vaccines against various diseases.[1]

I find the promising research using genetics to improve the health and production of chickens very exciting. "I have recently been finding myself thinking more and more about McEaster Valley and the opportunities there were to contribute my time and talents towards a good cause. I wonder if there was only one chance to accept an offer to live there?"[3]

1– *Application of Genetics & Genomics in Poultry, ScienceEdited by Xiaojun Liu, 2018.*
2– *TODAY, Katie Jackson, 07/19/2022.*
3– *Easter: Easter McEaster Valley, Walter R. Hoge, 2010.*
4– *Animals Make Us Human, Temple Grandin, pages 217-220.*

7

EXTEND THE SHELF LIFE

In 2010 I wrote a book about stories I told my very young children in the 1980s about traveling into a mystical valley in the Sierra foothills, I called it McEaster Valley. There I was shown a food preservation processes that have intrigued me to this day. Since then, I have followed scientific literature discussing the challenges of preserving fresh fruits and vegetables long enough to get it from the fields to the customer's table. I am amazed how Mr. McEaster and his colleagues in McEaster Valley used several materials and processes that have come into the fore front of research since I visited the valley.

"…my friend mentioned that there was a lot of demand for food at one particular time of the year. The demand could only be met by producing food year-round. The food items most in demand were chocolate and hard candy, plus soft, animal-shaped marshmallow treats. Many years ago, even though there were fewer people on the earth, there were never enough of these items available during the season when demand was high. He said that much of the food would spoil if it were stored for several weeks. Then, with a wink from his most always wide-opened eye, he said, 'Let me show you the technique we've found to store food for not only several weeks but several years.' We traveled into a darker part of the trail. Vines were growing above us and some large gourd-shaped fruit or vegetables clinging to the vines. I mentioned these and was told that they were vegetables and had been developed as a food source for the insect that produced the main ingredient for the food storage process. He stated that as they increased the size of the insects, they also had to find a plentiful, highly productive plant to feed them. The plant was able to do very well on some of the less productive ground that was near a warmer region of the valley.

The increased warmth stimulated the insects to grow rapidly and produce the "milk," as he called it, to add as a preservative to the food products being made. I was told that the insects resembled aphids and the "milk" they secreted from their bodies was a complex carbohydrate (sugar). This sugar is much like the sweet material produced by normal aphids that honeydew ants harvest for their food. The milk was collected during the cleaning process of the pens in which they were kept. I was told directly that I could not visit the aphid pens. However, he did allow me to go a little out of our way and see the large bees (not honey bees) that they had developed to make a special, very thin honeycomb, which was used in the storage process. I politely declined. Having allergies, I wasn't sure taking a chance of finding, allergenic pollen-producing plants or toxic stingers had any potential of improving the great day I was having.

...we entered what looked like a cave opening covered by a porous netting. Inside it smelled moist and like a potato cellar, and towards the rear of the cave, there was a dark glow penetrating the darkness. On either side of the cave, there were boxes filled with what looked like soil containing wormlike glowing larvae, and at the end of the cave, glowing insects were flying inside of a cage. I commented that these looked like glow worms and fireflies. My friend said that this was correct but had me notice that the light emitted was a different brightness and cautioned me to not get too close or the corneas of my eyes may be damaged. The light emitted from the insects caused some of my clothing to give off a greenish glow…He told me that the light these valuable insects were giving off had been developed to change the surface of food and form a thin airtight seal that would protect it from spoiling for years. When the food came in contact with water of any kind, the seal would dissolve away and not harm those eating it. He then informed me that our next stop would be the food preservation area.

We walked to the back of the cave and through a door, into a brightly lit white room. On one wall, I could see stainless steel countertop and a conveyer belt that entered through the wall. I was told that on the other side of the wall was where the food was prepared, and this side of the wall was where the food was preserved. He said that the milk produced by the aphid-like insects was mixed into the food before cooking. After the food passed from the other side of the wall into the preservation room, a very thin, honeycomb, waxy material (from the bees) was placed under and on top of the food. The food was then rolled on the conveyer belt to a covered chamber on the other side of the room, which contained the adult fireflies. The food would pass through this chamber in about four and a half seconds and then pass out through the wall behind the chamber. It was then placed deep within the mountain…in an area that was very warm and dry, which was necessary to keep the food fresh."[1]

Many techniques have been studied in order to extend the shelf life of fresh produce (fruits and vegetables), for example, low temperature and high relative humidity, controlled and modified atmosphere packaging/storage, etc. However, each has advantages and disadvantages. The maintenance of the quality of fresh produce is still a major challenge for the food industry.

Research on edible coatings and films has been intense in recent years. Edible coatings have many advantages over other techniques, but only when the coated produces are stored at proper temperatures, which depends on the commodity. They can act as moisture and gas barriers, control microbial growth, preserve the color, texture and moisture of the product and can effectively extend the shelf life of the product. All fruits and vegetables have a natural waxy coating on their surface, which conserves water. Wiping of fruits or abrasions by wrapping paper is sufficient to impair the protective action of waxy layers and increases the rate of respiration of fruits.

A protective coat on fruits and vegetables is given by application of extra continuous or discontinuous film on them. The idea of using edible coatings has also been obtained from the skin of fruits and vegetables. These are thin layers of edible materials which restrict loss of water, oxygen and other soluble material of food. The coating is an integral part of the food which can be eaten as a part of the whole food product.

1. Edible coatings can offer the following advantages to the fresh fruits and vegetables industry: a) improved retention of color, acids, sugar and flavor components; b) maintenance of quality during shipping and storage; c) reduction of storage disorders; and d) improved consumer appeal. Edible coatings have also a high potential to carry active ingredients such as anti-browning agents, colorants, flavors, nutrients, spices and antimicrobial compounds that can extend product shelf life and reduce the risk of pathogen growth on food surfaces.

   During the last few decades, a range of formulations of edible coating have been developed which are widely used in fruits and vegetable industries. In this review article the properties of main coating ingredients and use of diverse coating materials in fruits and vegetables to increase shelf life has been discussed.

2. Materials used for edible coatings can be divided into proteins, lipids and carbohydrates, alone or in combination. They act as barriers to moisture and oxygen during handling and storage and do not solely retard food deterioration but also enhance its safety due to their natural biocide activity or the incorporation of antimicrobial compounds.

   – Lipid based coatings include a group of hydrophobic compounds, which are neutral esters of glycerol and fatty acids. They also include "waxes", which are esters of long-chain monohydric alcohols and fatty acids. Lipid coatings are good barriers to moisture loss. In addition to preventing water loss, lipid coatings have been used to reduce respiration, thereby extending shelf life, and to improve appearance by generating a shiny product in fruits and vegetables. Coatings that include lipid solids can be used to improve coating performance without diminishing moisture-barrier properties.

– Sources of edible oils are paraffin oil, mineral oil, castor oil, acetylated monoglycerides, and vegetable oils, (peanut, corn, and soy) have been used alone or in combination with other ingredients to coat food products.

– Wax coatings are naturally found on fruit and vegetable surfaces, where they help prevent moisture loss, especially in the dry season. Preservation of fresh and dry fruits and nuts by wax coatings have been practiced since time immemorial. Paraffin, carnauba, beeswax and candelilla wax have been used to coat food products, alone or in combination with other ingredients.

Paraffin wax is a distillate of crude petroleum and is used for coating raw fruits and vegetables. Several attempts had been made to develop edible wax from bio-based materials. Its ability to preserve both the nutritional and sensory qualities for four months under low temperature of stored sweet oranges has been reported and its coated products may be considered safe for consumption from the elemental point of view. It may also be a good source of health beneficial minerals. Wax prevents some spoilage and preserves defense-related enzymes in sweet potatoes under ambient temperatures. Brazilian palm tree leaves has a very high melting point and is used as an additive to other waxes to increase toughness and luster. Beeswax or "white wax" is secreted by honeybees, and candelilla wax is exudates of the candelilla plant.

- Fatty acids and monoglycerides are used in coatings mainly as emulsifiers and dispersing agents. Fatty acids are generally extracted from vegetable oils, while monoglycerides are prepared by transesterification of glycerol and tri-glycerol.

- Resins are a group of acidic substances that are produced and secreted as a wound response by specialized plant cells of trees and shrubs. Synthetic resins are petroleum-based products. Shellac resins are secreted by the insect Laccifer lacca found in India. Shellac is compatible with waxes, and gives coated product a high gloss appearance. Shellac and other resins have relatively low permeability to gases and moderate permeability to water vapor. Application of shellac- based waxes reduces internal O_2 levels, and increases internal CO_2 and ethanol levels.

- Protein based coatings sources are used in edible coatings from plants including corn zein, wheat gluten, soy protein, milk proteins and animal derived proteins like collagen, keratin and gelatin. Most protein films are hydrophobic and, therefore, do not present good barriers to moisture. However, dry protein films such as zein, wheat gluten, and soy present relatively low permeability's to O_2. Protein-based films have impressive gas barriers and mechanical properties compared with those from lipids and polysaccharides. Milk proteins and especially sodium caseinate (NaCas) are effective as edible coatings since they provide a high nutritional added value, good taste, show excellent functional properties and are filmogenic. Sodium caseinate has been extensively investigated because of its emulsifying properties.

Furthermore, the mechanical and water barrier properties of sodium caseinate films might be considerably improved at the casein isoelectric point, by calcium cross linking, or by the addition of lipophilic molecules.

Whey is a byproduct of cheese manufacturing that contains approximately 7% dry matter. In general, the dry matter includes proteins, lactose, minerals, about organic acids, and less than 1% fat. In general, these whey proteins are used as additives in the agrofood industry, such as athletic drinks. Viable edible films and coatings have been successfully produced from whey proteins; their ability to serve other functions, viz. carrier of antimicrobials, antioxidants, or other nutraceuticals, without significantly compromising the desirable primary barrier and mechanical properties as packaging films, will add value for eventual commercial applications. For example whey protein coating helped to improve the shelf life of peanuts by retarding the lipid oxidation causing rancidity. In addition, those edible films were reported not to modify the sensory attributes of the coating or its aspect, reduced the growth of mesophilic aerobes, psychrotrophs, yeast and molds and maintained the growth of E. coli, Staphylococcus aureus, Salmonella species, while providing some health benefits for the consumer.[2]

Mr. McEaster used renewable energy and the plants and animals available in the area to care for all the needs in the valley including the preservation of perishable foods. In 2020 Rice University developed inexpensive coatings that can be used to protect fruits and vegetables. Plus, this eco-friendly, micron-thick coating solves problems both for the produce and its consumers. According to an estimate, more than 200 million eggs end up in landfills. Eggs that would otherwise be wasted can be used as the base of an inexpensive coating.

Reducing food shortages in ways that don't involve genetic modification, inedible coatings or chemical additives is important for sustainable living. The work is a remarkable combination of interdisciplinary efforts involving materials engineers, chemists, and biotechnologists from multiple universities across the U.S.A.

Despite being eco-friendly, this edible, multifunctional coating retards dehydration as well. It also offers antimicrobial protection and is mainly impermeable both to water vapor to retard dehydration and to gas to prevent premature ripening. The coating is all-natural and washes off with water.

Egg whites (aka albumen) and yolks account for nearly 70 percent of the coating. Most of the rest consists of nanoscale cellulose extracted from wood, which serves as a barrier to water and keeps produce from shriveling, a small amount of curcumin for its antimicrobial powers, and a splash of glycerol to add elasticity.

Scientists tested the coating on strawberries, avocadoes, bananas, and other fruits. All the fruits maintained their freshness far longer than uncoated produce. What's more, Compression tests showed coated fruit were significantly stiffer and more firm than uncoated.

They chose egg proteins because there are lots of eggs wasted, but it doesn't mean we can't use others. The team is testing proteins that could be extracted from plants rather than animal products to make coatings."[3]

The postharvest loss of fresh fruits and vegetables are estimated to be 20–30%. Given the perishable nature of fruits and vegetables, the use of cold storage is necessary to delay changes related to ripening, such as ethylene making, softening, pigment changes, respiration rate, acidity changes and decrease in weight. However, cold storage is not enough to preserve fruits and vegetables quality at optimum levels during transportation and marketing, often leading to the incidence of severe chilling injury symptoms. So, the appropriate postharvest technologies combined with cold storage are needed.

Today, due to the non-degradability of synthetic packaging materials, there have been growing study interests toward natural resources to making biodegradable edible coatings. These researches mainly focused on developing edible coatings and improving their properties to apply the main desired features of usual synthetic materials.[2]

I have now reached the point in my life where my children have left home and produced seventeen grandchildren that are being well cared for. My close family is more and more becoming the clients that call Camden Pet Hospital the place where their companion animals receive their health needs. I've been practicing in the same building for three years shy of fifty years and there is seldom a day when I don't share special moments with clients I've known over the years. There are days when I have thoughts of places and things I would rather be doing but at the end of a day my spirits are usually lifted by others and my experiences have helped sharpen my brain plasticity and reduce my brain fog.

However, there is one dream that crosses my mind more and more as the years are passing by. I find myself thinking about McEaster Valley and the opportunities that were available. A place where I could contribute my time and talents towards a good cause and work with people that had developed into the best they could be.

1– *Easter: McEaster Valley, 2010, Walter R. Hoge.*
2– *Application of Edible Coatings on Fruits and Vegetables Article in "Imperial Journal of Interdisciplinary Research (IJIR), December 2016.*
3– *Egg-based coating extends the shelf life of perishable fruits and vegetables Egg-based coating preserves fresh produce, Technology, by Pranjal Mehar, June 2020.*

8

LASERS

During my experiences in the Mystical valley in the Sierra Mountains I observed: "...The sun was very bright, and I saw several large rainbows in the area...The vine cable ended near the front door of a large building. The roof went up on all four sides and formed a large, circle. I couldn't tell if the circular structure was open or covered...the building was very large inside...In the center of the building, from the ceiling down, was a large structure that looked like a funnel. The large rim attached to the ceiling had a diameter about the same distance across as the circle I had seen on the roof. At the bottom of the funnel, several hoses were coming out from the circular rim. They came to a point on the end, with a bright light shining through. Several workers were carefully holding these tubes, and it looked like they were tracing or drawing. I was amazed at the speed and accuracy of the work. However, I had no idea what they were doing. My friend, anticipating my thoughts, told me that in this building they were cutting out materials for making toys. He went on to tell me that the large coned area on the roof was used to trap the sun's rays. It had been built in the valley where the sun shined the most throughout the year, and there were several buildings like this one in the area. They had developed cells within the cone that intensified the sun's energy and created an intensified light that cut through the material, similar to laser technology. However, the technology was simple and the cones were also used for heating and lighting if other energy sources were not available."[1]

A laser (Light amplification by stimulated Emission of Radiation) is created when electrons in the atoms in optical materials like glass, crystal, or gas absorb the energy from an electrical current or a light. That extra energy "excites" the electrons enough to move from a lower-energy orbit to a higher-energy orbit around the atom's nucleus.

A laser takes advantage of the quantum properties of atoms that absorb and radiate particles of light called photons. When electrons in atoms return to their normal orbit - or "ground" state - either spontaneously or when "stimulated" with a light or other energy source, even another laser in some cases, they emit more photons.

The idea for lasers goes back to the early 1900s and they have been produced in 1960. Today, lasers come in many sizes, shapes, colors, and levels of power, and are used for everything from surgery in hospitals, to bar code scanners at the grocery store, and even playing music, movies, and video games at home. You might have undergone LASIK surgery, which corrects your vision by using a tiny laser to reshape the cornea of your eye. Some lasers, such as ruby lasers, emit short pulses of light. Others, like helium–neon gas lasers or liquid dye lasers, emit light that is continuous.

Lasers can be tiny constituents of microchips or as immense as National Ignitions Facilities (NIF). The world's largest and most energetic laser is housed in a building 10 stories high and as wide as three football fields.[2] In 2023, Earth & Space reported about a group of scientists in France that have developed lasers capable of diverting lightning away from areas that can be damaged by strikes.

A solar-pumped laser (or solar-powered laser) is a laser that shares the same optical properties as conventional lasers such as emitting a beam consisting of coherent electromagnetic radiation which can reach high power, but which uses solar radiation for pumping the lasing medium. This type of laser is unique from other types in that it does not require any artificial energy source. There is even a hypothetical megastructure called a stellaser which uses a star as both the power source and the lasing medium.

Solar-pumped lasers are not used commercially because the low cost of electricity in most locations means that other more efficient types of lasers that run on electrical power can be more economically used. Solar pumped lasers might become useful in off-grid locations.

Since there is no 'grid' power in space, most spacecraft today use solar power sources, mostly photovoltaic solar cells. Powering lasers requires high levels of power, so the inefficiency of solar cells (usually less than 27% efficiency) motivates interest in solar pumping of lasers. Other potential benefits of solar-pumped lasers might be reduced weight and reduced number of components, affording higher reliability (reduced number of failure modes) versus an electrically pumped laser powered from solar cells. They can also be used for deep space communications, sensors for conditions on earth, detecting and tracking objects in space, as well as power transmission.[3]

According to scientists, sunlight-powered laser could be used instead of fossil fuels to kickstart chemical processes for the energy-intensive production of fertilizer. Conventional lasers are powered by electrical energy from a battery or the grid. Even if renewable generation electricity is used, this requires additional infrastructure and energy is invariably lost along the way.

Scientists outlined how a new sunlight-powered laser could work. Sunlight is abundant, but because it is dilute and variable, it is difficult to collect, store and harness. Nature has already found a way to do this through photosynthesis, when plants turn sunlight, water and carbon into food and energy.

They designed a bio-inspired blueprint for a new laser system that can upgrade natural sunlight into a coherent laser beam.

Other researchers have already started working on solar-powered lasers, but those demonstrated so far need elaborate systems and high levels of refrigeration. Scientists from Italy and Mexico turned to purple bacteria, a group of photosynthetic organisms found in ponds and lakes for inspiration for their new system. Purple bacteria have ring-like antennae which have a reaction center in their middle that allows them to convert sunlight to chemical energy.

If they can find a way to strip out the reaction centers and replace them with a much simpler structure, they could use a bunch of those modified photosynthetic structures to convert sunlight into a laser beam under ambient conditions.

Specifically, the design would be self-contained and neither require an external power source, nor complicated large surrounding lenses. It would be lightweight and portable and entirely natural, organic components. It would constitute the ultimate source of green energy.

They have all these ingredients available and need to find the best way to play molecular Lego and assemble the structures. The end result could be a solar-powered laser that would be low energy, but still useful for a range of applications.

Solar-powered lasers could be used to generate green energy or to bring about chemical processes.

This could tackle the carbon footprint of processes like the production of fertilizer, which is currently responsible for 1-2% of global energy consumption. They could use one of our most abundant resources to help reduce 1-2% of the world's energy consumption![4]

For decades, fusion energy has been a dream. 2022 it came closer to reality. The world's largest nuclear fusion device, which is currently being built in France by a collaboration of 35 nations including the U.S., is expected to be completed by 2025. Known as ITER (International Thermonuclear Experimental Reactor), the experimental device is poised to demonstrate that fusion energy can be a viable energy source. New advances in fusion technology have dramatically increased its chances of success.

With nuclear fission, an atom is split in two, creating enormous energy. Fission powers today's nuclear power plants (as well as atomic weapons). Fusion takes the opposite approach, fusing two atoms together, rather than ripping them apart.

Fusion is different from fission in other ways, as well. Fusion is relatively safe: It produces far less radioactivity and hazardous waste than fission. It doesn't risk out-of-control chain reactions and meltdowns. And it creates more energy than fission, without producing greenhouse gases. In short, fusion sounds like the perfect replacement for fossil fuels, and it would be - if it could be made to work.

The problem is not the science. Scientists understand the physics pretty well; they can make fusion. The obstacles that remain are engineering challenges. Creating fusion energy means making - and controlling and containing - something very like a small star. (After all, our sun is essentially a giant fusion reactor.)

To achieve this, ITER is the most complex engineering project ever built. And results from labs around the world are beginning to confirm this audacious pursuit might actually be possible. A team at the National Ignition Facility in Livermore, California, reported in January 2022 that, for the first time, they achieved a burning plasma condition - the state when the fusion reaction gets most of its energy from the nuclear reaction itself rather than from outside energy sources.

Meanwhile, in the U.K., scientists created 59 megajoules of sustained fusion energy, setting a new world record. In a press release announcing the achievement, project results are a strong indication that they were on the right track to demonstrating full fusion power.

The White House announced a set of initiatives intended to accelerate the development of fusion energy. The goal has changed. The U.S. government has gone from "Let's look at the science of this" to "Let's make some electricity.

Making fusion a practical and cost-effective source of energy will require continued improvements and innovation. But these recent advances suggest that, far from being a quixotic project, a world powered by fusion energy is a realistic goal. Thoughts are that we want to act on climate change and we don't have much time to wait. Fusion is considered the winning card that we must play.[5]

What energy does it take to produce fusion? What happens when 192 of the world's highest-energy lasers converge on a target the size of a peppercorn filled with hydrogen atoms? Answer: the same thing that happens inside the Sun and the stars: fusion!

National Ignition Facilities laser beams can create nuclear fusion in the laboratory by generating the same kinds of temperatures and pressures that exist in the cores of stars and giant planets and inside nuclear weapons. I'm sure that the lasers produced in McEaster Valley would not be able to produce fusion energy. However, I do suspect that their captured sun rays were used to produce enough energy for the production of the materials used for Easter and other heating and lighting to support their needs. I also suspect that some of that energy was produced by modified photosynthetic products from the large plants grown in the area. After all, McEaster Valley is probably the most carbon neutral place on earth.

1– *Easter McEaster Valley, Walter R. Hoge, 2010.*
2– *A Legacy of Lasers and Laser Fusion Pioneers, Lawrence Livermore National Laboratory.*
3– *Solar-pumped laser, from Wikipedia.*
4– *Sunlight could be used to power lasers, by Heriot-Watt's Institute of Photonics & Quantum Sciences University, New Journal of Physics, 2022.*
5– *Determining Nuclear Fusion's Future, Avery Hurt, Discover Magazine, January/February 2023.*

9

BIOLUMINESCENCE

Visiting the mystical McEaster Valley in the Sierra Mountains, "…we entered what looked like a cave opening covered by a porous netting. Inside it smelled moist and like a potato cellar, and towards the rear of the cave, there was a dark glow penetrating the darkness. On either side of the cave, there were boxes filled with what looked like soil containing wormlike glowing larvae, and at the end of the cave, glowing insects were flying inside the cage. I commented that these looked like glow worms and fireflies. My friend said that this was correct but had me notice that the light emitted was a different brightness and cautioned me to not get too close or the corneas of my eyes may be damaged…He told me that the light these valuable insects were giving off had been developed to change the surface of food and form a thin airtight seal that would protect it from spoiling for years…"[1]

I suspect the glow worms and fireflies developed in McEaster Valley were developed from the New Zealand Fungus Gnat. The scientific name *Arachnocampa luminosa* does a good job in describing this type of fly, as roughly translated it means "glowing spider bug." This is a reference to two of its more peculiar traits: its habit of glowing in the dark, and the method it uses to capture its prey. There are four basic stages within this fly's life: the egg, larvae, pupae, and finally adult (the larvae itself molts four times – there are 5 instars).

Adults are slightly larger than a mosquito, being just over ½ in (1.5 cm) in length. They have six long legs and, like all flies, have only one pair of wings. Organs known as halteres are located just behind the wings. They act as flight stabilizers, preventing the fungus gnats from flying upside down. One peculiar feature in the adults is that they lack mouths, and as a result cannot ingest food. Therefore, they have short life spans – upon emerging from the pupa, males have only 3-5 days to live and females have only 1-2 days. The adults, like the larvae, have the ability to glow, but females often lose their luminescence after laying their eggs.

The larvae are commonly known as glowworms – not to be confused with the larvae of fire flies, which are also known as glowworms (fire flies are actually a type of beetle). When the larvae hatch, they are voracious hunters and have large mandibles. Their bodies are relatively featureless. The larvae are brown in color, but the skin is transparent, allowing the bluish-green light to shine through.

All stages of the New Zealand fungus gnat, other than the eggs, glow. This bioluminescence is internal, and is brought about by chemical reactions that occur in a special organ located at the end of the excretory tube. These chemicals include luciferin, which is a waste product that the gnat produces; ATP (adenosine triphosphate), which is a molecule that even we rely on to keep us alive; and oxygen.

The fungus gnats also produce an enzyme known as luciferase. It causes a chemical reaction with luciferin that speeds a reaction that results in the production of light. This light is used to attract food and mates; the hungrier a larva is, the brighter it glows. Also, if no male is waiting on a female pupa when the she is ready to emerge and mate, the female will glow brighter, and will flash its lights on and off. The light turns off when any one of the chemicals needed to produce it is cut off from the light organ. Larvae also produce a brighter light when fighting, but the reason for this is not known.

New Zealand fungus gnats are common throughout New Zealand, and are often found in damp, sheltered areas such as caves, and are usually associated with streams. Although they are quite common, their habitat must meet some requirements: it must be humid, it must have hanging surfaces, it must be dark for a good portion of the day so that their glow can be seen, and the air must be protected from winds, which can tangle up their dangling homes.

The fungus gnats create their own homes from their very own mucous and silk. They can create vast networks of horizontal tubes that they suspend from branches or rock. During the day, they hide in crevices, but when night comes they enter these tubes and begin to hunt. Silk threads that can reach 20 in (50 cm) in length are suspended from these tubes and act as fishing lines.

New Zealand fungus gnat larvae are ingenious hunters. Suspended from their tubes are several dozen "fishing lines" made of silk and covered with globules of sticky mucous. When night comes and the larva begins to glow, various insects that are attracted to the light and fly near get caught in the sticky mucous of the fishing lines. Vibrations are sent up the line and sensed by the larva, which then begins to reel in its catch by swallowing the line. At the same time, certain chemicals within the mucous begins to paralyze the prey so that it doesn't try to break free, or get ensnared in other lines or damage the one it's on. When the prey has been reeled up, the larva bites it, kills it, and then either sucks out its juices or eats the entire thing. Since the adults lack mouths, the larvae must eat enough food to keep the adult alive during mating.

Fungus gnats can be cannibalistic, the larvae often eating other larvae or even adults that happen to fly into the fishing lines. They also catch and feed upon mosquitoes, moths, stone flies, sand flies, caddis flies, midges, ants, spiders, millipedes, and even snails.[2]

"I didn't see mosquitoes or other plant or animal pests during my day or night outdoor visits in McEaster Valley. I suspect the firefly and glow worms served two functions. Insect vector and crop pest control plus a source of energy to preserve food."

Bioluminescence is light produced by a chemical reaction within a living organism. Bioluminescence is a type of chemiluminescence, which is simply the term for a chemical reaction where light is produced.

(Bioluminescence is chemiluminescence that takes place inside a living organism.) Bioluminescence is a "cold light." Cold light means less than 20% of the light generates thermal radiation, or heat.

Most bioluminescent organisms are found in the ocean. These bioluminescent marine species include fish, bacteria, and jellies. Some bioluminescent organisms, including fireflies and fungi, are found on land. There are almost no bioluminescent organisms native to freshwater habitats.

The chemical reaction that results in bioluminescence requires two unique chemicals: luciferin and luciferase. Luciferin is the compound that actually produces light. The interaction of the luciferase with oxidized (oxygen-added) luciferin creates a byproduct, called oxyluciferin. More importantly, the chemical reaction creates light. Very few organisms can produce more than one color.

Some bioluminescent organisms produce (synthesize) luciferin on their own. Some organisms do not synthesize luciferin. Instead, they absorb it through other organisms, either as food or in a symbiotic relationship. Some organisms emit light continuously. Some species of fungi present in decaying wood, for instance, emit a fairly consistent glow, called foxfire. Most organisms, however, use their light organs to flash for periods of less than a second to about 10 seconds. These flashes can occur in specific spots, such as the dots on a squid. Other flashes can illuminate the organism's entire body.[3]

The last decade or so has seen great advances in protein engineering, synthetic chemistry, and physics which have allowed luciferins and luciferases to reach previously uncharted applications. The bioluminescence reaction is now routinely used for gene assays, the detection of protein–protein interactions, high-throughput screening (HTS) in drug discovery, hygiene control, analysis of pollution in ecosystems and in vivo imaging in small mammals.

Moving away from sensing and imaging, the more recent highlights of the applications of bioluminescence in biomedicine include the bioluminescence-induced photo-uncaging of small-molecules, bioluminescence based photodynamic therapy (PDT) and the use of bioluminescence to control neurons.

There has also been an increase in blue-sky research such as the engineering of various light emitting plants. This has led to lots of exciting multidisciplinary science across various disciplines.[4]

Bioluminescence is a "cold light." Cold light means less than 20% of the light generates thermal radiation, or heat. I know that when I was in McEaster Valley I noticed the light emitted from the glow worms and fire flies had a different brightness than I had ever seen. Mr. McEaster cautioned me to not get too close or the corneas of my eyes might be damaged…He told me that the light these valuable insects were giving off had been developed to change the surface of food and form a thin airtight seal. Do you suppose that the "cold light" produced from these organisms had been bioengineered to produce a light that generates much greater than 20% thermal radiation? If so, that would explain how the light could change the surface of the food and form a thin airtight seal that placed in the right place could preserve food for years.[1]

> Here come real stars to fill the upper skies,
> And here on earth come emulating flies,
> That though they never equal stars in size,
> (And they were never really stars at heart)

Achieve at times a very star-like start.
Only, of course, they can't sustain the part.
Robert Frost

1– *Easter: McEaster Valley, Walter R. Hoge, 2010.*
2– *The New Zealand Fungus Gnat known as the "glowing spider bug."*
3– *National Geographic Education: Bioluminescence—Living Light.*
4– *Applications of bioluminescence in biotechnology and beyond, Chem. Soc. Rev, 2021.*

10

YETI MYTHS LEGENDS

Letter from Michael Retford, DVM, 2020-11-07 Squatch (Sasquatch or Bigfoot): "While growing up in Southeast Idaho, I spent a lot of time on horseback in the river bottoms of the Snake River. I gained an appreciation for nature and formed a deep connection to the living things that surrounded me. Many of my friends were Native Americans belonging to the Shoshone Bannock tribe. My friendship with them added to my love for nature and respect for life in all its forms.

I had heard legends of a large man-like creature and figured they were talking about a Sasquatch. I had seen things on television and about the supposed creature but I had always remained curious yet skeptical. My formal education in zoology followed by attending veterinary school gave me a greater understanding of how little we actually know about all of the life forms on our planet. I gained a more open mind about many things but when I came to the subject of Bigfoot, I still remained a skeptic. Then one night that all changed.

A friend of mine owned property a few hundred yards from my cabin in the woods near Island Park, Idaho. Due to my background as a veterinarian and him having watched me track wild animals, he called me over to his property to inspect some strange tracks. It was an experience that shook me to the core!

When I first got to his property and saw the tracks, I immediately started trying to figure out how he could have pulled off such an elaborate hoax. The more I tried to reason that these giant footprints that looked just like a huge barefoot human's, the clearer it became that they were real! They looked exactly like a large (and I mean like 18 inches from toe to heal) human footprints. By the depth they penetrated the snow compared to my 230 pound size 12 prints, I estimated this animal weighed several hundred pounds. Even if I jumped up and then landed on one foot, mine only sank about 3 inches into the snow. These prints were a good 4-8 inches depending on the location (sunny versus shady etc). Give the amount of surface area these approximately 18 by 8 inch tracks covered, that's a lot of snow to pack down with each step. The spacing between each footfall varies between 4-6 feet. Even if I tried to jump between steps, in that snow, I couldn't come anywhere near that.

The prints paralleled moose tracks. I didn't know if it was tracking the moose or walking along with it. I followed the tracks through the forest until they came to a road where a snowplow had passed and couldn't find where they went from there.

I had thought of Sasquatch or Bigfoot as a legend, a myth, a scary campfire story up until that day. Every bit of my experience as a biologist, a scientist, an animal doctor, an outdoorsman, a hunter/tracker, and a realist could only come to one conclusion: These tracks were made by an animal weighing several hundred pounds with human like feet, HUGE stride, and the ability to walk through deep snow like no barefoot human could dream of."[1]

Traveling into the mystical McEaster Valley in the Sierra Mountains I recorded, "Here and there, I noticed large fur-covered footprints that had been placed there by an animal, the looks of which I couldn't imagine. I immediately thought of Big Foot of the Southwest, but these were not primate feet."[2]

Scientists suspect that the huge animal sizes living during the age of the dinosaurs were at least partially due to the increased oxygen levels in the atmosphere. Looking back at my experiences going into the valley I recall, "...a sense of euphoria...running down trail...feeling young and physically like I had never felt better. My mind was alive, I could see and hear and smell and taste and touch and feel things better than I ever had before."[2] Could there have been higher atmospheric levels of oxygen in the area that helped me experience this hyper state of my mind and my middled aged body?

I do know that I saw oversized plants and invertebrates with my own eyes and the descriptions of the foot prints found near Yellowstone Park by Dr. Retford fit the ones I saw. Over the years I have wondered if the foot prints were from a very large rabbit and not a Yeti (big foot).

The Yeti is a character in ancient legends and folklore of the Himalaya people. In most of the tales, the Yeti is a figure of danger, author Shiva Dhakal told the BBC. The moral of the stories is often a warning to avoid dangerous wild animals and to stay close and safe within the community.

Alexander the Great demanded to see a Yeti when he conquered the Indus Valley in 326 B.C. But, according to National Geographic, local people told him they were unable to present one because the creatures could not survive at that low an altitude.

In modern times, when Westerners started traveling to the Himalayas, the myth became more sensational. In 1921, a journalist named Henry Newman interviewed a group of British explorers who had just returned from a Mount Everest expedition. The explorers told the journalist they had discovered some very large footprints on the mountain to which their guides had attributed to "metoh-kangmi," essentially meaning "man-bear snow-man." Newman got the "snowman" part right but mistranslated "metoh" as "filthy." Then he seemed to think "abominable" sounded even better and used this more menacing name in the paper. Thus, a legend was born.

The Russian government took an interest in the Yeti in 2011, and organized a conference of Bigfoot experts in western Siberia. Bigfoot researcher and biologist John Bindernagel claimed that he saw evidence that the Yeti not only exist but also build nests and shelters out of twisted tree branches. That group made headlines around the world when they issued a statement that they had "indisputable proof" of the Yeti, and were 95 percent sure it existed based on some grey hairs found in a clump moss in a cave.

Bindernagel may have been impressed, but another scientist who participated in the same expedition concluded that the "indisputable" evidence was hoaxed. Jeff Meldrum, a professor of anatomy and anthropologist at Idaho State University who endorses the existence of Bigfoot, said that he suspected the twisted tree branches had been faked. Not only was there obvious evidence of tool-made cuts in the supposedly "Yeti-twisted" branches, but also the trees were conveniently located just off a well-traveled trail and hardly in a remote area.

Meldrum concluded that the whole Russian expedition was more of a publicity stunt than a serious scientific endeavor, likely designed to increase tourism in the impoverished coal-mining region. Despite quasi-official claims of "indisputable proof" of the Yeti, nothing more has come of the story.[3]

Truth is a property not so much of thoughts and ideas but more properly of beliefs and assertions. But to believe or assert something is not enough to make it true, or else the claim that 'to believe something makes it true' would be just as true as the claim that 'to believe something does not make it true.'

For centuries, philosophers have agreed that thought or language is true if it corresponds to an independent reality. For Aristotle, 'to say that what it is, and what is not is not, is true.' For Avicenna, truth is 'what corresponds in the mind to what is outside it.' And for Aquinas, it is 'the adequation of things and the intellect'. Unfortunately for this so-called correspondence theory of truth, the mind does not perceive reality as it is, but only as it can, filtering, distorting, and interpreting it. In modern times, it has been argued that truth is constructed by social and cultural processes, to say nothing of individual desires and dispositions.

According to the coherence theory of truth, a thing is more likely to be true if it fits comfortably into a large and coherent system of beliefs. It remains that the system could be a giant fiction, entirely detached from reality, but this becomes increasingly unlikely as we investigate, curate, and add to its components -assuming, and it is quite an assumption, that we are operating in good faith, with truth, rather than self-preservation or -aggrandizement, as our aim.

According to the pragmatic theory of truth, truth leads to successful action; therefore, successful action is an indicator of truth. Clearly, we could not have sent a rocket to the moon if our science had been wide off the mark. The truth is only the expedient in the way of our thinking, just as the right is only the expedient in the way of our behaving. If something works, it may well be true; if it doesn't, it most probably isn't. But what if something works for me but not for you? Is that thing then true for me but not for you?

That a thing fits into a system, or leads to successful action, may suggest that it is true, but does not tell us much about what truth actually is, while the correspondence theory of truth is so thin as to be almost or entirely tautological. And perhaps for a reason. It has been argued that to say that 'X is true' is merely to say that X, and therefore that truth is an empty predicate. Truth is not a real property of things. Rather, it is a feature of language used to emphasize, agree, or hypothesize, or for stylistic purposes. For example, it can be used to explicate the Catholic dogma of papal infallibility: 'Everything that the pope says is true.' But this is merely shorthand for saying that if the Pope says A, then it is the case that A; and if he says B, then B.

For some thinkers, something can only be true or false if it is open to verification, at least in theory if not also in practice. The truth of something lies at the end of our inquiry into that thing. But as our inquiry can have no end, the truth of something can never be more than our best opinion of that thing. If best opinion is all that we can have or hope for, then best opinion is as good as truth, and truth is a redundant concept. But best opinion (whether it be science or religion) is only best because, at least on average, it is closest to the truth, which, as well as instrumental value, has deep intrinsic value.[4]

Dr. Thomas Burnett, a philosopher and science historian, aptly put it this way: It is one thing to celebrate science for its achievements and remarkable ability to explain a wide variety of phenomena in the natural world. But to claim there is nothing knowable outside the scope of science would be similar to a successful fisherman saying that whatever he can't catch in his nets does not exist. Once you accept that science is the only source of human knowledge, you have adopted a philosophical position (scientism) that cannot be verified, or falsified, by science itself. It is, in a word, unscientific.

Likewise, we find extreme orthodoxy within religion that rejects all other avenues for seeking truth, claiming that truth can only come from revelation concerning the creation of our beautiful world and all other aspects of human life. Both worldviews put limits upon human inquiry.

Neither reality is a healthy place in which to live and to learn and to progress. We must become more comfortable with uncertainty. Think about it: From a spiritual standpoint, how many of you would claim that you know everything there is to know about the gospel of Jesus Christ? I certainly wouldn't claim that! Likewise, no self-respecting scientist who truly understands the nature of science would claim that we know all truths about the natural world. We still don't fully understand all the causes of cancer or how to cure it. If we thought we knew everything, the scientific enterprise would come to a screeching halt! Thankfully, the more I learn about science, the more I understand the depths of that which we are yet to know.

Dogmatism in science or in religion closes down your ability to learn and progress. If something seems to conflict between what science reveals and what you have learned through your religious faith, don't abandon one or the other. Hold off judgment, be patient, and keep an open mind to truth from both sides.

When he was an apostle, President Russell M. Nelson said at the dedication of the BYU Life Sciences Building, "There is no conflict between science and religion. Conflict only arises from an incomplete knowledge of either science or religion, or both."[5]

Dr. Retford further wrote: "We sent the pictures of the 'giant footprints' to Dr Jeff Meldrum at Idaho State University. He is without a doubt one of the world's leading crypto zoologists and a well-respected scientist and professor. He said he had no doubts as to their authenticity and agreed with my conclusions.

Take it as you will but for me, there is no longer doubt in my mind, there are large ape-like animals in the forest who mean us no harm and it appears they are herbivores based on there never being any signs found of them killing another animal.

Don't fear them. I still frequently walk alone in the woods. I make noise and carry bear spray but if I ever have the chance to meet one of these creatures, I shall do so as if I were meeting a silverback gorilla in his territory. With meekness, gentleness, non-threating body language. I will drop my head and avoid eye contact, and slowly extend my hand palm up and hope it will recognize this as a universal friendly request for acceptance and submission amongst the primates worldwide.

I just hope it doesn't desire to take me home and make me a pet..."[1]

In 2007, American TV show host Josh Gates claimed he found three mysterious footprints in snow near a stream in the Himalayas. Locals were skeptical, suggesting that Gates — who had only been in the area for about a week — simply misinterpreted a bear track. Nothing more was learned about what made the print, and the track can now be found not in a natural history museum but instead in a small display at Walt Disney World.

The lack of hard evidence despite decades of searches doesn't deter true believers; the fact that these mysterious creatures haven't been found is not taken as evidence that they don't exist, but instead how rare, reclusive, and elusive they are. Like Bigfoot, a single body would prove that the Yeti exists, though no amount of evidence can prove they don't exist. For that reason alone, these animals — real or not — will likely always be with us.[3]

1– *Letter written by my brother-in-law Michael Retford, DVM following a discussion we had about "Squatch" during a visit to his home in Island Park Idaho (near Yellowstone Park) Memorial Day weekend 2020…*

2– *Easter: Easter McEaster Valley, Walter R. Hoge, 2010.*

3– *Live Science, The Yeti: Asia's Abominable Snowman, Benjamin Radford, BS, MS, Bad Science columnist, 2017.*

4– *Psychology Today, What Is Truth, Jessica Schrader, 2019.*

5– *Faith and Science: Symbiotic Pathways to Truth, Jamie L. Jensen, Associate Professor of Biology, BYU Devotional address, 11-03-2020.*

11

LIGHT

Moaning Caverns is a solutional cave located in the Calaveras County, California, near Vallecito, California in the heart of the state's Gold Country. It is developed in marble of the Calaveras Formation. It was discovered in modern times by gold miners in 1851, but it has long been known as an interesting geological feature by prehistoric peoples. It gets its name from the moaning sound that echoed out of the cave luring people to the entrance, however expansion of the opening to allow access for the public disrupted the sounds. The portion of the cave developed for tourists consists of a spacious vertical shaft 165 feet tall, which is descended by a combination of stairs and a unique 100-foot-high (30 m) spiral staircase built in the early 1900s. It is open to the public for walking tours and spelunking. Including the off-trail areas, the cave reaches a depth of 410 feet (124 m).

Moaning Caverns is also an archaeological site. There are many human bones in the cave. Some are at least 12,000 years old. The cave has long been the resting spot for the bodies of prehistoric people and animals who fell into its opening. *Wikipedia*.

I have been into the caverns several times with my boys as a scout leader and with my brother-in-law, Michael Retford, and his two sons. I will never forget the unique experience of total darkness in Moaning Caverns after we shut off our flashlights for several minutes, with a child in front and behind me crawling through tight tunnels in the cave. I also remember being grateful that none of us had a panic attack trapped behind and in front of another person. My son Brad, remembers when Hal Stephens found himself in this situation with his sons in the Moaning Caverns tunnels.

We take natural light for granted. We don't realize it, but it gets us up in the morning, takes us through our regular day, and its absence sends us into our nightly slumber. So, what happens when our body is deprived of light? Very strange things, indeed.

Two cave explorers, Josie Laures and Antoine Senni, took on a particularly gloomy mission in the name of science — living alone in a dark, desolate cave for months to test the effects of isolation, loneliness, and darkness. They didn't even have the company of one another; they resided in separate caves a few hundred yards apart.

The only people they stayed in touch with were researchers at a control point who tracked their sleeping and eating habits, as well as memory and vital signs. Laures and Senni weren't given any insight about how time was passing outside of their dark living holes. When they finally emerged, they had to wear dark goggles to shelter their eyes from the bright sunlight, and their senses of time were warped.

Laures spent 88 days in the cave, while Senni spent 126. When Laures came out of her cave on March 12, 1965, she thought the date was February 25. Senni's sense of time was even more distorted — just a few days before emerging from his cave on April 5, he thought it was February 4. In their minds, they'd lost months.

The researchers reported that Senni would sleep for stretches of 30 hours at a time, but wake up believing he had just taken a quick nap. Further research done on human physiology in total isolation reveals that humans can even stretch their sleep cycles out for 48 hours.

Our body's natural cycle and circadian rhythm rely on natural light, and without it, our physiology and mind can be adversely affected. The same goes for living in complete isolation — being deprived of interaction of any sort can result in psychosis.

In fact, Laures and Senni turned to animals most of us would reject: rodents. Senni spread jam on the cave floor to try and attract a mouse he could keep as a pet. His attempt went awry after he tried to trap the mouse in a dish and, due to poor aim, accidentally crushed the rodent instead. Laures, reported that a white mouse was her sole companion throughout the whole ordeal.

Since this type of sensory deprivation is often used as a torture technique during wartime, a British study locked up six volunteers in dark, solitary confinement for 48 hours to test its effects. Adam Bloom, an extroverted stand-up comic, fared particularly terribly. He says at one point, he started singing and then suddenly burst into tears, feeling as if his emotions were running out of control. He found himself suspecting the whole experiment was a trick. He wondered how did he know who these people really were? What if they'd gone home and he was trapped down there forever? The utter darkness caused him to completely lose his sense of time. He'd doze off and then wake up not knowing whether it was night or day, and even meals didn't help restore a feeling of normalcy. In fact, he and some of the other volunteers actually started hallucinating — a heap of 500 oysters, tiny cars, snakes, zebras, fighter planes, mosquitos, and even the sensation of the room taking off.

The BBC went on to produce a documentary using footage of these six volunteers called *Total Isolation*.

Bottom line: humans need light and interaction to stay sane. Without light, we lose our sense of time, and without interaction, we become consumed with loneliness and boredom. With this sensory deprivation comes the strangest, most unimaginable psychological effects.[1]

When you think of light, you probably think of what your eyes can see. However, the light our human eyes can detect is only a sliver of the total amount of light that's out there. The electromagnetic spectrum is the term scientists use to describe the entire range of light that exists. From radio waves to gamma rays, most of the light in the universe is, in fact, invisible to us.

Light is a wave of alternating electric and magnetic fields. The propagation of light isn't much different than waves crossing an ocean. Like any other wave, light has a few fundamental properties that describe it. For example, one is its frequency, measured in hertz (Hz), which counts the number of waves that pass by a point in one second. Another closely related property is its wavelength: the distance from the peak of one wave to the peak of the next. In fact, these two attributes are inversely related. The larger the frequency, the smaller the wavelength, and vice versa.

The electromagnetic waves your eyes detect – visible light – oscillate between 400 and 790 terahertz (THz). To put it another way, that's several hundred trillion times a second. As an illustration, the wavelengths are roughly the size of a large virus: 390 – 750 nanometers (1 nanometer = 1 billionth of a meter; a meter is about 39 inches long). Our brain interprets the various wavelengths of light as different colors. For example, red has the longest wavelength, and violet the shortest. When we pass sunlight through a prism, we see that it's actually composed of many wavelengths of light. The prism creates a rainbow by redirecting each wavelength out at a slightly different angle.

But light doesn't stop at red or violet. Indeed, just like there are sounds we can't hear, there is an enormous range of light that our eyes can't detect. In general, the longer wavelengths come from the coolest and darkest regions of space. Meanwhile, the shorter wavelengths measure extremely energetic phenomena.

Astronomers use the entire electromagnetic spectrum to observe a variety of things. Radio waves and microwaves are the longest wavelengths and lowest energies of light. With this in mind, they are used to peer inside dense interstellar clouds and track the motion of cold, dark gas. Radio telescopes have been used to map the structure of our galaxy. Additionally, microwave telescopes are sensitive to the remnant glow of the Big Bang.

Infrared telescopes excel at finding cool, dim stars, slicing through interstellar dust bands. Plus, they even measure the temperatures of planets in other solar systems. The wavelengths of infrared light are long enough to navigate through clouds that would otherwise block our view. By using large infrared telescopes, astronomers peer through the dust lanes of our galaxy into the Milky Way's core.

The majority of stars emit most of their electromagnetic energy as visible light, the tiny portion of the spectrum to which our eyes are sensitive. Because wavelength correlates with energy, the color of a star tells us how hot it is: red stars are coolest, blue are hottest. The coldest of stars emit hardly any visible light at all; they can only be seen with infrared telescopes.

At wavelengths shorter than violet, we find the ultraviolet, or UV, light. You may be familiar with UV from its ability to give you a sunburn. Astronomers use it to hunt out the most energetic of stars and identify regions of star birth. When viewing distant galaxies with UV telescopes, most of the stars and gas disappear, and all the stellar nurseries pop into view.

Beyond UV come the highest energies in the electromagnetic spectrum: X-rays and gamma rays. Our atmosphere blocks this light, so astronomers must rely on telescopes in space to see the X-ray and gamma ray universe. X-rays come from exotic neutron stars, the vortex of superheated material spiraling around a black hole. Or from diffuse clouds of gas in galactic clusters that are heated to many millions of degrees.

Meanwhile, gamma rays – the shortest wavelength of light and deadly to humans – unveil violent events. These include supernova explosions, cosmic radioactive decay, and even the destruction of antimatter. Gamma ray bursts are among the most energetic singular events in the universe. They are a brief flickering of gamma ray light from distant galaxies when a star explodes and creates a black hole.

The electromagnetic spectrum describes all the wavelengths of light, both seen and unseen.[2]

The scientific law of the universe is well supported by our belief that you cannot create something from nothing and that all things come from previously existing constituents. Hence, light is generated from some source. This is also related to the fact that light is a wave, which means it is always in motion. Waves cannot be stored, whether they are of light, oceanwater, sound, or anything else. Expressed in scriptural terms: "There is no such thing as immaterial matter. All spirit is matter, but it is more fine or pure, and can only be discerned by purer eyes; We cannot see it; but when our bodies are purified, we shall see that it is all matter" (Doctrine & Covenants 131:7-8).

When considering spiritual light, this scientific reality – that light cannot be stored – becomes of great significance. Since light must be generated from a source, even spiritual light that radiates from (and is within) us must come from a light source. Whether it be within us or at some place at the center of the universe, is the Light of Christ.

Jesus declared, "I am the true light that lighteth every man that cometh into the world" (Doctrine & Covenants 93:2). "which light proceedeth forth from the presence of God to fill the immensity of space – the light which is in all things, which giveth life to all things, which is the law by which all things are governed, even the power of God who sitteth upon his throne, who is in the bosom of eternity, who is in the midst of all things" Doctrine & Covenants 88:12-13. Often the importance of the Light of Christ is oversimplified when this unseen power is defined as a person's conscience. While there is scriptural support that the Light of Christ aids us in the determinations of right versus wrong, it is also clear that such light is intended to lead one to the gospel, wherein the more constant guidance from the Holy Ghost can be obtained.[3]

We should also endeavor to discern when we "withdraw [ourselves] from the Spirit (light) of the Lord, that it may have no place in [us] to guide [us] in wisdom's paths that [we] may be blessed, prospered, and preserved" (Mosiah 2:36). Precisely because the promised blessing is that we may always have His Spirit to be with us, we should attend to and learn from the choices and influences that separate us from the Holy Spirit.

The standard is clear. If something we think, see, hear, or do distances us from the Holy Ghost, then we should stop thinking, seeing, hearing, or doing that thing. If that which is intended to entertain, for example, alienates us from the Holy Spirit, then certainly that type of entertainment is not for us. Because the Spirit cannot abide that which is vulgar, crude, or immodest, then clearly such things are not for us. Because we estrange the Spirit of the Lord when we engage in activities we know we should shun, then such things definitely are not for us.

As we gain experience with the Holy Ghost, we learn that the intensity with which we feel the Spirit's influence is not always the same. Strong, dramatic spiritual impressions do not come to us frequently. Even as we strive to be faithful and obedient, there simply are times when the direction, assurance, and peace of the Spirit are not readily recognizable in our lives. In fact, the Book of Mormon describes faithful Lamanites who "were baptized with fire and with the Holy Ghost, and they knew it not" (3 Ne. 9:20).

The influence of the Holy Ghost is described in the scriptures as "a still small voice" (1 Kgs. 19:12; see also 3 Ne. 11:3) and a "voice of perfect mildness" (Hel. 5:30). Thus, the Spirit of the Lord usually communicates with us in ways that are quiet, delicate, and subtle.[4]

Clayton Christensen, whose theory of disruptive innovation made him a key influence on Silicon Valley powerhouses like Netflix and Intel and twice earned him the title of the world's most influential living management thinker, died Jan. 23, 2020 at age 67 from complications from cancer in Boston, Massachusetts, where he had been a notable part of the Latter-day Saint community for over 40 years.

Clay was the most influential business theorist of his generation. But his legacy goes well beyond the books he wrote and the speeches he gave. Clay was absolutely one of a kind…in intellect, generosity, compassion and depth of faith…

Among the world's most influential business leaders and dignitaries, Clay was always the smartest person in the room—but also, incredibly, humble. His loyalty to his faith was not carefully separated out from his teaching or consulting life. People knew where Christensen stood and as The New York Times noted, "A deeply religious man and a member of the Church of Jesus Christ of Latter-day Saints, he incorporated his musings on religion into his academic work."

In fact, in his book "The Power of Everyday Missionaries", he is very clear about his conviction to let his faith vitally invigorate every aspect of his life, without political correctness or stashing it away as not fit for polite company.[5]

Every human being has had many spiritual light experiences. Some are not recognizable and most come in quiet, delicate, subtle ways and maybe the light comes as a warm feeling that you experienced from helping others or as a confirmation that you were making a correct discission in your life. Clayton relates a spiritual light experience that was a pivotal in his life:

In his last year of college, Christensen won a Rhodes Scholarship, and he went to Oxford to study econometrics. Being a Mormon at Oxford, it was soon clear, was going to be extremely inconvenient. He had already served a two-year mission to Korea, and thought he was certain of his beliefs, but now he decided he'd better figure out for sure whether his was the true church. Each night at eleven, he knelt down and told God out loud that he needed to know whether the Book of Mormon was true. After praying, he sat and read one page, and then he stopped and thought about it. Then he knelt and prayed out loud again, asking God to tell him whether the book was true. Then he read another page. He did this for an hour each night for many weeks.

"I told God how desperate I was to find out if this was a true book, and I told Him that if He would reveal to me that it was true, that I then intended to dedicate my life to building this kingdom. And I told Him if it wasn't true that I needed to know that for certain, too, because then I would dedicate my life to finding out what was true. Then I would sit in the chair, and I read the first page of the Book of Mormon, and when I got down to the bottom of the page, I stopped, and I thought about what I had read on that page, and I asked myself, 'Could this have been written by a Charlatan who was trying to deceive people, or was this really written by a prophet of God? And what did it mean for me in my life?' And then I put the book down and knelt in prayer and verbally asked God again, 'Please tell me if this is a true book.' Then I would sit in the chair and pick up the book and turn the page and read another page, pause at the bottom, and do the same thing. I did this for an hour every night, night after night in that cold, damp room, at the Queen's College Oxford.

By the time I got to the chapters at the end of 2nd Nephi, one evening (October 1975) when I said my prayer and sat in my chair and opened the book, all of a sudden there came into that room a beautiful, warm, loving spirit that just surrounded me and permeated my soul, and enveloped me in a feeling of love that I just had not imagined I could feel. And I began to cry, and I didn't want to stop crying because as I looked through my tears at the words in the Book of Mormon, I could see truth in those words that I never imagined I could comprehend before. And I could see the glories of eternity and I could see what God had in store for me as one of His sons. And I didn't want to stop crying. That spirit stayed with me the whole hour, and then every evening as I prayed and sat with the Book of Mormon by the fireplace in my room, that same spirit returned and it changed my heart and my life forever.

I look back in the conflict that I experienced, wondering whether I could afford to spend an hour everyday apart from the study of applied econometrics to find if the Book of Mormon was true, and you know, I use applied econometrics maybe once a year, but I use my knowledge that the Book of Mormon is the word of God many times every day of my life. In all of the education that I have pursued, that is the single most useful piece of knowledge that I ever gained."[5]

In the mystical McEaster valley I mention… "Many years ago, during the early light of day, I was walking in the Sierra foothills with my Labrador retriever, Beau. As the sun began to rise in the east, I noticed a passageway into a valley that shone like gold, much the same as the sun's reflection appears when it sets at the end of the day and reflects off the windows to the east. I didn't think much about it and continued walking eastward on the south side of the valley entrance. Approximately twenty minutes later, I again looked toward the valley. The color of gold had changed to the various colors of vegetation, with a beautiful blue cloudless sky marking the horizon. However, the colors were bright and seemed to glow, more like a painting than the familiar California countryside to which I had become accustomed…"

After my visit to Mc:Easter Valley I awoke: "…I slowly rose to my feet and looked towards the valley I thought I had visited. The valley was there, but its colors were not any brighter or showing more of a painted glow than the surrounding Sierra foothills. There were too many vivid experiences and too many things I saw that I could not have created or imagined in a three-hour dream..."[6]

Yes, every human being has had many spiritual light experiences. Some are not recognizable and most come in quiet, delicate, subtle ways and maybe the light comes as a warm feeling that you experienced from helping others or as a confirmation that you were making a correct decision in your life.

In McEaster Valley I felt both the physically detectable electromagnetic waves and the spiritually scientifically undetectable spectrum of light. Like Clayton Christensen, "And I could see the glories of (people living for all) eternity and I could see what God had in store for me (all of us) as one of His sons (or daughters)." I observed the warmth, love and light available to all mankind as I traveled in McEaster Valley.

I will also never forget the unique experience of total darkness in Moaning Caverns I experienced after we shut off our flashlights for several minutes and the studies of humans living in total darkness and isolation.

I have learned if we are engulfed completely by the darkness of the universe or we feel that the gates of hell are about to engulf us – it is not enough to put out the flame of the small electromagnetic photons of a candle or the spiritual photons of light from Christ, which can engulf us and penetrate any darkness that can ever come our way.

I bear witness that darkness cannot stand before the brilliant light of the Son of the living God!... Even after the darkest night, the Savior of the world will lead you to a gradual, sweet, and bright dawn that will assuredly rise within you. Elder Dieter F. Uchtdorf

"God does notice us, and he watches over us. But it is usually through another person that he meets our needs." Spencer W. Kimball.

1– *Isolation in the Dark Drives Humans to Brink of Insanity, Kelly Tatera Brain and Body, Science Explorer, 2015.*

2– *What is the electromagnetic spectrum? Earth Sky community, 2022.*

3– *The Spiritual Physics of LIGHT, Aaron D. Franklin PhD Pages 148-149, 2021.*

4– *That We May Always Have His Spirit to Be with Us, by Elder David A. Bednar, April 2006.*

5– *Clayton Christensen in His Own Words: Decisions for Which I've Been Grateful, Meridian Magazine, by Maurine Proctor. January 27, 2020.*

6– *Easter: McEaster Valley, Walter R. Hoge, 2010.*

12

KEEPING THE
EARTH WARM

To effectively separate and quantify human impacts on climate change, it is important to understand the natural impacts. Scientists have discovered what they think may be one of these natural impacts contributing to Greenland's ice melt: A thin spot in Earth's crust is enabling underground magma to heat the ice. They have found at least one earth crustal "hotspot" in the northeast corner of Greenland - just below a site where an ice stream was recently discovered. The researchers don't yet know how warm the hotspot is. But if it is warm enough to melt the ice above it even a little, it could be lubricating the base of the ice sheet and enabling the ice to slide more rapidly out to sea.[1]

Below the earth's crust is the mantle, the partially molten rocky layer that surrounds the Earth's core. The crust is the absolute outermost layer of the Earth, which constitutes just 1% of the Earth's mass. The thickness of the crust varies depending on where the measurements are taken, ranging from 30 km (16 miles) thick where there are continents to just 5 km thick (3 miles) beneath the oceans. The mountains of Tibet have the thickest crust (40 miles) and in 1981 scientists thought they had discovered the thinnest portion of the Earth's crust - a 1 mile thick, earthquake-prone spot under the Atlantic Ocean where the American and African continents connect.

Where the crust is thicker, things are cooler, and where it is thinner, things are warmer. And under a big place like Greenland or Antarctica, natural variations in the crust will make some parts of the ice sheet warmer than others. In the western continental United States, there are thin crust areas and in Yellowstone National Park not only is the earth's crust thinner but in various areas the surface is very warm.

The temperature of the Earth's crust ranges considerably. At its outer edge, where it meets the atmosphere, the crust's temperature is the same temperature as that of the air. So, it might be as hot as 35 °C (95 F) in the desert and below freezing in Antarctica. On average, the surface of the Earth's crust experiences temperatures of about 14°C (57 F). The hottest temperature ever recorded was 70.7°C (159°F), which was taken in the Lut Desert of Iran. The coldest temperature ever recorded on Earth was measured at the Soviet Vostok Station on the Antarctic Plateau, which reached an historic low of -89.2°C (-129°F) on July 21st, 1983.

The majority of the Earth's crust lies beneath the oceans. Far from the sun, temperatures can reach as low as 0-3° C (32-37.5° F) where the water reaches the crust. Still, a lot warmer than a cold night in Antarctica![1,2]

In the mystical McEaster Valley in the Sierra mountains of California there are areas where the earth's crust is thinner and that means in those areas things are warmer.

"...I noticed that the deeper we traveled, the warmer the ground and walls of the tunnel became. I again became a little concerned, because the warmer ground could mean that we were getting farther into the earth, near the magma layer, where all the molten rock can be found. I also knew that the earth's core is kept very hot due in part to radioactive decay...I was told that on the other side of the wall was where the food was prepared, and this side of the wall was where the food was preserved...It (the food) was then placed deep within the mountain, near the tunnel I passed through the day before. This area was very warm and dry, which was necessary to keep the food fresh..."[3]

Geologists have known for some time, if you dig down into the continental crust, temperatures will go up. For example, the deepest mine in the world is currently the TauTona gold mine in South Africa, measuring 3.9 km deep. At the bottom of the mine, temperatures reach a sweltering 55 °C (131 degrees F), which requires that air conditioning be provided so that it's comfortable for the miners to work all day.

Temperature of Earth's crust varies considerably. It's average surface temperature which depends on whether it is being taken on dry land or beneath the sea. And depending on the location, seasons, and time of day, it can range from sweltering to freezing cold!

And yet, Earth's crust remains the only place in the solar system where temperatures are stable enough that life can continue to thrive on it. Add to that our viable atmosphere and protective magnetosphere, and we really should consider ourselves to be the lucky ones![2]

The newly discovered hotspot in Greenland is just below the ice stream, and could have caused it to form. But what caused the hotspot to form? It could be that there's a volcano down there, but it's probably just the way the heat is being distributed by the rock topography at the base of the ice. Recent observations indicate that the Greenland Ice Sheet is much more active than has been expected. There have been rapid changes in outlet glaciers that are critically linked to conditions at the ice bed. To measure actual temperatures beneath the ice, scientists must drill boreholes down to the base of the ice sheet-- a mile or more below the ice surface. The effort and expense make such measurements prohibitive for now, researchers are combining theories of how heat flows through the mantle and crust with the gravity and radar data, to understand how the hotspot is influencing the ice.[1]

If you looked back at Earth 170 million years ago, you'd find a very different planet. The world's continents were all linked up into one vast 'supercontinent' called Pangaea, and according to a study in 2016, the outermost layer of the planet was 1.7 km (1 mile) thicker than it is today.

Researchers have found that since the break-up of Pangaea, Earth's inner mantle has been cooling twice as fast as they thought, and it looks like its crust has been thinning out ever since.

The outermost crust of Earth is formed by the mantle, which sits between the scorching hot core and the crust, spanning some 2,900 km (1,802 miles), and making up a whopping 84 percent of the planet's total volume. Magma produced in the mantle forms the outer oceanic crust when it rises to the surface and cools into rock.

Based on chemical analyses of lava rocks, about 2.5 billion years ago, the mantle had been cooling at a rate of 6 to 11 degrees Celsius every 100 million years. But then something happened around 170 million years ago to bump that cooling rate up to as much as 20 degrees per 100 million years ever since.

Scientists expected the mantle to cool over time as heat left over from Earth's formation and from radioactive decay dissipating. However, this degree of cooling was surprising. The researchers suspect that plate tectonics - the theory that Earth's 'outer shell' is divided into several plates that glide over the mantle - could explain the cooling. The supercontinent Pangaea may have acted as an insulating blanket and when the continents started opening up the deeper mantle was exposed to the atmosphere and the ocean it started cooling much master.

The study could not only explain why Earth's crust appears to be getting thinner with age - it could also explain why Pangaea split up in the first place: all the heat below that giant 'insulating blanket' might have eventually broke through and split the landmass apart.[2]

Earth measurements suggest radioactive decay provides more than half of its total heat, estimated at roughly 44 terawatts based on temperatures found at the bottom of deep boreholes into the planet's crust. The rest is left over from Earth's formation or other causes yet unknown, according to the scientists. Some of that heat may have been trapped in Earth's molten iron core since the planet's formation, while the nuclear decay happens primarily in the crust and mantle. But with fission still pumping out so much heat, Earth is unlikely to cool—and thereby halt the collisions of continents—for hundreds of millions of years thanks to the long half-lives of some of these elements. And that means there's a lot of geothermal energy—or natural nuclear energy—to be harvested.[4]

1– *Heat From Earth's Magma Contributing To Melting Of Greenland Ice, Ohio State University, 2007.*

2– *Earth's Crust Is Getting Thinner Than Ever, Thanks to a Rapidly Cooling Interior, Bec Crew, Environment, 2016.*

3– *Easter McEaster Valley, Walter R. Hoge, 2010.*

4– *Nuclear Fission Confirmed as Source of More than Half of Earth's Heat, Scientific American, David Biello, 07/18/2011.*

13

LONELINESS

From my mystical experiences in Easter McEaster Valley "…I have now reached the point in my life where my children have pretty much-left home and they are taking good care of themselves. I also recently became unexpectedly alone. I've found that as the family grows, the parents find themselves needed more and more for the care and well-being of their children. Then suddenly, their family is gone and they begin to feel unneeded. You still have something to contribute, but no one seems to be reaching out in need.

I have recently been finding myself thinking more and more about McEaster Valley and the opportunities there were to contribute my time and talents towards a good cause. I wonder if there was only one chance to accept an offer to live there. I would like to again be able to run like the wind and feel, as a youth, that all is good and nothing can or will prevent me from being what or whom I want to be."[1]

A heavy feeling on the chest. A throat that's leaden, as if to physically push down emotions as they bubble up. An unrelenting and overwhelming feeling of isolation.

Loneliness hurts - and over time, it can put the body into a vicious inflammatory state that increases our risk of everything from heart attack and stroke to diabetes and cancer.

Stephanie Cacioppo, an assistant professor of psychiatry and behavioral neuroscience at the University of Chicago Pritzker School of Medicine, says that countless studies have helped researchers formulate a holistic purpose for loneliness. "Our social structures evolved hand in hand with neural, hormonal and genetic mechanisms to support these social structures (couples, tribes and communities) that help us survive and reproduce."

Because while loneliness may be painful to experience today, for our prehistoric ancestors it would've been a far better alternative to being caught alone with a saber-toothed predator on the prowl. Though being social had its downsides even back then - competition for food, for example, or contribution to the spread of pathogens - we evolved to feel loneliness because it was more important to work with one another to accomplish tasks and protect everyone. The pain of loneliness prompted us to renew the social structure so we could survive and promote key features like trust, cooperation and collective action.

For years, researchers thought of loneliness as a "disease with no redeeming features." But now, they're realizing that it's more of a biological hunger signal that reminds us when it's time to reconnect with those around us to promote our short-term survival. If the outcomes of loneliness were entirely negative, it would no longer be a part of our DNA. Hunger and thirst protect our physical body while loneliness protects our social body.

Interestingly, while loneliness sends a signal to the brain that it's time for connection, at the same time it's also looking for danger. This "paradoxical signal", reminds us to be wary of whether the people we are connecting with are foes or friends. She calls this need to be vigilant even as we're socializing a "self-protection mechanism." That means in situations where you feel lonely even when surrounded by others, you're subconsciously thinking that this crowd might not be a good evolutionary fit for your survival.

Loneliness triggers the body's fight-or-flight response when we're by ourselves and in self-preservation mode. Picture it: An early human decides to hunt or gather alone one day, when all of a sudden loneliness sets in. They're anxious, scared and hyper-vigilant - traits that could come in handy if they encounter a giant sloth, a dire wolf or a beaver the size of a Bullmastiff.

That said, loneliness impacts us all differently. While it is universal and we're all vulnerable to it some of us may find certain situations lonely though others don't. Our brain is our main social organ for cultivating and maintaining relationships and because of that, the feature of loneliness is subjective. The removal of social structures can make us feel differently from person to person.

There's also a genetic component: Some of us are born to feel lonelier than others. According to Nathan Spreng, director of the Laboratory of Brain and Cognition at the Montreal Neurological Institute, the way we were treated as children - including how much attention we were given - can also play a role in how lonely we feel as adults. Reading loneliness signals helps us stave off the long-term damage that it can do to our mental and physical health.

Spreng says that over time, loneliness is a self-fulfilling prophesy. Lonely people spend most of their time deep within their own imaginations; they may conceptualize social encounters so much, in fact, that this part of their brain is in overdrive. That means when they're around other people, they're actually less likely to be present. "People who are really lonely may be desperate to form connections, but they aren't as present when they're with people so they might miss the social cues necessary to form deeper connections."

It's clear that loneliness has a nasty impact on our mental health, but there is a bright side. It's an annoying biological signal that reminds us our primal selves and our modern selves are in need of a friend, and that our social body needs to tend to these relationships. The feeling is a lot like that light on your car dashboard that warns when it's time for a trip to the gas station or a mechanic — and like that light, it only works if you listen to it.[2]

Who among us has not felt lonely at times? A loved one dies, friends and family move away, visits come to an end, and silence is all we hear. The quiet of loneliness can be deafening.

At other times we may feel alone even when surrounded by people. Perhaps our loneliness stems from the nagging feeling that we're not liked or appreciated. It may be that we're discouraged. Or maybe jealousy and animosity have led us to detach ourselves from others. To one degree or another, all of us will feel lonely at some time. Whatever the reason, the continuum of loneliness can range from feelings of momentary sadness to the crushing weight of despair.

At such times, know this: there is a way to the other side of loneliness. The Lord taught that the peacemakers, the pure in heart, the meek and merciful would be blessed here and hereafter with comfort and joy. Purposeful work, worthwhile endeavors, service to others, family, and friendship and fellowship with the good people of this earth will help us feel less lonely. And remember, some loneliness must be lived with. As we patiently wait upon the Lord, He will not leave us comfortless. Loneliness is never permanent when we walk on with faith.

You've had such faith during your life; and you can be inspired by the examples of so many you know. A woman who has suffered great loss could brood about her loneliness and feel sorry for herself in her heartache. Instead, in time and with great willpower, she has chosen to lift and bless others. She knows that while she hasn't changed the world, she has made a difference. She has been a friend. She has listened and been kind.

You know people like her, people who reach out to God and to others while in the midst of loneliness. The Lord blesses them and each of us—for if we walk with Him, we'll never walk alone.[3]

1– *Easter McEaster Valley, Walter R. Hoge, 2010.*
2– *Humans Evolved To Be Lonely, Sara Novak, Discover Magazine, 2022.*
3– *In Times of Loneliness, Music & the Spoken Word, program #3917, 2004.*

PART II

THOUGHTS SHARED
WITH FAMILY
AND FRIENDS

14

KEEPING FAITH

The summer of 1968 I started attending graduate school in the Department of Animal Science at Purdue University. One of the tasks my assigned professor asked me to do was think about how I could design a bathing solution that would create an environment that could maintain the vitality of harvested graph tissue until they could be placed under the kidney capsule of a rat. The kidney is used because the overlying capsule holds the tissue in place next to the good blood supply of the kidney. The graft placed here has an excellent opportunity to survive. This procedure is still used for research.

At the time, magnetic stirrers, rockers & rollers with motions in various planes and small pumps (like used for aquariums) were available with and without solution temperature regulation. For some reason I got into my head using a clock. I envisioned extending a devise from the hour hand with a small paddle at the end. On the hour the hand would penetrate the incubation solution and cause enough current to be sure fresh nutrients came in contact with the harvested tissues.

I don't know if my major professor gave me this assignment to get to know my thought processes or just something to keep me busy during my first summer session. All I do know is that the thoughts about keeping alive tissue cultures resulted in me placing a lot of stress on my mind. Until this day I still remember this assignment and have periodically experienced night mares trying to find a solution to this assignment.

In 2016, Sarah Olson's son Levi was born with spina bifida, undergoing more than a half-dozen surgeries in the first years of his life. When Levi was just three years old, surgeons created an opening called a stoma in his abdomen to provide a way for his bladder to drain without invasive catheterization through the urethra. A stoma is an opening on the abdomen that can be connected to either your digestive or urinary system to allow waste (urine or feces) to be diverted out of your body. It looks like a small, pinkish, circular piece of flesh that is sewn to your body. Over the top of your stoma you will wear a pouch, which can either be closed or have an opening at the bottom.

To keep the stoma open while it healed, they insert a temporary catheter through the newly formed opening and into the bladder. Hopefully, within a month, the temporary catheter will no longer be needed.

Though the stoma surgery had gone perfectly, the catheter proved to be a nightmare for Levi. It resulted in recurring infections, excruciating bladder spasms, and additional surgery. And because of all the complications the stoma hadn't been healing well and there seemed to be no relief in sight. Levi was just a toddler and after six unbearable months, Sarah demanded that doctors give Levi a break.

He removed the catheter after warning Sarah that within a short period of time she would find herself back at the doctor's office pleading to get some help for Levi. She knew that her four-year old needed to use a catheter again but refused using the accustomed Foley catheter. In frustration she commented, "There's got to be another solution."

Her doctor's reply was, "I've been doing this a long time. I wish there were something else, but this is the best option we have for this condition. Nothing else exists. If you want something different, you would have to invent it yourself."

The first thing she did was go home and start praying. Raised in a Christian family, she had believed in Jesus from the time she was four years old and talking to God had always been an important part of her life.

She admitted that when she started praying, she was angry. "I was throwing a temper tantrum with the Lord," she recalled. "I told him, Look, I'm not okay with this solution. It seems this catheter works for other people, but it's not working for Levi. Why is this happening to my little boy? And if you love him more than I love him, why are you allowing this?"

A college dropout, Sarah had no training in engineering, the medical field, or the development of new devices – not anything close to those subjects.

Her prayer continued: "What am I supposed to do, Lord? Invent something? I think I'm a good mom, but I wouldn't have the slightest idea how to invent something. I'm so inadequate to do anything like that."

Sarah described what happened next as being like a lightning bolt. Instantly, in the that moment, she knew exactly how to solve the problem. In fact, she saw an image in her head of a device and knew God wanted her to do something with what he was showing her.

"People think I'm crazy when I say this but it was like God speaking into my ear. I knew what he was saying."

What Sarah heard God saying to her was this: "Sarah, Levi isn't the one struggling like this. It's like when the Israelites were crying for help, and I sent Moses to deliver the message that set them free. I need you to be my Moses, because there are a lot of people struggling just like Levi, and I'm going to use you.

I'm going to ask you to do a lot of things that are far beyond your natural abilities, so it can't be explained away. And I need you to say yes. I need you to be all in. If Medtronic or 3M or any other medical device company came up with this idea, it would make sense, but I'm not going to use them. I'm going to use you, Sarah Olson. It won't make sense, but just do what I tell you to do. Have faith in me to guide you."

Sarah sketched he image onto paper. She watched YouTube videos to try to figure out how to make a CAD design to be printed by a 3D printer. Finally, she enlisted a friend who helped her complete the drawing and located a 3D printer.

When she had a proto-type in hand, she made an appointment to see Levi's doctor. Sitting in his office once again, she asked, "Remember when you told me I had to invent something?" He told her that he remembered, but was joking. "But I wasn't," she responded. "I promised you we're not going to use that Foley again. So, I invented something." She slid the device across the desk toward him. The doctor looked at the device and then at Sarah. "Really? You invented something?"

She nodded and told the urologist what he already knew: that the Foley catheter uses in internal stabilizer, a liquid-filled balloon at the end of it, to keep it from slipping out of the bladder. That means there's something foreign inside the bladder. "And the bladder doesn't like that," Sarah explained. "It leads to infections and bladder spasms. Miserable for anyone, especially kids." She explained that by stabilizing the stoma from the outside of the abdomen you don't need liquid-filled balloon irritating the bladder. She asked the doctor if he wouldn't try the new invention instead of the Foley catheter on Levi.

His reply was that he could not place the device until it had been patented. Her child was scheduled for surgery in thirty-days, she found a patent developer that worked day and night writing applications for a patent and the device was approved for a provisional patent two days before Levi's surgery.

The new device was placed on Levi, and the results were nothing short of miraculous. After Levi's first stoma surgery, complications from the Foley catheter had resulted in his spending two and a half weeks in the hospital, six surgeries, a significant number of drugs – and the stoma still hadn't healed up after six months.

This time, wearing the device his mother had invented for him, Levi spent one night in the hospital for observation, went home, and healed in ten days with no infection, complications, or bladder infections.

A few weeks later Levi's doctor told Sarah that her work had just begun. She now owned the patent on a device that could help people, save lives all over the globe, and she now had a huge responsibility to somehow take this device to market. The doctor mentioned that producing the device would not be an easy task.

"If the big medical device companies caught wind of what she was doing, they wouldn't be pleased because they don't want anything competing with the Foley. The Foley catheter is a seven-billion-dollar industry – just that one catheter – because it's the only device that has been used. Until now. So, you've got to do this yourself. And nobody in the world has done that before."

Sarah continued praying – and asking everyone she met if they knew someone who could help her get the device into the marketplace. She began referring to her invention as the LECS, for Levi's External Catheter Stabilizer.

She learned that an acquaintance knew the CEO of a medical device corporation. Treading carefully, she asked to meet with him to see if he had any advice. Sitting in front of the CEO's expansive, burnished desk, Sarah told her story, ending with a passionate plea: "What do I do next? How do I take a medical device to market?" The CEO started laughing. Feeling put off, she asked, "What are you laughing at?"

He replied, "You're so excited about something that's never going to happen," he continued. "You're in over your head. Just stop. Now. This isn't something that individuals do on their own. You're going to waste time. You're going to ruin your reputation. The medical device field is brutal. They'll chew you up and spit you out."

As he was talking, Sarah was praying. Would this be the moment she would run into defeat? Or would she trust God to use her and her invention to bless others? Calmly standing up, Sarah put her hands on the edge of the giant desk and leaned in. "You know what?" she said defiantly. "You might be the owner of a medical device company. You might know a lot more than I do. But you put your pants on the same way I do every morning, and if you can do it, so can I. And what you are saying to discourage me is only lighting a fire in me. I'm going to get this done. This medical device will be in hospitals someday, I promise you that. So, I'm not mad at you. In fact, I thank you. Thank you for lighting a fire that is going to burn in my gut for the rest of my life." Picking up her purse and file folders, she turned and walked out of the office.

Six months later, Sarah had attracted enough investors to put together a small team of consultants, accountants, and lawyers. Sitting around a boardroom table, they debated which of four types of elastomer – a rubbery, flexible material – the LECS should be made from. It was a make-or-break decision. The wrong choice could cost tens of thousands of dollars that Sarah didn't have. She had a few investors, but there as always only enough to be able to take the next step, never more than she needed; never enough to absorb an expensive mistake.

As the men and women around the table explained why one manufacturing material was the best, Sarah was struck by the irony of the situation. she thought, *I'm sitting at the head of this table, a mom with pink hair, surrounded by very smart people who know what they're doing, and I have no idea what they're talking about. And I'm going to have to make the final decision.*

After the members of the team finished their discussion about how to produce the product, Sarah said, "I'm going to step outside for five minutes, and when I come back, I'll tell you what we're going to do."

When Sarah returned, she said, "All right, everyone, we're going to go with option C. I can't tell you why, except that I prayed about it, and I know we're supposed to go with C. My faith is important to me, and I pray about every decision. And then I do what God tells me to do. And you're probably thinking, 'Why did she even hire us if she's not going to follow our advice?' Or maybe you're thinking, 'She's raised thousands of dollars of other people's money, and this is how she runs her business?' I get it. But God asked me right from the start to listen to Him and do what He tells me to do. And if that sounds crazy to you, you're free to go. No hard feelings."

A couple of weeks later, the team reassembled, and one of the members informed her that the company they recommended to make the elastomer wouldn't have provided the medical grade they needed. The material wouldn't have worked long term. Looked like option C was the right choice.

Sarah believes that God worked overtime to make sure that Levi got what he needed – and is still working miracles within her company to make sure other children and adults get help, too. Within five years, Sara's company, Levity Products, obtained a certificate of biocompatibility on the first attempt, meaning that the material used does not cause complications when applied to the body. The device passed clinical trials with no problem or delays, and she received patents on two additional medical devices.

"Big corporations spend ten years and ten million dollars to get where we are today," Sarah said. "God got us here in half the time with half the capital."[1-2]

Levity Products web site 2023: *We began our journey with the dream of helping one child and quickly realized that we weren't dreaming big enough. Through our innovative New Product Development process, we've made that dream available to patients of all shapes and sizes.*

Levi was recently diagnosed with a rare spinal disease unrelated to spina bifida. Sarah says that despite living with debilitating pain, her ten-year-old is one of the most faith-filled, resilient people she's ever met.

One day she asked him, "How do you do it, buddy? How do you deal with this kind of pain and keep smiling?"

"Well, Mama," he answered, "Life goes the way the corners of your mouth turn." She asked what he meant. He nodded. "If you smile, life goes better. So, if I have the choice, why wouldn't I smile? And if I have the choice to complain or not to complain, I'm going to choose not to complain, because if my mind is complaining, my body is going to complain, too."

When days are hard for Levi or for Sarah, she remembers his sage advice and adds a twist of her own:

"If I have the choice to pray and trust God - or the choice not to pray or trust Him – I'm going to pray and trust. Faith is a choice. And my journey has proved that faith in God is always the right choice."[2]

Who knows? Maybe if I had of pushed forward as hard as Sarah Olson, I might have been successful in clocks to nourish tissue cultures. Maybe in my early 20's if I spent more time on my knees, I might have been successful.

However, if I had of been successful, I may not have thought more seriously about veterinary school. I wouldn't have had the wonderful experiences of practicing veterinary medicine. But, if I had spent more times addressing my Heavenly Father during graduate school, I might not still be troubled at times with those night mare dreams of clocks helping feed tissue grafts.

As the years have gone by, I've become a lot like Sarah Olson in my philosophy of life: "If I have the choice to pray and trust God - or the choice not to pray or trust Him – I'm going to pray and trust. Faith is a choice. And (hopefully) my journey (will also prove) that faith in God is always the right choice."

1– *Mom demonstrates medical invention in Central Florida, Mike Holfeld, Investigative Reporter, 2017.*
2– *Faith still moves mountains, Harris Faulkner, 2022, 59-68.*

15

DONALD R. DOOLEY

Don's wife, Sharon, died from dementia, a condition characterized by progressive and persistent loss of intellectual functioning, with impairment of memory and abstract thinking, and with a personality change, resulting from organic disease of the brain. This was a loss that he never got over.

Another event that tested his faith was the loss of a grandson who was killed from a motor cycle accident. His wife's body was stored in a mausoleum, he had the casket opened and his grandson's cremains container placed in her casket.

In 2004 he was diagnosed with cancer in the bone marrow, he told me chemotherapy would make his remaining life miserable and the course of the disease often ended with a hemorrhagic bleed out from the internal organs and a miserable death.

Evaluating his options, discussing these with his minister and asking him if in God's eyes choosing starvation would be considered suicide - he decided to stop eating and starve himself to death.

He placed himself in a care facility and planned on dying by Thanksgiving. He missed that mark and passed shortly before Christmas. He continued to have weekly staff meetings in his care facility with veterinary hospital staff members he had consulted with for years.

I planned visits with him on a weekly basis, tried to lift his spirits, but mostly he lifted mine. He told me that the worst part of starving was headaches. So, I purchased some tea, placed it in a special container with paper to make a joint, and labeled it - *Marijuana for medicinal headache use only*. We had some fun with it and it seemed to lighten his day. After he passed, his assistant manager mentioned that she couldn't believe I was so bold as to take marijuana into a building so casually.

One day Don mentioned that he had discussed with his doctor whether a small amount of food could be taken. The doctor told him that he had been without food for so long that eating could have uncomfortable ramifications on his digestive system and advised against it. To help lift his spirits, the next visit I brought an IV bag full of brown liquid labeled chocolate milk and I told him I was prepared to give it to him intravenously. I told him that if he couldn't put food in his stomach why not try some good tasting milk placed through his veins.

November 9, 2004, about a month before he died, I sent Don this letter:

> "First of all, I must spend a moment to thank you for your friendship and the positive council and guidance you have given me in my professional and personal

life. You have not influenced me by the typical written or spoken message of 'to be successful in.........you must.....' Your transfer of knowledge and wisdom to me has come from light hearted stories about your experiences with your family, friends or professional contacts. You have helped my practice be successful beyond my wildest dreams and when crisis came encouraged me to keep everything in perspective. However, most of all you have helped me in my personal life. Your willingness to share with me your inner feelings and family experiences, especially during Sharon's illness and since her passing, has helped me more personally than any other effort you could have made in my behalf.

You and I both know from personal experience that the task ahead will not be easy. When I think about the struggles Sheryl went through, I think of two statements that have been of assistance. The first one is a quote placed on a picture of Christ that I have hanging on my bedroom wall. It states, 'I didn't say it would be easy......I only said it worth it.' The other one is recorded communication between Joseph Smith and the Lord. It can be found in the Doctrine of Covenants section 122. At this time Joseph was in prison at Liberty, Missouri (March 1839). Verse 4 '...because of thy righteousness; and thy God shall stand by thee forever and ever. v5 If thou art called to pass through tribulation; if thou art in perils among false brethren; if thou art in perils among robbers; if thou art in perils by land or sea; v6 If thou art accused with all manner of false accusations; if thine enemies fall upon thee; if they tear thee from the society of thy father and mother and brethren and sisters; and if with a drawn sword thine enemies tear thee from the bosom of they wife, and of thine offspring and thine elder son, although but six years of age, shall cling to thy garments, and shall say, My father, my father, why can't you stay with us? O, my father, what are the men going to do with you? And if then he shall be thrust from thee by the sword, and thou be dragged to prison, and thine enemies prowl around thee like wolves for the blood of the lamb; v7 And if thou shouldst be cast into the pit, or into the hands of murderers, and the sentence of death passed upon thee; if thou be cast into the deep; if the billowing surge conspire against thee; if fierce winds become thine enemy; if the heavens gather blackness, and all the elements combine to hedge up the way; and above all, if the very jaws of hell shall gape open the mouth wide after thee, know thou, my son, that all these things shall give thee experience, and shall be for thy good'.

Don, I know that we both know there is more and better waiting for us on the other side of the veil. We can each give testimony to this truth by way of the experiences we've had during our times of need over the last few years. I also know that we have talked about how trials help us find out who we really are. And, how challenges give us the opportunity to stretch ourselves to be the best we can be and are good for our 'experience.'

In Isaiah 32:17 it says, 'And the work of righteousness shall be peace; and the effect of righteousness quietness and assurance forever.' You are one of the most righteous men that I have known. Your honesty and integrity in the work place, love of family and charity extended to those around you should give you peace, quietness and assurance as to who you are in the eyes of God and the honor and glory awaiting you and Sharon on the other side.

Now let's fight the good fight, get you back on your feet and go to lunch for some more light hearted stories containing wisdom for my soul. And, above all please let me help you in any way I can. After all you have mostly served me and I would like some blessings from having the opportunity assisting you in your time of need."

Donald R. Dooley's career began as a farmer, then representative of several veterinary drug companies, and finally a veterinary practice manager, public speaker and writer.[1] My file contains copies of *The Dooley Letter* he wrote for the years 1984 to the year he passed in 2004. His monthly letters contained an introduction explaining his reasoning for the subject of that month, a page for the veterinary staff and one to the practice leader. Contained in these letters are many insightful quotes."

Let me share a few of Don's ideologies and the methods used to help veterinary practitioners and their staff recognize their potential at work and in their private lives. Just a few of Don's many 'isms:

"We are told that experience is a great teacher. If this is true, why does experience make some veterinarians better diagnosticians, while it makes others worse? part of the answer is found in the old saying, 'You can have 20 years of experience or one year of experience twenty times.' To be improved by experience requires an open mind."

"There is a continual battle raging within most practice leaders. It is the battle between the mind and the heart. Minds re pretty good leaders. Hearts guide us in doing what we feel is the 'right' thing. The mind figures out what needs to be done and how to do it, and then the heart gets in the way of getting it done."

"Nothing has greater influence on our accomplishments than our imagination. We simply can't accomplish or achieve that which we can't imagine. The reason is quite simple. Without being able to visualize a finished product, we can't visualize the steps need to achieve the desired result."

"Clients come to a veterinary practice because they want the services of a veterinarian. Sometimes veterinarians get confused and think clients are seeking friendship. They really want an authoritative professional they can respect and trust to care for their animals. Most clients already have friends, it is veterinary service they need when they come to a veterinary practice."

"Life teaches us many valuable lessons and one of the most important is that the occasional victory or outstanding performance is soon forgotten. When you point to past victories or performances, the response is always the same. What have you done lately? If you want rewards, you have to be consistent in your performance. Of course, you have your 'up's' and 'down's' and bad days are your problem and if you want to be successful, you will also be consistent."

"It has been my experience that some of the best answers to management problems in a veterinary practice come from the receptionists, technicians and assistants. I've also noticed that sometimes management problems remain unresolved for long periods of time because these people with the answer are reluctant to offer their suggestions."

"It appears that many veterinarians have forgotten what their degree stands for. D.V.M. is supposed to stand for Doctor of Veterinary Medicine. Unfortunately, many practice owners think it stands for Director of Veterinary Minutia. Rather than lead the practice and practicing medicine, far too many practice owners insist on managing the practice right down to the most minute detail. This, of course, interferes with the medical work they could be doing and frustrates the owner to the point of complaining about 'burnout'."

"If you want to be a happier person there is something you can do that will bring you a great deal of happiness. Each night when you go to bed, before you go to sleep, ask yourself, 'What did I do today that made someone happy?' It will give you the opportunity to relive a pleasant experience. You will be thinking pleasant thoughts as you go to sleep, which is certainly better than going to sleep thinking about the news of the day."

"The primary difference between humans and other animals is the ability of the humans to think. Both animals and humans act and react instinctively and intuitively, but only humans have the ability to think. Unfortunately, this is a greatly underutilized ability. Those who study these things disagree about whether humans are using 5% or 10% of their minds' capabilities. Even if both groups are underestimating by 50%, we still have a tremendous ability available to use that we aren't using.

Nobel prize winning author, George Bernard Shaw, attributed his success to his thinking a couple of times each week. He felt that thinking two hours each week gave him a great advantage over his peers."

"To a leader, what is accomplished is more important than who gets credit for it. Many times there is no obvious evidence of leadership when good things are accomplished. The important word there is 'obvious' because when good things are accomplished, they happen as a result of strong leadership. Great accomplishments do not occur in a vacuum. People are guided in their dealings with others by one of two philosophies. Some are guided by a desire to help *others*, while the rest are concerned only about helping *themselves*. Most of you who work in veterinary hospitals are the fortunate ones who are guided by the desire to help others."

"As an enjoyable thing to do, taking an animal to a veterinarian ranks pretty near the bottom of the list. It is just below taking the car in for repairs and just above going to the dentist. It is both out of the normal routine and it costs money, two of the things any of us dread most."

"In the most extreme cases, air, water or ground pollution can cause death. Death, of course, is bad, but the effect of *attitude pollution*, may be even worse. It is possible that people who die from air, water or ground pollution may have had a good life before their contact with the pollution. Unfortunately, many who suffer from *attitude pollution* have never lived or at least aren't presently living. Many who suffer as a result of a *polluted attitude* may never have known the pleasure of a truly enjoyable day. Living life with a good attitude is worth whatever effort it takes to avoid *attitude pollution!*"

"You can improve your chance of having a good day by starting it right. Whether we will have a good day or a bad day depends a great deal on how it starts. Days that start well tend to get progressively better, and days that start poorly often get worse as they go on."

"The latest 'buzz' word in business management today is '*team*.' All over the country, seminars are being given on '*the team concept*', '*how to create a team*', etc. A great deal of excitement is being caused by an '*invention*' that has been around nearly forever. Working together as a team is just as important to the individual team members as it is to the leader. Therefore, if it is important to each member, working together as a team is everyone's responsibility."

"Knowledge is acquired through the education process. Initially it is acquired in a series of schools, then it is continued through seminars, workshops, reading, contact with specialists, etc. Wisdom is acquired from the lessons taught by life. It is the ability to discern between what is right and what is wrong. Wisdom also enables us to tell the difference between what is important and what isn't. To the young, everything seems extremely important, but with age, fewer and fewer things are still worth the effort. Part of this comes from being old, tired and worn out, but much of it is wisdom."

"The attitude with which we begin our work day will determine what we are able to accomplish. We can look good and feel good physically and still have a bad day, or we look and feel less than our best and still have a good day. The difference is in our mind."

"According to those who have made a study of it, communication is made up of three components. They are: body language (70%), tone of voice (15%), and verbal content – what we actually say (15%). The old cliché 'Actions speak louder than words' is apparently true. Body language and one of voice often drown out what we are trying to say."

"Yes, the things that will make you stand out as an employee are the same traits that make you an entertaining and enjoyable human being to be with. Competence is very desirable in an employee, but only when it is combined with a very likable human being. Ability will get you a job, but it will take likability to keep it. Being both competent and likable is an unbeatable combination."

"Finally, anything said or done in the presence of a client to make the receptionist look bad, will cost you clients. If you will keep in mind that the receptionist is your primary client and the clients with the animals have been referred to you by the receptionist, and treat the receptionist accordingly, you will see your client count increase."

"Yes, anything worthwhile in life that is eventually accomplished, started with a dream. That dream was then converted into a specific goal. Several interim goals may have been required to achieve the overall goal. It is also quite common for the dream to change a time or two before the ultimate goal is achieved. Changing a goal from time to time isn't a problem. Not having a goal is a serious problem."

"Every change we encounter has the possibility of damage, and it also carries with it the seed of an opportunity. We need to see the possible danger, so we can deal with it if necessary. However, if all we do is evaluate the possible danger, and try to build a defense against it, we will completely miss the benefit of the change."

"It was explained that managers are 'fixers' and 'solvers'. They spend their time fixing things and solving problems. This sounds great, after all, things do have to be fixed and problems do need to be solved. The problem is that managers tend to get too deeply involved in fixing and solving. They can get so involved in fixing small things and solving small problems that they lose tract of the purpose of the practice."

"I used to feel that there was only one thing you should do, and that was to be happy. Then I realized, I had no right to suggest that you should be happy. If you really wanted to be miserable, what right did I have to make you feel guilty about it. So, I concluded that you can be happy if you want to, but there is no reason that you should if you don't want to."

"Most of us like to hear and read things that affirm our beliefs. It makes us feel as if we are right, because someone else agrees with us. We need this affirmation from time to time so we can feel good about ourselves and what we do. However, if all we choose to hear or read are things that affirm what we already know and believe, we won't learn very much."

"There are some things your clients probably won't say about you. They probably won't talk about beautiful sutures, straight incisions, placing catheters, reading radiographs, analyzing lab reports, or any other medical procedures. They relate to you as a person not as a provider of medical services. Providing medical services is what you do, but it isn't who you are."

"So, there is one other ingredient in a healthy self-esteem. That other ingredient is our contribution to society. In all of us there is a hope that the world is just a little bit better because we are here. To accomplish this, we not only need to do well what we do, we also need to feel that what we are doing is making a contribution to humanity."

I wish he had lived long enough to organize his many *words of wisdom* to share with the world.

1– *God Sends Answers We Can Understand, Walter R. Hoge, 12/19/2022.*

2–

16

PEER PRESSURE

One morning during my 7th or 8th grade in high school I recall as I walked off the bus that I was feeling great because there were no assignments due or tests to be taken. However, one of my friends mentioned that "I didn't look so good and wondered if I hadn't been ill." Heading into the school building I let my friend know that I was having a good day, thank you very much.

During my classes several more of my friends came by mentioning that I didn't look well and before lunch I wasn't feeling good. At the end of the morning period my friends came by, mentioned again to me how sick I looked and started to laugh about the joke they had played on me. For the rest of the day I didn't feel well.

Years ago, Jack S. Marshall taught a high school seminary class filled with the "stars" of the senior class: Mr. Macho, the all-state quarterback, a heart-stopper of every young lady in school; little Miss Pep, the head varsity cheerleader; Mr. President, our student body leader; Mr. Most-Likely-to-Succeed; and Mr. Brains, a young man who had already been offered several full-ride scholarships to some pretty prestigious universities. One day we all learned a sorry lesson that almost any of us can bend to peer pressure. Here's how it happened.

Mr. Marshall had read a magazine article on negative peer pressure. The article described an experiment that he was tempted to try on his class of "achievers." The experiment was designed to show, in a very convincing way, how powerful peer pressure can be. It didn't really occur to me that the experiment might have some negative consequences.

In class the next morning I did as instructed for the experiment. On the chalkboard I drew a star, a circle, an oval, and a square. I told my class that for the next 50 minutes, the objects on the board were to be identified as a star, a circle, an oval, and a triangle, even though the square was obviously a square. It was now to be called a triangle and nothing else! In a moment they would have an opportunity to convince an unsuspecting visitor that the square was actually a triangle.

Six-fold-out seats were set in front of the classroom. Mr. Quarterback, Miss Pep, Mr. President, Mr. Most-Likely-to-Succeed, and Mr. Brains were invited to take their seats, leaving one vacant chair. I then invited a freshman student into the classroom. He immediately recognized that he was among the "elite" of the high school. The students made him welcome. In no time he was feeling right at home. He was with the "Who's Who" of the school and was thriving on it.

I invited him to take a seat in the one remaining chair in front of the class. I explained that when it came his turn, he was to simply identify the objects drawn on the board. He agreed. The others smiled. The lesson began.

Mr. Quarterback, was asked by me to identify the objects on the board. In a deep, macho voice he said, "Star, circle, oval," and then, coming to the square, he confidently said, "Triangle."

Our visitor, forgetting himself, let out a laugh that conveyed the idea, "You've been sacked a few too many times." But the rest of the people in the room were absolutely silent.

The freshman quickly searched the faces of those present for acknowledgement of Mr. Quarterback's obvious mental fumble, but my students were playing their parts. To them that square was nothing more than a triangle. Mr. Freshman had a bewildered expression.

I then turned to Miss Pep and asked her to please identify the objects on the board. She enthusiastically replied, "Star, circle, oval, triangle."

The freshman fidgeted in his seat. The class remained silent and nonchalant. Twice more the question was asked. Mr. President and Mr. Most-Likely-to-Succeed answered in perfect form. By now our visitor looked slightly ill and had that "may-I-please-be-dismissed" expression on his face.

"Star, circle, oval, triangle," Mr. Brains answered. Now it was Mr. Freshman's turn. With each object his voice grew weaker, shakier, and less confident. "Star … circle … oval …" Then silence. We looked at him. He looked at us. "What's the last object?" I asked. Silence. "Come on, what is it?" Then finally, quietly he spoke. "Triangle."

I thought we'd all break the tenseness with a good laugh. The experiment had worked. But instead, there was silence. I searched the students' faces. They were all deep in thought. Some heads hung.

Then it hit me. Each one in the class could relate to the embarrassed freshman. Each in a foolish moment, wanting so badly to be accepted or to be part of the group, had in his own way called a square a triangle, had committed a wrong when there was no misunderstanding. Even I could add my name to the list. And we all realized, especially me, that we had been unkind to put Mr. Freshman in such an awkward situation.

We spent the remainder of our class time sharing feelings and regrets, but more importantly sharing desires, hopes, and longings to be more courageous. Mr. Quarterback put his arm around Mr. Freshman, and we all reassured him that we'd made the mistake of bowing to pressure before, too. By the end of the class he was accepted by his peers—not because he'd given in, but because we'd all come to see the importance of never surrendering, of calling a square a square despite the consequences.

When the bell rang, we left as a group, wiser, more hopeful, and with a greater resolve to fight a good battle amid the pressures of the world."[1]

Philipp Freiherr von Boeselager (6 September 1917 – 1 May 2008) was the second-last surviving member of the 20 July Plot, a conspiracy of Wehrmacht officers to assassinate the German dictator Adolf Hitler in 1944. Peer pressure did not prevail against him when he realized people were being killed in cold blood because of their ethnicity and to prevent further slaughter of the innocent Hitler needed to be assassinated.

When Boeselager was a 25-year-old field lieutenant, he was part of Operation Walküre, a plan developed to take control of Germany once Hitler had been assassinated. Boeselager's role in the plan was to order his troops, who were unaware of the plot, to leave the front lines in Eastern Europe and to head west, where they would be airlifted to Berlin to seize crucial parts of the city in a full-scale coup d'état after Hitler had been killed.

Boeselager's opinion turned against the Nazi government in June 1942, after he received news that five Roma people had been shot in cold blood solely because of their ethnicity. Together with his commanding officer, Field Marshal Günther von Kluge, he joined a conspiracy to assassinate Hitler. The first attempt was in March 1943, when both Hitler and Heinrich Himmler were coming to the front to participate in a strategy meeting with Kluge's troops.

Boeselager was given a Walther PP with which he was to shoot both Hitler and Himmler at a dinner table in the officers' mess. However, nothing ever came of this plan because at the last minute, Himmler left Hitler's company, and the risk of leaving him alive to succeed Hitler was too great.

The second assassination attempt was in summer 1944. No longer caring about Himmler, the conspiracy planned to kill Hitler with a bomb when he was attending another strategy meeting in a wooden barracks. When the assassin's bomb failed to kill the Führer, Boeselager was informed in time to turn his unexplained cavalry retreat around and return to the front before suspicions could be aroused.

Because of Boeselager's fortunate timing, his involvement in the operation went undetected, and he was not executed, unlike the majority of the conspirators. Philipp's brother Georg was also a participant in the plot, and likewise remained undetected, but was later killed in action on the Eastern Front.

Shortly before the end of the war, Boeselager overheard General Wilhelm Burgdorf saying, "When the war is over, we will have to purge, after the Jews, the Catholic officers in the army". The devoutly-Catholic Boeselager noisily objected, citing his own decorations for heroism in combat. Boeselager then left before Burgdorf could respond.

After the war, Boeselager's part in the failed attempt on Hitler's life became known. He was regarded as a hero by many in Germany and France and received the highest military medals that both countries could provide. He studied economics and became a forestry expert. Even in his old age, Boeselager still had nightmares about the conspiracy and the friends whom he lost during the war. He urged young people to become more involved in politics, as he felt apathy and the political inexperience of the German masses had been two of the key reasons why Hitler was able to come to power. In 2009, the film *Valkyrie* starring Tom Cruise and directed by Bryan Singer, addressed these events.

The entrance to his residence in Kreuzberg bears the Latin motto Et si omnes ego non ("even if all, not I") or in other words, "Even if everybody does it, I will not." *Wikipedia*

Peer pressure and suggestions that may not be in our best interest are powerful especially in our pre adult years. I remember in my youth when I desired something my parents didn't feel I should have or do the comment coming out of my mouth all too often was – so and so has or does so why can't I.

If Boeselager's Latin motto, "(just because) everybody does it, I (may) well not", were applied universally in our decision process, think of the reduced "sorry I did it" to the increased glad "I could of but didn't" choices made during our lives.

"If you expect something to happen—if someone or something suggests to you a specific outcome—your expectations of that outcome play a major role in its occurrence. The expectation or suggestion alone, often unconsciously, changes your behavior and your responses to help bring into reality the outcome you are expecting."[2]

The wisdom of the prudent is to understand his way: but the folly of fool's deceit. Proverbs 14:8

1– *Jack S. Marshall, New Era, September 1987.*
2– *4 ways the power of suggestion can change your life, Psychology Today, 04/21/2015.*

17

POSITIVE CONSEQUENCES FROM KINDNESS

Scientists who study happiness know that being kind to others can improve well-being. Acts as simple as buying a cup of coffee for someone can boost a person's mood. Everyday life affords many opportunities for such actions, yet people do not always take advantage of them.

In studies published in the Journal of Experimental Psychology: Nicholas Epley, a behavioral scientist at the University of Chicago Booth School of Business, and I examined a possible explanation: people who perform random acts of kindness underestimate how much recipients value their behavior.

Across multiple experiments involving approximately 1,000 participants, people performed a random act of kindness—that is, an action done with the primary intention of making someone else (who isn't expecting the gesture) feel good. Those who perform such actions expect nothing in return.

From one situation to the next, the specific acts of kindness varied. For instance, in one experiment, people wrote notes to friends and family "just because." In another, they gave cupcakes away. Across these experiments, we asked both the person performing a kind act and the one receiving it to fill out questionnaires.

We asked the person who had acted with kindness to report their own experience and predict their recipient's response. We wanted to understand how valuable people perceived these acts to be, so both the performer and recipient rated how "big" the act seemed. In some cases, we also inquired about the actual or perceived cost in time, money or effort. In all cases, we compared the performer's expectations of the recipient's mood with the recipient's actual experience.

Across our investigations, several patterns emerged. For one, both performers and recipients of the acts of kindness were in more positive moods than normal after these exchanges. For another, it was clear that performers undervalued their impact: recipients felt significantly better than the kind actors expected. The recipients also reliably rated these acts as "bigger" than the people performing them did.

We initially studied acts of kindness done for familiar people, such as friends, classmates or family. But we found that participants underestimated their positive impact on strangers as well. For example, in one experiment participants at an ice-skating rink in a public park gave away hot chocolate on a cold winter's day. The experience was more positive than the givers anticipated for the recipients, who were people who just happened to be nearby. Although the people giving out the hot chocolate saw the act as relatively inconsequential, it really mattered to the recipients.[1]

Recently, when I pushed on our garage door button the door would start to lift and then stop and close. We also were at times having a hard time getting one of our other garage doors to open or close when the opener button was pushed. I had arranged to have a repairman from the company who installed the garage door controls to help us. Several days had gone by and there had been no response.

It just so happened that friends, we had known since we moved to San Jose in 1976, were in town waiting for a flight to see their son Cris in Okinawa. During our visit with the Wikstroms the garaged doors were mentioned. The next day their son Cory called us and arranged to come over the next afternoon and look at our garage doors. He came, realigned one garage door, greased and examined all three of our doors and replaced a defective opener. Cory had been in Boy Scouts and other youth church activities during my tenure as an adult leader. We had a wonderful visit about his parents and family. He was a very active young man and had some fun that made me silently question how he was going to handle adult life.

When mentioned that I needed to run in the house and get my checkbook – he told me that there was no charge and that he was happy to return some of the favors I'd extended him in the past. Thoughts of him trying to care for a family and my more stable financial situation made me feel guilty accepting his generosity. He insisted and I thanked him for his kind act.

His actions have crossed my mind several times and more intensely since I read the article on the consequences of kindness: "both performers and recipients of the acts of kindness were in more positive moods than normal after these exchanges. For another, it was clear that performers undervalued their impact: recipients felt significantly better than the kind actors expected. The recipients also reliably rated these acts as "bigger" than the people performing them did."

The research also revealed one reason why people may underestimate their action's impact. For example, when we asked one set of participants to estimate how much someone would like getting a cupcake simply for participating in a study, their predictions were well calibrated with recipients' reactions. But when people received cupcakes through a random act of kindness, the cupcake givers underestimated how positive their recipients would feel. Recipients of these unexpected actions tend to focus more on warmth than performers do.

Missing the importance of warmth may stand in the way of being kinder in daily life. People know that cupcakes can make folks feel good, but it turns out that cupcakes given in kindness can make them feel surprisingly good. If people undervalue this effect, they might not bother to carry out these warm, prosocial behaviors.

And kindness can be contagious. In another experiment, we had people play an economic game that allowed us to examine what are sometimes called "pay it forward" effects. In this game, participants allocated money between themselves and a person whom they would never meet. People who had just been on the receiving end of a kind act gave substantially more to an anonymous person than those who had not. The person who performed the initial act did not recognize that their generosity would spill over in these downstream interactions.

These findings suggest that what might seem small when we are deciding whether or not to do something nice for someone else could matter a great deal to the person we do it for. Given that these warm gestures can enhance our own mood and brighten the day of another person, why not choose kindness when we can?[1]

President Abraham Lincoln led America through the ravages of the Civil War with dignity and grace. In his second inaugural address, as the South was collapsing in the last of the battles, Lincoln called for "malice toward none" and "charity for all." In essence, he spoke of showing kindness in the most difficult of circumstances.

Kindness is relatively easy to practice when all is going well. To show kindness at difficult and stressful times is to allow the heart to govern what we do. Kindness is a language of its own, a power, a strength of character, a way of life—and these days it seems so often in short supply.

President Lincoln did more than just speak publicly of kindness; it guided his private interactions as well. He once instructed an army commander regarding the punishment of a Confederate officer: "My dear General, . . . do nothing in reprisal for the past—only what is necessary to ensure security for the future. I remind you," he continued, "that we are not fighting against a foreign foe, but our brothers, and that our aim is not to break their spirits but only to bring back their allegiance. Conquer them with kindness—let that be our policy."[2]

The study on kindness and consequences that, "These findings suggest what might seem small when we are deciding whether or not to do something nice for someone else could matter a great deal to the person we do it for. Given that these warm gestures can enhance our own mood and brighten the day of another person, why not choose kindness when we can?" This statement made me feel remised and I wished I could have let Cory really know how he made me feel during our encounter with my garage doors. I recently texted him the following letter:

"I've thought several times about the kindness you extended coming over and taking care of our garage door needs. Then to do it out of the goodness of your heart had a further impact. They call this behavior Charity or the pure love of Christ and loving your fellow man.

You came from good seed, found good soil to sprout and grew into a man of good character. Thank you for your expression of love you made to me and my family…"

I'm in hopes that my placing Cory on the receiving end that he will better understand, "it was clear that performers undervalued their impact: recipients felt significantly better than the kind actors expected. The recipients also reliably rated these acts as 'bigger' than the people performing them did."

Thank you, Cory Wikstrom

1– *Kindness Can Have Unexpectedly Positive Consequences, Scientific American By Amit Kumar (Credit Chanelle Nibbelink), 2022.*

2– *Conquer with Kindness, Music & The Spoken Word, #4321, July 08, 2012.*

18

LIFE LONG SECRET

Dr. Joseph Linsk grew up on Atlantic Avenue in the uptown section of Atlantic City, N.J., in the early 1930s. It's an area where he's spent most of his life and where he practiced medicine starting in the 1940s, specializing in cancer and blood diseases. Now 94 years old, the former hematologist and oncologist is failing in health, as he battles Parkinson's disease. This grave illness, however, is only one part of a perennial struggle Linsk faces. For more than 80 years, he has kept a secret. And it's one about which we're kindly requesting your help.

At his Atlantic City home over the Thanksgiving weekend, Linsk was recorded by his son, Richard, as part of StoryCorps' annual effort called the Great Thanksgiving Listen. During that recording, Dr. Linsk shared that well-guarded secret he had held onto for almost his entire life.

I was smitten with grief at what I had done. I kept that secret to the age of 94, which is hard to believe, but the event never left me: "When I was 8 years old, I was running in the schoolyard and my arm struck the eyeglasses of one of the students. And he began to cry," he recalls. "He was going to tell his father. It would cost $2 to fix the glasses. And I was frightened to death — where was I going to get the $2?

We had a cleaning lady by the name of Pearl, a black woman. And I knew that every week, she'd get $2 for her services. On this particular day, I was so terrified, I took the $2, and took it to the teacher and settled the problem of the broken glasses."

"When Pearl finished her day's work, she went for the $2 and they weren't there. And my mother said there was no question that Pearl took the $2 and didn't admit it. And my mother was so angry that she told Pearl not to come back anymore."

His action had a domino effect. Word leaked out that Pearl was a thief. Pearl, who had several children, couldn't get another job, Linsk says. "I was the only one who knew the true story. And I didn't tell anyone. And I was smitten with grief at what I had done. I kept that secret to the age of 94, which is hard to believe, but the event never left me."

This is only half the story. Linsk doesn't remember Pearl's last name and doesn't know what happened to her or her family. That's where you come in. Considering Dr. Linsk's Atlantic City origin, if you have information regarding Pearl or know someone related to her, please email StoryCorps.org.[1]

It has sometimes been assumed that truth pertains only to what one says or writes—that if we give a wrong impression with the right words, we are still within the truth. But words are not the only way of conveying meanings. And whether or not we are truthful depends not only upon the words we use but also upon the intentions we have and the impressions we give. The truth has not been told unless there is an honest transference of thought, an honest conveyance of meaning, regardless of what we say in words.

Indeed, the untruth of actions can be more misleading than the untruth of words. A picture or a gesture may tell a thousand lies without a word being spoken. And what is left unsaid may be more misleading than what is said. It is a relatively easy matter to convict a man of a spoken or a written lie, but it is often difficult to convict him of deliberately making a false impression. We can read words; we can record them; we can define them; we can hear the true or false ring of the voice that speaks them. But an unspoken lie is an illusive deception. It is akin to the kind of lying a man does when he falsely wears a uniform, which, without his saying so, gives the impression that he is something which he is not. For this kind of false impression there are specific penalties. But for some kinds of false impressions, the penalties are difficult to invoke. Nevertheless, he who acts a lie, he who lives a lie, or he who knowingly permits a deception, is guilty on moral grounds with him who deliberately speaks a lie, because both contrive to mislead the minds of men.

To those with many years ahead of them—to youth, especially—let this be said: We are not wholly truthful when we offer a half-truth to anyone who has a right to the whole truth. We are not wholly truthful when we warp facts with words or in any other way. Deception is much more than a mere matter of words. He who falsifies without words is guilty with him who does it with words. And even though the rules of legal evidence may not always be able to hold him accountable, the rules of moral evidence will.[2]

Before my teenage years I was staying with my parents at a dude ranch in the mountains near our home in southeastern Idaho. We had our own cabin, horses to ride and I will always remember a cloud burst of rain, hail, lightening, and thunder's crashing sounds echoing in the mountains around us. It was a wonderful trip having one on one moments with my mom and dad.

I also have not forgotten the candy bar dispensing machine that was at the lodge. I placed a nickel in the machine and got a candy bar and a nickel for change. I kept going back to the machine and ate several candy bars during our stay. Near the end of our vacation, I "bought" another candy bar and left the nickel in the change receptacle. Love of candy squelched my guilt and fear of being caught for the moment. Conscience and guilt caught up with me after I wasn't able to repent and give restitution for my actions.

Portion of Dr. Linsk's obituary in October 2018:

> "Dr. Joseph Linsk passed away today, age 95, after a prolonged illness. He follows his beloved wife of 69 years, Doritt, who passed in October. They were high school sweethearts and knew each other for 80 years. Joe was a lifelong resident of Atlantic City, where he practiced medicine and raised his family.
>
> The Linsk home was loving and welcoming, always full of family and friends. Joe and Doritt cared for everyone, providing a second home for the children of Doritt's

sisters, Ruth and Sheila, who died prematurely of cancer.

Joe had a rich interior life and nurtured his passion for literature. He often could be found in his den listening to Beethoven and reading - in many instances rereading – the classics. He was a published poet and a playwright. He had a joke for everyone.

He gave to charities just about every day. Most of all he was a master clinician and pioneer who wrote two textbooks introducing Fine Needle Aspiration to American physicians."[3]

If conscience smite thee once, it is an admonition; if twice, it is a condemnation. What other dungeon is so dark as one's own heart! What jailer so inexorable as one's self! *Nathaniel Hawthorne*

1– *A Lifelong Secret: Can You Help This Ailing 94-Year-Old Man Make Amends? Stefanie Campolo, Press of Atlantic City, December 2016.*

2– *Music & The Spoken Word, On Lying Without Speaking, #1,067, 1950.*

3– *Roth-Goldsteins Memorial Chapel, LLC, Pacific & New Hampshire Avenues, Atlantic City, New Jersey.*

19

ABANDONING AMBITIONS

Since the 19th century, when motivational science had its start, scientists have focused on what makes us persist through difficulties and achieve what we want. Only recently have they zeroed in on how we can relinquish our cherished aspirations—and why we should. They term this process "goal disengagement," and research psychologist Gabriele Oettingen says it has been treated as the "black sheep" of the field.

Why is that so? Western cultural bias celebrates persistence and achievement, so abandoning goals is seen as "failure," says psychologist Cathleen Kappes co-editor of the December 2022 issue of Motivation and Emotion, which is devoted entirely to advances in goal disengagement science. The issue exemplifies a swelling movement to correct this neglect.

This work mainly focuses on long-term goals central to our lives or identity: getting a degree, finding a spouse, becoming a homeowner. Some aims may be shorter-term, such as training to run a marathon, but they all require commitment, effort and sacrifice.

Endless research and everyday experience tell us that overcoming obstacles to eventually succeed is essential for our well-being. Such initiatives can be anything from a toddler falling on her butt until she learns to walk to a law school graduate finally passing the bar.

But trying and trying again is not the whole story. What the latest science shows us is the importance of abandoning ambitions when they become too costly or their feasibility plunges, or both. Given the long-running emphasis on the value of persistence, an immediate question arises: Is letting go as critical as persisting? It's hard to know. What matters most for our well-being, Kappes says, "is rather the optimal interplay between both processes."

The ability to set goals, pursue them despite setbacks and then quit them as circumstances change is adaptive and healthy. So is finding and committing to meaningful new aspirations. Some of us are much better at doing one or both of these things, and how well we do them dramatically affects our emotional and physical health.

To measure how our natural abilities to do both these things affect people's lives, psychology professor Carsten Wrosch, developed the Goal Adjustment Scale (GAS). It asks people how they react when forced to stop pursuing an important goal. One self-rating component declares, "I stay committed to the goal for a long time; I can't let it go." Another says, "I seek other meaningful goals."

The GAS measures both people's ability to disengage and their ability to find and commit to new objectives. Wrosch says these are complementary but differing capabilities. Letting go means withdrawing both commitment and effort - it prevents repeated failures and leads to less stress, depression and intrusive thoughts. Committing to and working toward new ambitions create a sense of purpose in life and reduce the sense of failure.[1]

God has a way of forcing one to stop pursuing his/her perceived important goals. My first hint that I was mortal and the need to change some of my goals came at the age of forty (1986) when I had a ruptured disk in my back, had my first root canal and passed a calcium oxalate kidney stone. The root canal and kidney stone pain passed and were soon forgotten. However, I was advised by a pharmacist friend that the state of the art of surgery on my back was risky and that I should not have surgery until the pain drove me to the surgery suite. I strengthened my back muscles riding a bicycle and was able to work and do physical activities with my family and serve as an assistant scout master and a cub master until I was released in 2020. I rode my bike with a youth group from San Jose to Disney Land two times and from the Oregon border to San Francisco.

Riding a bike for exercise and working as a veterinarian is a difficult task. Early morning exercise often in the dark and with commute traffic was not wise and in the evening after work I was tired, hungry and the demands of my family made riding difficult. Being a weekend warrior had its strain on family, Sunday activities and proper physical rest preparing for the coming week.

When my kid's mom was diagnosed with terminal cancer in 2001 riding a bike slowly tapered off and eventually became non-existent. I needed to be home more and who would come to my rescue if I had problems alone on the side of the road 10 miles away from home.

At the suggestion from my secretary/business manager, Nance Itri, I began walking with my Labrador retriever, Maui, after my wife's passing. In 2004 I had a goal of walking at least 1000 miles a year. That meant that I needed to walk an average of at least 20 miles a week rain or shine or work or vacations etc. With an average walking speed for humans of 2.5 to 4 miles per hour, I found myself getting up as early as 3:30 AM to reach my goal of 5 miles per day. It wasn't long before Maui started limping on her right front leg during these walks and I became a lone walker.

One morning I noticed a mountain lion near where a creek crosses under the road. Here I was out in the dark of early morning, seeing a lion walking near a street light, the hair raising on the back of my neck and stupidly continuing to walk past the spot where the lion went into the bushes in order to complete my morning route.

It has been said that it takes only three times missing Sunday meetings at church to become inactive – I was so intense reaching my walking goal it became more important than sleep or breakfast. It took fairly extreme weather events to keep me from my walks. For cruises with my family, I bought a hand counter, while in dock used my iPhone to calculate the distance around the hallway on our deck, and would get up early to walk laps around the ship's empty hallway keeping track of my mileage – the outside track was closed at night. During this time in my life, missing three Sunday meetings caused a lot less anxiety than not walking three days in a row. It only took a few years before I was forced into getting my priorities in order.

My flat feet have always bothered me when standing too long and eventually they began hurting when I was walking during exercise. A podiatrist recommended inserts which did not help, recommended my feet be injected with cortisone for plantar fasciitis which I rejected and finally a client recommended that I try her success using Z-coil shoes. These shoes have a spring attached under the heal of the foot that elevates it much like a women's high heels. The Z-coils helped make it possible for me to continue walking without much discomfort.

In 2013-2014 I was treated for prostate cancer, 2017 I had surgery on my right knee for a torn meniscus which failed the next year, high blood and a stroke in April 2019, and in the same year finally had a fusion of my lumbar back, that had bothered me since 1986, with screws, a lumbar disk spacer and two rods. If I only had heeded what I was doing to Maui on our walks I may have backed off, became less aggressive and more realistic as to what I was doing to my body.

My goal adjustment scale over the years has progressively told me that I could not continue the physical and work activities I was accustomed to. I have had to slow down and learn to enjoy the pleasantries around me. I have needed to disengage from intense physical activities and now engage in the medical needs of my body. The mental anxieties have changed to more a state of peace of mind, wonderment of the beauty of God's creations and the engagement with friends I've become close to over the years. Especially, there's the joy and satisfaction of watching my offspring conquer the challenges coming their way and the fulfillment of their dreams and aspirations.

No more dreams about 1000 mile a year walking goals. I have found and committed to new objectives that complement my more realistic capabilities. This has reduced my anxiety of failure, helped me have new ambitions, restored a sense of purpose in life and reduced the sense of failure.

In his younger days, Miracle was a member of Rockledge High School's state championship 4x800 relay team in the 1999-2000 school year. Through the years the youth soccer and football coach and father of four had done his best to stay in shape.

It was New Year's Eve in 2019 when Gary Miracle's life and goals changed forever. The father of four from Rockledge, Florida, suffered a blood infection and septic shock that led to cardiac arrest. At the hospital, his life was saved by a cardiac surgeon who just happened to be nearby when he coded.

The surgeon saved Gary's life using an extracorporeal membrane oxygenation (ECMO) machine, but unfortunately, his limbs could not be revived. After spending 10 days in a coma and 117 days in the hospital, Gary was ultimately discharged having lost all four limbs below his elbows and knee joints. Through it all, the one thing he never lost was his faith!

A devout Christian, Gary set out to live up to his last name: Miracle. Not content to merely learn to walk again, he was determined to get back to the athletic world he's always loved, like running and coaching youth soccer.

He received an outpouring of love and support from his friends, family, and community, including the Christian rock band MercyMe, who wrote a song called "Say I Won't" in his honor. Gary refused to allow anyone to feel sorry for him, choosing instead to use his condition as a teachable moment for others. "Everyone has my permission to stare and ask questions," he said. "If I can show 7- or 8-year-old kids another side of life, to show them that they can overcome all obstacles, I'm happy." His goal was to ditch his electric wheelchair for good, and he worked hard in rehab to get there.[2]

Committing to and working toward new ambitions and goals, a sense of purpose in life and reducing the sense of failure requires certain personality traits. Optimists may feel, "My life will be good again," which makes it easier to let go and to reengage with new goals. People who are habitual planners (if-then thinkers) sometimes have more trouble letting go but, once free, are better at finding and going after new endeavors.

Armed with a scale to measure goal-adjustment capacities, scientists have studied their impact. A 2019 meta-analysis of 31 samples overwhelmingly shows that people who are better at letting go have better functioning endocrine and immune systems, better health behaviors and fewer physical problems. Those better at pursuing new goals are healthier and function better physically under emotional distress.

In this context, two studies are particularly striking. Two groups of parents were compared: the first group's children had cancer, and the second group's children were healthy. The parents of healthy children had generally low depression. The parents of children with cancer, however, reported high depression if they were unable to disengage or reengage. Their counterparts who were able to disengage and reengage, by contrast, had low depressive symptoms, similar to the parents of healthy children.

Another study followed 135 adults, aged 64 to 90 years, over about six years at a time of life when physical declines often make certain desired pursuits no longer possible. For those who scored high in disengagement abilities, depressive symptoms were generally low and did not worsen. Those who scored low became more depressed over time, and at the end of the multiyear period, they reached a level of depression that warranted clinical evaluation and possible intervention.[1]

When Gary's custom prosthetic limbs were finally ready to use, he celebrated by completing his first one-mile jog on a treadmill.

The next step was to participate in an even longer race, so Gary signed up to run in the Tailgate Two Miler, a 2-mile footrace in Viera, Florida. "Yeah, you don't usually see guys without arms and legs (in footraces)," he joked.

On August 15, Gary accomplished his mission by crossing the finish line on his "brand new pair of legs!" His "Say I Won't" team was comprised of over 200 others, many of whom have limb differences of their own.

While Gary could have gotten stuck in regret and grief, his chosen goal is to inspire, motivate, and educate others instead. He's acutely aware of how close he came to dying, and he's not going to waste his second chance at making an impact in life. "I could have lost my (hands and feet), but I could have lost everything," he said. "Now I get emails from people across the world, people who want to tell their stories, and the most humbling part is that God has kept me in this position, a position in which I am able to speak and listen. At the end of the day, we all have our struggles. Mine are just more visible."

Gary is literally a walking miracle! His positive attitude is helping so many others overcome their struggles, and we are in awe!

While these things happened, Miracle's family and friends remained steadfast. And Miracle has some prominent friends. A sales professional, years ago Miracle worked in Texas with the Oklahoma-based contemporary Christian music group MercyMe, and they have remained "lifelong friends."

The group is known best for its 1999 hit "I Can Only Imagine." Being like the Miracles, devout Christians, the group prayed for him. Being entertainers, they created a song inspired by him.

"Say I Won't" (Keep on saying I won't and I'll keep proving you wrong) comes with a video of Miracle during his struggles and thereafter, as well as lead singer Bart Millard, like Miracle, mainly in a chair. It is, in large part, responsible for Miracle's story having been told worldwide. I can do all things.[2]

> "Through 'Christ' who gives me strength,
> So keep on saying I won't. And I'll
> keep proving you wrong,
> I'm gonna run. No, I'm gonna fly,
> I'm gonna know what it means to
> live, And not just be alive,"
> *"Say I Won't", MercyMe*

Mircale said, "From the moment I came home, my wife and I have prayed for purpose. I could have lost my (hands and feet), but I could have lost everything. Now I get emails from people across the world, people who want to tell their stories, and the most humbling part is that God has kept me in this position, a position in which I am able to speak and listen."[2]

"No man, with a man's heart in him, gets far on his way without some bitter, soul-searching disappointment. Happy he who is brave enough to push on another stage of the journey, and rest where there are "living springs of water, and three-score and ten palms." *Jean Fleming Brown, educator (1881-1950).*

1– *The Best New Year's Resolution Might Be to Just Let Go of an Unfulfilled Life Goal Leaving aside a cherished objective may benefit psychological and even physical health, by Francine Russo, 2022.*

2– *"I Could Have Lost Everything." Dad Who Lost All 4 Limbs Inspires Millions By Taking On 2-Mile Race, Beverly L. Jenkins, 2021.*

20

DON'T LET THE DAM BREAK

I have a rock in my museum dated June 1994 that was collected on the Mendenhall glacier near Juneau, Alaska during an inside passage cruise with my family. We were flown by helicopter 12 miles from Juneau to the surface of the glacier and did a guided walking tour on the surface. During this tour the two lasting memories are that the rocks on the surface of the glacier were forming deep holes in the ice the diameter of the rock (the sun heated the rocks enough to slowly melt the ice underneath and the weight of the rock sank deeper and deeper into the ice). The other thing I noticed was there was the sound of water flowing under the ice. It reminded me of a rapidly flowing mountain stream. The Mendenhall Glacier drains into Mendenhall Lake which drains into the Mendenhall River.

Igneous quartz-rich, dioritic rocks known as tonalite are commonly eroded by the Mendenhall Glacier and are found in glacier sediments around Mendenhall Lake. The rocks contain magnetic minerals, which makes the darker sands around the Mendenhall Lake attractive to magnets. The rock I have reminds me of granite in the Sierra Mountains in California and magnets are attracted to it.

Another memory about this trip occurred after a formal dinner on the cruise ship when I was walking through the casino. There was my 19-year-old son preparing to embark on a mission for his church to Argentina and his about to become 18-year-old brother sitting at a black jack table all dressed up in their Sunday best gambling.

A glacial lake is a body of water that originates from a glacier. It typically forms at the foot of a glacier, but may form on, in, or under it. As Earth's climate warms, the world's glaciers are shrinking, increasing freshwater outputs to all kinds of glacial lakes. Some communities depend on glacial meltwater for seasonal irrigation or domestic use, but as the balance shifts toward more melt, this water source may not be reliable in the long term and comes with new risks.

As glaciers move, they erode the terrain under them, leaving depressions and grooves on the land. When they churn up rock and soil, they etch ridges of debris known as moraines. Most glacial lakes form when a glacier retreats and melt water empties into the hole left behind.

Natural dams, formed out of ice and terminal moraines, can also form glacial lakes. An ice dam forms when a surging glacier, which can move up to 100 times faster than an average glacier, may dam up meltwater as it closes off a valley or fjord and prevents it from draining. Dams formed by moraines can be dense and stable, holding sizable lakes behind them for years. They can also be leaky, allowing the lake to drain slowly into nearby rivers.

However, prolonged melting or abrupt bursts of intense melting can wreak havoc. Too much meltwater in a short period of time might overflow a lake or (pent-up closely confined or held water) may burst through natural barriers, flooding lands downstream, washing away communities, and damaging roads and infrastructure. Lakes held back by moraines pose a serious threat because the porous moraine walls can destabilize easily. A rise in the amount of meltwater from glaciers increases the water pressure on the moraine barriers, which can quickly give way and threaten inundation.

The hazards of a moraine-dammed pent-up glacial lake and potential triggers include: contact glacier calving; icefall from hanging glaciers; rock/ice/snow avalanches; dam settlement and/or piping; ice-cored moraine degradation; rapid input of water from on top of, inside, or subglacial (including subaqueous) sources; earthquakes.

Conditioning factors for dam failure include pent-up large lake volume; low width-to-height dam ratio; degradation of buried ice in the moraine structure; limited dam freeboard.

Key stages of a Glacial Lake Outburst Flood (GLOF) include (1) propagation of displacement or seiche waves in the lake (similar in motion to a seesaw, a seiche is a standing wave in which the largest vertical oscillations are at each end of a body of water with very small oscillations at the "node," or center point, of the wave), and/or piping through the dam; (2) breach initiation and breach (gap or break) formation; (3) propagation of resultant flood wave(s) down-valley.

Alaska currently lacks a warning system to notify communities of impending glacial lake outburst floods.

While they constitute a growing concern, glacial lakes are a natural part of the glacial process. However, in a world of increasing temperatures and human population, flooding is a growing concern.[1]

We all experience the feeling of being angry. Maybe it is anger directed at a situation or another person, or perhaps it's your go-to response to a perceived threat, real or not. Regardless of what causes you to feel angry, it's how you handle it that matters most.

But what happens when anger takes over and you can't find a way to address and release these feelings? When this occurs, the result is what experts often refer to as pent-up anger, or anger that's been withheld and not expressed -similar to a pent-up ice-dammed glacier that needs some of the pressure released. This type of anger can affect your mental and physical health. That's why it's important to identify, address, and move past these feelings.

While the triggers for each person may vary, there are some common causes of pent-up anger, such as feeling unheard or unappreciated, lack of acceptance of a situation, or unmet needs. Some people may also experience anger when they're hurt. Instead of feeling vulnerable to the pain of feeling the hurt, they instead feel anger and often feel a desire to hurt others.

Depression and anxiety are examples of unexpressed anger, because anger turned inward often results in self-hatred, which causes depression.

What all of these situations have in common is an experience of anger without expressing or coping with the feelings. When this happens, the anger is allowed to simmer internally, resulting in pent-up anger.

While anger is a valid emotion, most of the time it doesn't serve us or help us to hold onto it."[2]

August 6, 2023 at least two homes in Juneau, Alaska, collapsed into a river and were swept away over the weekend as fast-moving flash flood waters from a melting glacier cascaded through the city. Water rushed down the river so quickly that it eroded the bank, leaving additional homes and condo buildings condemned and displacing dozens of people. The city issued a state of emergency in response to the disaster, the scale of which, Aaron Jacobs, senior service hydrologist for the National Weather Service experts, said they didn't even think this was possible.

Mendenhall Glacier, located about 13 miles from Juneau, is one of the city's most popular attractions. The awe-inspiring, 3,000-year-old mass is moving slowly downhill toward Mendenhall Lake, the headwaters of the Mendenhall River, which runs through Juneau. But climate change is causing the glacier to recede.

As Mendenhall and another nearby glacier melt, the water collects in a lake called Suicide Basin. Since 2011, this side basin has been periodically releasing pent-up retained surges of water called glacial lake outburst floods. Usually, Mendenhall Glacier traps water in the basin, like a dam. But eventually, the dam breaks, and water surges out from underneath the glacier and toward the city.

These glacial dams are no different to construct than a dam. If you take the Hoover Dam, for instance, you've got a massive lake behind it, but if you suddenly remove the

Hoover Dam, that water has to go somewhere, and it's going to come cascading down a valley in massive flood waves.

Over the years, the floods from Mendenhall Glacier have become more frequent and more destructive. The recent flooding was a result of water discharging at about 25,000 cubic feet per second, a staggeringly high rate of flow that the Federal Emergency Management Agency had previously predicted had less than a 1 percent chance of happening.[3]

The English dramatist, John Webster, observed that, "There is not in nature a thing that makes man so deformed, so beastly, as doth intemperate anger." He was not alone in his observation. In virtually every culture and time, wise men and prophets have noted how destructive anger is. In the words of a Chinese proverb, "The fire you kindle for your enemy often burns yourself more than him."

And yet, how many times have we excused our anger, or excused our actions because of it? Like a pent-up glacier bursting from the dammed water within it,[5] many people treat anger as though it were some sort of unavoidable consequence, an emotion that cannot be controlled. They say, "I couldn't help myself," or "I blew up," as though anger were an emotion thrust upon them and for which they have no personal responsibility.

But the scriptures are clear about our responsibility concerning anger. "Cease from anger," the Psalmist writes, "and forsake wrath." Why? Because we cannot control our lives unless we do. Anger is not an "active" emotion but is "reactive." In a very real sense, it depends on the actions of others, and it makes us submissive to those actions. Someone hurts or offends us, and we become angry. Thus, the angry person is forever the "effect" of some other "cause."

There is no profit in anger—no peace, no joy, no love. There are those who presume to be angry because of love or concern, but in truth, anger springs from fear and weakness, from an inability to control what has been given us to control. True love, and the peace and joy that spring from it, overcome anger; they make us "effective" rather than mere "effects."

"Cease from anger," the Psalmist writes, "For…those that wait upon the Lord, they shall inherit the earth."[4]

The USDA Forest Service Mendenhall Glacier Visitor Center is located in the Mendenhall Valley, 12 miles from downtown Juneau. The visitor center provides amazing views of the glacier and lake. During the week of the 4th and 11th of June 2023 our family took the tour to Mendenhall Lake. We were able to walk around the lake and pick up glacier ice. I wander what we would have observed if we had of been on that tour on August 6th 2023? Would we have expressed anger if we had been caught in the rising waters in Mendenhall Lake?

1– *What are glacial lakes?, National Snow & Ice Data Center, 02/15/2022.*

2– *How to Deal with Pent-Up Anger, Medically reviewed by Timothy J. Legg, PhD, PsyD — By Sara Lindberg on May 20, 2019.*

3– *Two Buildings Collapse, Others Damaged in Record-Setting Glacial Floods in Alaska, Smithsonian, 08/11/2023.*

4– *Cease From Anger, Music & the Spoken Word, Broadcast# 2778, 11/14/1982.*

5– *Added by book author.*

Igneous quartz-rich, dioritic rocks known as tonalite are commonly eroded by the Mendenhall Glacier and are found in glacier sediments around Mendenhall Lake. The rocks contain magnetic minerals (note magnet lower right corner). Found on glacier June 1994…

21

THE SPIRIT TO BE WITH US

All men know they must die. And it is important that we should understand…the designs and purposes of God in our coming into the world, our sufferings here, and our departure hence. What is the object of our coming into existence, then dying and falling away, to be no more? It is but reasonable to suppose that God would reveal something in reference to the matter, and it is a subject we ought to study more than any other. We ought to study it day and night, for the world is ignorant in reference to their true condition and relation. If we have any claim on our Heavenly Father for anything, it is for knowledge on this important subject.[1] (ch1#3)

We should never forget that we have been promised, if worthy, to always have His Spirit with us…it is a grand privilege…to have the manifestations of the Spirit every day of our lives. So we should be careful not to judge too quickly, deny "the power of God" and "quench the Holy Spirit". We trust the Lord will help us discern the truth.[1](ch1#7)

The light of Christ, which is in the sun, moon, stars, and earth, and which constitutes the power thereof by which they were made "proceedeth forth from the presence of God to fill the immensity of space." Most Near-Death Experience beholders often encounter this light in the spirit world. They find it difficult to define, but their feelings are consistent with the light of Christ: comfort, joy, love, warmth and belonging, reassurance, peacefulness, and understanding.[1](ch16#170)

It appears that every human being that has ever lived on the earth was privileged to have spiritual light of Christ experiences. Some are not recognizable and most come in quiet, delicate, subtle ways and maybe the light comes as a warm feeling that you experienced from helping others or as a confirmation that you were making a correct discission in your life. Short answers as to the conditions in which we qualify for spiritual enlightening experiences were given by Christ in The New Testament called the Beatitudes:

1– Blessed are the poor in spirit who come unto me: We can all agree that being poor economically is not usually a desired blessing, but the Savior is talking about something entirely different. He is talking about humility and subjecting oneself to the Lord in all things.

2– Blessed are they that mourn - for they shall be comforted: It is through suffering that one discovers the difference between those things that are important and that which is unimportant in the eternal perspective. It is in the midst of mourning that one discovers the personal closeness of his Heavenly Father and his Savior Jesus Christ and the comfort of the Holy Ghost.

3– Blessed are the meek for they shall inherit the earth: I don't feel the Savior wanted us to be doormats to be walked on. You can be strong, enthusiastic, talented, spirited, zealous, and still be "meek" by being obedient and well trained. I can seek to be that kind of a meek person and be proud to have that as my goal—obedient and well trained—and still coexist in the success-oriented world in which we live.

4– Blessed are they which do hunger and thirst after righteousness - for they shall be filled with the Holy Ghost: The highest blessings of the gospel are not for the fainthearted, lukewarm, coolly rational, theoretical philosopher, nor for the intellectually curious. The highest blessings are for those stouthearted souls who are on a noble quest, a crusade for greater personal righteousness. They hunger and thirst for righteousness.

5– Blessed are the merciful - for they shall obtain mercy: If ye forgive men their trespasses, your heavenly Father will also forgive you: But if ye forgive not men their trespasses, neither will your Father forgive your trespasses. (Matthew 6:14–15)

6– Blessed are the pure in heart - for they shall see God: It is probable that this beatitude requiring we be clean and pure of heart requires the greatest degree of self-examination of all the Beatitudes. It really means, "Blessed are those whose thoughts are pure and clean and untainted by ulterior motives or conflicts of interest or anything spiritually degrading." This person's heart must be absolutely genuine and sincere. The self-examination must be honest and humbling. All pride and self-gratification must be eliminated. Therefore, sanctify yourselves that your minds become single to God, and the days will come that you shall see him; for he will unveil his face unto you, and (but) it shall be in his own time, and in his own way, and according to his own will.

7– Blessed are the peacemakers - for they shall be called the children of God: The term "peace" is used almost one hundred times in the New Testament and seems to always be closely identified with Christ as the Prince of Peace. The Savior had no material wealth to give to others, but he frequently gave them blessings of peace—a kind of legacy. In this beatitude, those who are blessed are not particularly those who love peace but rather those who seek peace and who produce peace. The blessed ones are those who are the doers of the word, not just passive listeners.

8– Blessed are they which are persecuted for my name's sake - for theirs is the Kingdom of Heaven: This beatitude is often referred to as the blessing of the martyrs. In the days of the New Testament and later days, the meaning of "witness" and "martyr" at times have been virtually synonymous. Bearing testimony always has brought persecution.[2]

Contemplating if man really has received revelation from God, Jesus Christ or the Holy Ghost throughout the history of the human animal, I ran across a book about a man who "held one of – if not the most- powerful positions in the world during his time." I feel the only way he could have lived the way he did was if he was influenced by the Holy Spirit of God during a time when the term "god" in his culture meant something very different than described in the scriptures.

Marcus Aurelius was a Roman emperor, born nearly two millennia ago (121–180). Marcus became the Emperor of the Roman Empire in 161 and ruled for nearly two decades until his death in 180. It is important to realize the gravity of that position and the magnitude of power that Marcus possessed. He held one of—if not the most—powerful positions in the world at the time. If he chose to, nothing would be off limits. There is a reason the adage that power in absolute absolutely corrupts has been repeated throughout history—it unfortunately tends to be true. And yet, as the essayist Matthew Arnold remarked, Marcus proved himself worthy of the position he was in.

Marcus has only one core work, which was actually never intended for publication: His Meditations (originally titled "To Himself"). This is not only one of greatest books ever written but perhaps the only book of its kind. It is the definitive text on self-discipline, personal ethics, humility, self-actualization and strength. *Daily Stoic*

Below is a fairly lengthy list of thoughts I found during the reading of the *Meditations of Marcus Aurelius* that I feel personally were influenced by God's spirit and light:

- Be tolerant with others and strict with yourself.
- You don't have to turn this into something. It doesn't have to upset you.

- To live a good life: We have the potential for it. If we learn to be indifferent to what makes no difference.
- It's silly to try to escape other people's faults. They are inescapable. Just try to escape your own.
- Think of yourself as dead. You have lived your life. Now take what's left and live it properly.
- Because most of what we say and do is not essential. Ask yourself at every moment, 'Is this necessary?'
- The impediment to action advances action. What stands in the way becomes the way.
- It's unfortunate that this has happened. No. It's fortunate that this has happened and I've remained unharmed.
- You're better off not giving the small things more time than they deserve.
- If it is not right, do not do it, if it is not true, do not say it.
- Waste no more time arguing what a good man should be. Be one.
- It's all in how you perceive it. You're in control. You can dispense with misperception at will, like rounding the point.
- It's a disgrace in this life when the soul surrenders first while the body refuses to.
- The best revenge is not to be like your enemy.
- Just that you do the right thing. The rest doesn't matter.
- Your mind will take the shape of what you frequently hold in thought, for the human spirit is colored by such impressions.

- You shouldn't give circumstances the power to rouse anger, for they don't care at all.
- Take a good hard look at people's ruling principle, especially of the wise, what they run away from & what they seek out.
- Accept the things to which fate binds you and love the people with whom fate brings you together but do so with all your heart.
- Dig deep within yourself, for there is a fountain of goodness ever ready to flow if you will keep digging.
- Yes, keep on degrading yourself, soul. But soon your chance at dignity will be gone. Everyone gets one life.
- If there were anything harmful on the other side of death, they would have made sure that the ability to avoid it was within you.
- Don't waste the rest of your time here worrying about other people – unless it affects the common good.
- Never regard something as doing you good if it makes you betray trust, or lose your sense of shame, or makes you show hatred, suspicion, ill will, or hypocrisy, or a desire for things best done behind closed doors...If it's time for you to go, leave willingly – as you would to accomplish anything that can be done with grace and honor.
- Your ability to control your thoughts – treat with respect. It's all that protects your mind from false perceptions.
- Nowhere you can go is more peaceful – more free of interruptions – than your own soul.

- People who are excited by posthumous fame forget that the people who remember them will soon die too.
- Don't be hard on yourself. Practice the virtues you can show: honesty, gravity, endurance, seriousness, high-mindedness. Don't you see how much you have to offer – beyond excuses like "can't"?
- Some people, when they do someone a favor, are always looking for a chance to call it in. And some aren't, but they're still aware of it – still regard it as a debt. But others don't even do that. They're like a vine that produces grapes without looking for anything in return.
- In a sense, people are our proper occupation. Our job is to do them good and put up with them. But when they obstruct our proper tasks, they become irrelevant to us – like sun, wind, animals. Our actions may be impeded by them, but there can be no impeding our intentions or our dispositions. Because we accommodate and adapt. The mind adapts and converts to its own purposes the obstacle to our acting. The impediment to action advances action. What stands in the way becomes the way.
- So other people hurt me? That's their problem. Their character and actions are not mine.
- When you think you've been injured, apply this rule. If the community isn't injured by it, neither am I. And if it is, anger is not the answer. Show the offender where he went wrong.
- Don't be irritated at people's smell, or bad breath. What's the point? With that mouth, with those

armpits, they're going to produce that odor. Use your logic to awaken his. Show him. Make him realize it. If he'll listen, then you'll have solved the problem. Without anger.

— Consider all that you've gone through, all that you've survived. And that the story of your life is done, your assignment complete. How many good things have you seen? How much pain and pleasure have you resisted? How many honors have you declined? How many unkind people have you been kind to?

— Pride is a master of deception: when you think you're occupied in the weightiest business, that's when he has you in his spell.

— Treat what you don't have as nonexistent. Look at what you have, the things you value most, and think of how much you'd crave them if you didn't have them. But be careful. Don't feel such satisfaction that you start to overvalue them – that it would upset you to lose them.

— The gods live forever and yet they don't seem annoyed at having to put up with human beings and their behavior throughout eternity. And not only put up with but actively care for them.

— Give yourself a gift: the present moment.

— External things are not the problem. It's your assessment of them. Which you can erase right now.

— A man standing by a spring of clear, sweet water and cursing it. While the fresh water keeps on bubbling up. He can shovel mud into it, or dung, and the stream will carry it away, wash itself clean, remain unstained.

- We speak of the sun's light as "pouring down on us," as "pouring over us" in all directions. Yet it's never poured out. Because it doesn't really pour; it extends. Its beams get their name from their extension. What doesn't transmit light creates its own darkness.
- Don't look down on death, but welcome it. It too is one of the things required by nature. Like youth and old age. Like growth and maturity. Like a new set of teeth, a beard, the first gray hair. Like sex and pregnancy and childbirth. Like all the other physical changes at each stage of life, our dissolution is no different.
- And you can also commit injustice by doing nothing.
- Either all things spring from one intelligent source and form a single or there are only atoms, joining and splitting forever, and nothing else.
- Either the gods have power or they don't. If they don't, why pray? If they do, then why not pray for something else instead of for things to happen or not to happen? Pray not to feel fear. Or desire, or grief. If the gods can do anything, they can surely do that for us.[3]

In more a fatherly way, Marcus wrote a thought that reminded me of my youngest son – Jeremy. On Sunday mornings, while lying in bed, he would respond to my pleas that he needed to get ready for church with the "pat" answer, "I'll be ready". This response continued until I needed to leave, without him, for the meetings I was expected to attend.

He couldn't get up for early morning seminary classes. The instructor was nice enough to let him do "home study." Home study meant that his dad went through and found the answers to the study questions and wrote them down for him. His struggles through seminary involved reading his dad's writing and copying it into his study guide.

For his Boy Scout Eagle Award Project he remodeled a room assigned to the vocational agriculture department (their organizational club was FFA – Future Farmers of America). The department housed and cared for numerous animals – including exotic and endangered species. An engineer from GE, Ron Simons, was his project advisor and he had several friends help build a lab to help care for the animal's health needs. The goal of these projects is to contribute to the community with worthwhile service and learn leadership organizing and how to successfully complete a project. Jeremy learned the leadership by giving out assignments, using Ron's experience and showing up periodically like a project manager to evaluate the progress. Being there to do the work with his friends was seldom accomplished. Other "more important" things seemed to get in the way – mostly sports.

To make a long story short – Jeremy is active in his faith and raising a family with the admirable goals, he graduated from seminary, he received his Eagle Award and seems to be doing "everything right" to have a happy productive life.

I wished I had come across Marcus Aurelius' Meditations book during my son's informative years. Copies of Marcus' quote below would be taped to Jeremy's bathroom mirror, both sides of the front and his bedroom door in our house, on the inside side window of his car and as book marks in several places in his scriptures:

At dawn, when you have trouble getting out of bed, tell yourself: "I have to go to work – as a human being. What do I have to complain of, if I'm going to do what I was born for – the things I was brought into the world to do? Or is this what I was created for? To huddle under the blankets and stay warm?"

– But it's nicer here...?

So, you were born to feel "nice"? Instead of doing things and experiencing them? don't you see the plants, the birds, the ants and spiders and bees going about their individual tasks, putting the world in order, as best they can? And you're not willing to do your job as a human being? Why aren't you running to do what your nature demands?

– But we have to sleep sometimes...

Agreed. But nature set a limit on that – as it did on eating and drinking. And you're over the limit. You've had more than enough of that. But not of working. There you're still below your quota.

You don't love yourself enough. Or you'd love your nature too, and what it demands of you. People who love what they do wear themselves down doing it, they even forget to wash or eat. Do you have less respect for your own nature than the engraver does for engraving, the dancer for the dance, the miser for money or the social climber for status? When they're really possessed by what they do, they'd rather stop eating and sleeping than give up practicing their arts.

Is helping others less valuable to you? Not worth your effort?[3]

1– *Postmortal Spirit World, Compendium of Questions & Answers, Mark W. Sheffield, June 2011.*

2– *The Christ-Focused Beatitudes, Robert E. Wells, First Quorum of the Seventy, 05/20/1986.*

3– *Meditations, Marcus Aurelius (emperor of Rome 121-180), 2003.*

22

WORTH OF A SOUL

In the early 1930's Stalin in the name of a failed principle of collectivization of Ukrainian farmland, he took away the citizen's food and starved to death 3.9 million (13%) people. Nearly 100 years later the same country is attempting to destroy the same country with their military. Without needed energy many citizens and those from their surrounding countries stand to face freezing and starvation. Sad thing is that the Ukraine has one of the richest crop soils in the world and as in all aggressions -the reason given for all this destruction is like all wars - for the establishment of peace.

I never thought I would ever see people having protest marches for the right to kill their babies. Since 1973-2006 63.6 million abortions have been performed in this country. One of the arguments favoring abortions was to help reduce the cost to the welfare system raising these children.

In 1973 I graduated from college, I found employment, my wife and I moved into our first house, she began her nesting behavior by decorating a bedroom with a child's theme and we were not able to have children. We were not having much luck with a fertility clinic, an adoption service, at the time you could not foster care children and adopt, and we had a friend that worked for a hospital in Oakland, CA that offered abortions. My heart ached from the stories he told me about how many abortions the hospital performed and what was done with the fetus'. We didn't care about the sex of the child, where they came from or the color of their skin. The yearning was strong to share our lives with any child.

From the country south of us large quantities of Fentanyl, looking like skittles to attract youth, flood across the border. One taste or direct contact with the body, intentional or not, can result in addiction or death. From February 2021 to February 2022 108,000 victims did not receive a reversal drug in time before death. Transnational criminal organizations (TCOs) are the primary sources responsible for fueling the deadly overdose epidemic.

On 10/27/2022 the assistant director of Homeland and Security Dept of the U.S. Immigration & Customs Enforcement Dept. reported on Homeland Investigations (FHI) of the fentanyl flow entering the United States through Mexico. TCOs manufacture these drugs using precursor chemicals sourced from China and other foreign nations.

At my work we used Fentanyl for dogs in the 1990's. It was a great anesthetic, the drug was easily reversed, no patients that I remember died and since the patient couldn't consciously seek out the drug -there was no addiction. We stopped using the Fentanyl fearing employee abuse and the paper work needed by the FDA to monitor its use.

From the north 3% of Canada's total deaths are from assisted suicides. Those killed were supposed to show "reasonable foreseeable death" -whatever that is? Canada recently signed a new bill allowing mentally distressed individuals, including depression, to also be euthanized starting in 2023.

On 12/12/2022 Canada's MAID (Medical Assistance In Dying) system continued to alleviate the pain of patients and the financial strain on the nation's healthcare system, by an innovation expected to further improve results: Parliament just announced a punch card that allows patients to receive a free suicide after 10 doctor visits.

"From a small-scale maple syrup overdose to a full-blown moose attack, you receive a punch on your card every time you are admitted for an injury or sickness." The Canadian Healthcare website published a blog outlining the new program. "Filling out your punch card is mandatory, for data tracking purposes. No one sick person can be allowed to drain more than their share of the taxpayer's dollars!"

Trudeau praised the new initiative, positioning it as a way to better engage citizens and prevent any one citizen from becoming a burden on the system. "Canadians are team players," said Trudeau. "It's important for every citizen to make sure he's not wasting taxpayer money to sustain a life that's not worth living. And now with this punch card, they know that with each hospital visit they're one step closer to the end!" (I have a punch card for my car wash. Ten washes and I get a car wash for free – in Canada 10 doctor visits on your card and you get an all-expense paid suicide.)

Critics have contended that the new approach preys on disabled and impoverished Canadians who may see assisted suicide as their only option, but the criticism has already been quieted since Canadian Prime Minister Justin Trudeau froze the bank accounts of anyone who spoke out against his regime's policies in the comments section of the healthcare website's blog, or on Twitter, or elsewhere.

At publishing time, the burden on Canada's healthcare system was further alleviated when Parliament announced that the policy would retroactively apply to people who had already been admitted for 10 prior hospital visits. Looks like they will be the first in line to save Canada from "wasting taxpayer money."

These events have led me to ponder Gordon B. Hinckley's comment, "In all of living, have much fun and laughter. Life is to be enjoyed, not just endured." He lived to be 97 years of age and contributed to society until the day he died. Why does society place such little value on the souls that "get in their way" on this earth?

What motivated Henry Wadsworth Longfellow to write the poem "Christmas Bells" in 1863 that later became the famous song "I Heard the Bells on Christmas Day" that contains the words "hate is strong and mocks the song of peace on earth, good will to men?" And, after much anguish and despondency the carol concludes with the bells ringing out with resolution that "God is not dead, nor doth He sleep" and there will ultimately be "…peace on earth, good will to men."

In 1861, two years before writing this poem, Longfellow's personal peace was shaken when his second wife of 18 years, to whom he was very devoted, was fatally burned in an accidental fire. Then in 1863, during the American Civil

War, Longfellow's oldest son, Charles A. Longfellow, joined the Union Army without his father's blessing. Longfellow was informed by a letter dated March 14, 1863, after Charles had left. Charles was soon appointed as a lieutenant but he was severely wounded in the Battle of Mine Run. Charles eventually recovered, but his time as a soldier was finished.

Henry was traumatized from the loss of the woman he loved, an injured young son who left home without his knowledge that would have permanent scars from Civil War, and anguish and despondency from the loss of life and misery tearing up the United States of America.

What is the real worth a human's life and soul? Many seem to place little concern for those who don't directly affect them and if they do – it's okay to let them freeze or starve from war, have their lives terminated before they even have a chance at life, not be concerned about dangerous drugs killing their youth or if they are causing a burden on society having them removed by euthanasia.

"Remember the worth of souls is great in the sight of God; For, behold, the Lord your Redeemer suffered death in the flesh; wherefore he suffered the pain of all men, that all men might repent and come unto him" (D&C 18:10–11.)

The impact of this statement that Christ suffered "the pain of all men," here given by the Lord to emphasize his high appraisal of the worth of human souls, is sharpened by the realization of the intensity of that suffering. Of it, Luke wrote, speaking of Christ's prayer in Gethsemane: "And he … kneeled down, and prayed, saying Father, if thou be willing, remove this cup from me: nevertheless, not my will, but thine, be done. And there appeared an angel unto him from heaven, strengthening him. And being in an agony he prayed more earnestly: and his sweat was as it were great drops of blood falling down to the ground." (Luke 22:41–44.)

Now the answer to this profound question - What is man that he should be of such inestimable worth? It comes only by direct revelation from heaven. So important is it that it is communicated to men by God himself and angels sent by him. It was thus revealed in the very beginning to Adam and Eve. In each succeeding gospel dispensation, it has been likewise revealed to "chosen vessels of the Lord" (Moro. 7:31)—that is, to his prophets.

These prophets have faithfully borne testimony of the truth revealed to them. This they have done that the residue of men, those who will qualify themselves to obtain it, by the power of the Holy Ghost may come to a knowledge of it. (See Moro. 7:32.)

In this manner we ourselves have learned who and what man is. For such a knowledge we give the Lord great full thanks and adoration. Thus, knowing the truth, we bear the following witness:

Man is a dual being—a living soul—composed of a body of spirit and a physical body. His spirit existed as an individual personal entity in a premortal life long before the earth was created. As a matter of fact, this earth was expressly created as a place for the spirits of men to take on mortality.

The spirits of men, by their conduct in pre-earth life, earned a two-point destiny: (1) the privilege to be tabernacled in a body of flesh and bone; and (2) immortality as living souls.

The plan to bring about this two-point destiny provides for (1) mortal birth, through which man's spirit receives a body of flesh and bone, thus becoming a soul; (2) mortal death, by which man's spirit and body are temporarily separated—his soul dissolved; (3) redemption of the soul by resurrection—in which the spirit and body are inseparably reunited.

In this way the Lord brings to pass that immortality of which he spoke to Moses when he said, "This is my work and my glory—to bring to pass the immortality and eternal life of man" (Moses 1:39). Through his victory over death, Christ has already secured the immortality here spoken of. *The Worth of Souls,*

President Marion G. Romney, November 1978.

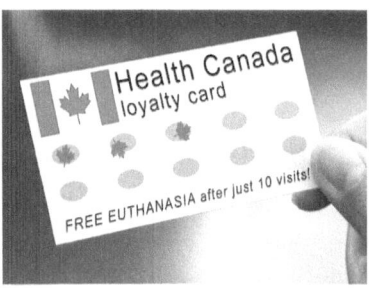
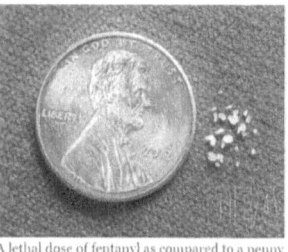

A lethal dose of fentanyl as compared to a penny
—U.S. Drug Enforcement Administration

23

POUND IS A POUND

There was once a farmer who, each week, sold a pound of butter to a baker. After several weeks of buying a pound of butter from the farmer, the baker decided to weigh the butter that he was receiving to ensure it was indeed a full pound. When the baker weighed it, he learned that the butter was under a pound, which enraged him. He felt he was being cheated and he decided to take the farmer to court.

When in court, the judge asked the farmer how he was weighing the butter. The farmer said, "Your Honor, I am poor. I do not own an exact measuring tool. However, I do have a scale."

The judge then asked if the farmer uses the scale to measure the butter. The farmer said, "Your Honor, I have been buying a one-pound loaf of bread from the baker since long before he began purchasing butter from me. Whenever the baker brings bread for me, I put it on the scale and then measure out the same weight in butter to give him in return. So, if the baker is not getting a pound of butter, he is also not giving a pound of bread as he promised." *(original author unknown)*

On July 23, 2023 Steve Hunter gave the following talk during our sacrament meeting: Recently I've been doing a lot of landscaping work in my front yard. While at The Home Depot getting supplies, I put 3 small bags of drip line drippers in my pocket, while I continued shopping. I went through self-checkout, and it wasn't until I got home and emptied out my pockets that I realized I forgot to pay for the 3 bags of drippers, still in my pocket.

Today I've been asked to talk about honesty. I hope to share a few ideas and principles to help us better understand had far-reaching the word "Honesty" really is. And why honesty is so important as disciples of Christ.

Honesty Is a Principle of Salvation. The 13th article of faith says, "We believe in being honest." Complete honesty is necessary for our salvation. President Brigham Young said, "If we accept salvation on the terms it is offered to us, we have got to be honest in every thought, in our reflections, in our meditations, in our private circles, in our deals, in our declarations, and in every act of our lives."

God is honest in all things. We too must be honest in all things to become like Him. The brother of Jared testified, "Yea, Lord, I know that thou … art a God of truth, and canst not lie". In contrast, the devil is a liar. In fact, he is the father of all lies. "Those who choose to cheat and lie and deceive and misrepresent become slaves of Satan."

Here are a few forms of Dishonesty: 1. Lying. Lying is intentionally deceiving others. Bearing false witness is one form of lying. The Lord gave this commandment to the children of Israel: "Thou shalt not bear false witness against thy neighbor" (Exodus 20:16). Satan would have us believe it is ok to lie. He says, "Yea, lie a little; … there is no harm in this".

Satan encourages us to justify our lies to ourselves. Honest people will recognize Satan's temptations and will speak the whole truth, even if it seems to be to their disadvantage.

2. Stealing is dishonest. Jesus taught, "Thou shalt not steal" (Matthew 19:18). Stealing is taking something without permission that does not belong to us. Taking merchandise or supplies from an employer is stealing. Copying music, movies, pictures, or written text without the permission of the copyright owners is dishonest and is a form of theft.

When I was 5 years old my mom took me shopping with her. When she wasn't looking, I stole a pack of gum. When she found out I had gum she marched me right back to the store and I had to tell the clerk what I did and say that I was sorry for stealing the pack of gum and then pay for it. I felt so bad about this, I knew I was never going to steal again. Kudos to parents that live their lives based on the principle of honesty and teach their children how to repent like my mom did!

3. Cheating is dishonest. We cheat when we give less than we owe, or when we get something we do not deserve. Some employees cheat their employers by not working their full time; yet they accept full pay. Some employers are not fair to their employees; they pay them less than they should. Taking unfair advantage is a form of dishonesty.

One of my brothers told me about a study he recently read about people using a vending machine that was broken. It would take your dollar, give you the candy and then give you your dollar back. It also had a sign on it that said, "If this machine malfunctions please call this number. Without exception, dozens of people took multiple candies over and over and not one of them called the phone number.

WALTER R. HOGE, DVM

What happens to us spiritually when we excuse our dishonesty? People use many excuses for being dishonest. People lie to protect themselves and to have others think well of them. Some excuse themselves for stealing, thinking they deserve what they took, intend to return it, or need it more than the owner. Some cheat to get better grades in school or because "everyone else does it". To the Lord, there are no acceptable reasons. When we excuse ourselves, we cheat ourselves and the Spirit of God ceases to be with us. We become more and more unrighteous.

I Googled: What is honesty? "Honesty is the quality of always speaking the truth and being totally authentic, straightforward, and transparent in our words and actions. It involves a few key practices: never lying, never hiding the truth, and never purposefully omitting or misdirecting people from the truth."

What does it mean to be completely honest? To become completely honest, we must look carefully at our lives. If there are ways in which we are being even the least bit dishonest, we should repent of them immediately.

Back to my stolen dripper story. Did I steal those 3 bags of drippers I put into my pocket? Accidental stealing is still stealing, so I did need to repent. So, I returned to the store and paid for 3 packages of dripper, and I told the store attendant what had happened.

When we are completely honest, we cannot be corrupted. We are true to every trust, duty, agreement, or covenant, even if it costs us money or friends. Then we can face the Lord, ourselves, and others without shame. President Joseph F. Smith counseled, "Let every man's life be so that his character will bear the closest inspection, and that it may be seen as an open book, so that he will have nothing to shrink from or be ashamed of."

In what ways does our honesty or dishonesty affect how we feel about ourselves? When we bought a used car for our youngest daughter Taylor, the man we bought the car from asked me what price I wanted him to write on the DMV Bill of Sales. I said the price I'm paying, the full price. He said, "Don't you want me to mark it down so you can save on sales tax?" I said, "no, my integrity is worth much more than a few hundred dollars. Then to my surprise he said, "Here is $200 back, I noticed the back seats needs cleaning." It felt like I was being immediately rewarded for doing the right thing.

What is the advantage of being honest? 1. An honest person feels good about himself, he can hold his head up high. 2. People are more likely to trust you. If you're always truthful, people will know that they can rely on you. They'll feel comfortable being your friend or doing business with you, because they know that you won't try to deceive them.

Honesty, integrity, and truth are eternal principles that significantly shape our experience in mortality and help determine our eternal destiny. For a disciple of Christ, honesty is at the very heart of spirituality.

When you live your life based upon the principles that Jesus Christ taught, like honesty. You have the advantage of direction and purpose in life that is greater than yourself. The principle of honesty will improve all your relationships because it builds trust with yourself, others and with God. Being honest is showing God that you trust and love him. In my experience, there is no better feeling than knowing you are right with God. It brings a feeling of peace, victory and love to your life, like nothing else can. It's not easy, but it's so worth it. Christ told us so and he cannot lie either. May we all do a little self-evaluation and see where we can improve in the honesty department. It' is the best policy. In the name of Jesus Christ. Amen.[1]

A traditional Chinese Mandarin fairy tale tales about a king who is old and childless and worried about an heir. He sends out a proclamation inviting anyone who would like to be king to enter a competition. All the knights and nobles come to the castle and prepare themselves for a war-like tournament. Among the crowd is a farmer's son. He enjoys the competition; but, is not interested in fighting or war.

It turns that the competition isn't a tournament. Instead, the king gives everyone a seed and asks him to return in a year with what he's grown and then he'll decide on the winner. The farmer's son tries everything: compost, manure, sun, water, shade – but nothing works. When the year is up he returns sadly to the castle. Everyone else has wonderful flowers to show. The farmer's son has to tell the king that, although he's tried everything, nothing has grown.

The king reveals a secret. He boiled the seeds so that they wouldn't grow. All the other competitors have cheated and the farmer's son is the only person to tell the truth. The king is looking for somebody with the courage and honesty to tell the truth to succeed him, and he chooses the farmer's son. *(like story that was referenced by Steve Hunter during his talk)*

You get what you give. If you try to cheat others out of what you promise them, you will be cheated in return. The more honest you are, the easier it is to trust other people and not suspect they may be cheating you in some way. When you're honest, not only will other people trust you, but you will also feel more confident in your trust with others. Honesty is always the best route–especially if you want others to be honest with you as well.

1– *Honesty Sacrament talk, Steve Hunter, Almaden Ward, Church of Jesus Christ of Latter-Day Saints, 7/23/2023.*

24

WHO'S THE HAPPIEST

Few choices are more important than whether to have children, and psychologists and other social scientists have worked to figure out what having kids means for happiness. Some of the most prominent scholars in the field have argued that if you want to be happy, it's best to be childless. Others have pushed back, pointing out that a lot depends on who you are and where you live. But a bigger question is also at play: What if the rewards of having children are different from, and deeper than, happiness?

The early research is decisive: Having kids is bad for quality of life. In one study, the psychologist Daniel Kahneman and his colleagues asked about 900 employed women to report, at the end of each day, every one of their activities and how happy they were when they did them. They recalled being with their children as less enjoyable than many other activities, such as watching TV, shopping, or preparing food. Other studies find that when a child is born, parents experience a decrease in happiness that doesn't go away for a long time, in addition to a drop in marital satisfaction that doesn't usually recover until the children leave the house. As the Harvard professor Dan Gilbert puts it, "The only symptom of empty nest syndrome is nonstop smiling."

After all, having children, particularly when they are young, involves financial struggle, sleep deprivation, and stress. For mothers, there is also in many cases the physical strain of pregnancy and breastfeeding. And children can turn a cheerful and loving romantic partnership into a zero-sum battle over who gets to sleep and work and who doesn't.

But, as often happens in psychology, although some research provided simple findings—in this case, "having children makes you unhappy"—other efforts arrived at more complicated conclusions. For one, the happiness hit is worse for some people than for others. One study finds that fathers ages 26 to 62 actually get a happiness boost, while young or single parents suffer the greatest loss. And crucially, there are geographic differences. A 2016 paper looking at the happiness levels of people with and without children in 22 countries found that the extent to which children make you happy is influenced by whether your country has child-care policies such as paid parental leave. Parents from Norway and Hungary, for instance, are happier than childless couples in those countries—but parents from Australia and Great Britain are less happy than their childless peers. The country with the greatest happiness drop after you have children? The United States.

Children make some happy and others miserable; the rest fall somewhere in between—it depends, among other factors, on how old you are, whether you are a mother or a father, and where you live. But a deep puzzle remains: Many people would have had happier lives and marriages had they chosen not to have kids—yet they still describe parenthood as the "best thing they've ever done." Why don't we regret having children more?

One possibility is a phenomenon called memory distortion. When we think about our past experiences, we tend to remember the peaks and forget the mundane awfulness in between. Our experiencing selves tell researchers that we prefer doing the dishes—or napping, or shopping, or answering emails—to spending time with our kids ... But our remembering selves tell researchers that no one—and nothing—provides us with so much joy as our children. It may not be the happiness we live day to day, but it's the happiness we think about, the happiness we summon and remember, the stuff that makes up our life-tales.

But other theories about why people don't regret parenthood actually have nothing to do with happiness—at least not in a simple sense. One involves attachment. Most parents love their children, and it would seem terrible to admit that you would be better off if someone you loved didn't exist. More than that, you genuinely prefer a world with your kids in it. This can put parents in the interesting predicament of desiring a state that doesn't make them as happy as the alternative.

When one person said raising her sons was the best thing she'd ever done, she was not saying that they gave her pleasure in any simple day-to-day sense, and not saying that they were good for her marriage. She's talking about something deeper, having to do with satisfaction, purpose, and meaning. It's not just her. When you ask people about their life's meaning and purpose, parents say that their lives have more meaning than those of nonparents. A study found that the more time people spent taking care of children, the more meaningful they said their life was—even though they reported that their life was no happier.[1]

The 2022 edition of the General Social Survey (GSS)—the nation's preeminent social barometer—reveals that marriage and family are strongly associated with happiness. The GSS shows that a combination of marriage and parenthood is linked to the biggest happiness dividends for women. Among married women with children between the ages of 18 and 55, 40% reported they are "very happy," compared to 25% of married childless women, and just 22% of unmarried childless women.

Nevertheless, it is important to note that unmarried mothers are the least likely to be very happy: with just 17% of them indicating they are very happy. These results parallel findings from 2020 and 2021 during the pandemic that we reported last year in The Atlantic. In earlier surveys, we found that women who were married with children were generally the happiest and the least lonely.

But what about men? Is the link between happiness, marriage, and parenthood similar for men? Indeed, the 2022 General Social Survey indicates that marriage is also linked to greater happiness for men ages 18-55. And here again, married fathers are happiest.

Specifically, 35% of married men ages 18-55 who have children report being "very happy," followed by 30% of married men who do not have children. By contrast unmarried childless men, and especially unmarried fathers are the least happy—with less than 15% of these men saying they are "very happy." In other words, married men (ages

18-55) in America are about twice as likely to be very happy, compared to their unmarried peers.

These results parallel other recent research from the University of Chicago indicating that for both men and women, marriage is "the most important differentiator" of who is happy in America. Meanwhile, falling marriage rates are a chief reason why happiness has declined nationally, according to that same study. The research found an astounding 30-percentage-point happiness gap between married and unmarried Americans.

Other factors do matter—including income, educational achievement, race, and geography—but marital status is most influential when it comes to predicting happiness in the study. What's more, other research indicates that the United States is witnessing a growing happiness divide between the most educated and least educated Americans, and marriage is likely the biggest driver of that decline.

Social psychologist Jean Twenge attributes the growing happiness divide in America along class lines to a faster decline in marriage among those with less education and income. In Twenge's view, the growing class divide in happiness clearly has many causes, including income inequality. Still, relationships are also crucial for happiness, and for many people, marriage is their primary and most stable relationship.

This new research provides further evidence that happiness is linked to American family life. In particular, and contrary to the views articulated by many on social media, the mainstream media, and the American public, marriage and parenthood do not appear to be obstacles to living a happy life. Instead, these two traditional markers of adulthood are associated with a happier life. As difficult as marriage and parenthood can be, in general, men and women who have the benefit of a spouse and children are the most likely to report that they are "very happy" with their lives, according to the most recent round of the General Social Survey.[2]

Raising children, then, has an uncertain connection to pleasure but may connect to other aspects of a life well lived, satisfying our hunger for attachment, and for meaning and purpose. The writer Zadie Smith describes having a child as a "strange admixture of terror, pain, and delight." Smith, echoing the thoughts of everyone else who has seriously considered these issues, points out the risk of close attachments: "Isn't it bad enough that the beloved, with whom you have experienced genuine joy, will eventually be lost to you? Why add to this nightmare the child, whose loss, if it ever happened, would mean nothing less than your total annihilation?" But this annihilation reflects the extraordinary value of such attachments; as the author Julian Barnes writes of grief, quoting a friend, "It hurts just as much as it is worth."[1]

When my kid's mom was diagnosed with terminal cancer her primary thoughts of disappointment was that she wasn't going to have the opportunity to see her grandchildren born or be involved with their growing experiences. She spent the last two and one-half years of her life visiting, buying gifts, and going on vacations with our children and grandchildren. Unfortunately, only one was old enough to still remember her. At home she would spend most of her free time finishing scrap books, blankets etc. for her children and future grandchildren.

There are two plaques on our wall that say, "Home is where your story begins", "Live, laugh and love" and one that is nearby is a picture of Christ that says "I never said it would be easy – I only said it would be worth it." One of our family's favorite songs that ties together, at least for me, "Who's the Happiest" is "Families can be together forever" found in Mormon Hymnal #300:

"I have a fam'ly here on earth. They are so good to me. I want to share my life with them through all eternity. Fam'lies can be together forever, through Heav'nly Father's plan. I always want to be with my own family, and the Lord has shown me how I can. The Lord has shown me how I can.

While I am in my early years, I'll prepare most carefully, so I can marry in God's temple for eternity. Fam'lies can be together forever through Heav'nly Father's plan. I always want to be with my own family, and the Lord has shown me how I can. The Lord has shown me how I can."

Fairy tale, I don't think so…my faith, hope and the pure love of Christ (Charity) helps keep me plugging along with a smile on my face even though raising a family has often felt like "It hurt just as much as it was worth it."

1– *What Becoming a Parent Really Does to Your Happiness, The Atlantic, adapted from the Book "The Sweet Spot: The Pleasures of Suffering and the Search for Meaning", Paul Bloom, 11/02/2021.*

2– *Who Is Happiest? Married Mothers and Fathers, per the Latest General Social Survey, By W. Bradford Wilcox | Wendy Wang, Institute for Family Studies, 09/13/2023.*

25

LITTLE BY LITTLE WE BECOME WHO WE ARE

Thomas Carlyle was born on 4 December 1795 in a village in southwest Scotland. His parent James Carlyle was a stonemason, later a farmer, who built the arched house where Thomas was born. His maxim was that "man was created to work, not to speculate, or feel, or dream.

Thomas pursued mathematics and science for a time, but after he started reading German literature, his career path shifted to that of a translator, writer, and critic. He began his writing career translating German texts.

In 1834, the philosopher John Stuart Mill discovered that, although he had signed a contract with his publisher to produce a general history of the French revolution, he was actually too busy with other commitments to come up with the promised work. So, he proposed to his friend Thomas Carlyle that Carlyle write it instead. Carlyle, struggling to make ends meet, and unwilling to stoop to mere journalism, took on the project with a fury — it was, he hoped, the work that would make his literary reputation.

Throughout 1834, Carlyle slaved over his history of the French Revolution with passion late into the night. When he had completed Volume One, he sent it to Mill for his review.

On the evening of the 6th of March, 1835, Mill turned up at Carlyle's house in Cheyne Walk, looking, Carlyle later wrote, "the very picture of desperation". Mill had left the manuscript at the house of his friend, Mrs. Taylor. Her servant, who could not read, had used it to light the fire. All that was left of Carlyle's passion and fury were a few charred leaves. Mill brought the leaves, as confirmation.

While most of us would greet this circumstance with hysteria and retribution, Carlyle was the epitome of politeness. Mill was beside himself with grief and self-recrimination. Carlyle probably offered him some tea. Mill offered to pay Carlyle for the damage, but Carlyle refused, saying that he could simply start again. Mill stayed very late, meaning that Carlyle, and his wife, Jane, had to stay up late, too, to comfort him.

When Mill left, Carlyle's first words to Jane were: "Mill, poor fellow, is terribly cut up. We must endeavor to hide from him how very serious this business is for us." And it was serious. The Carlyle's had no money, and Thomas knew he could never write that book again. He had destroyed his notes and could not remember what he had written: "I remember and can still remember less of it than of anything I ever wrote with such toil. It is gone." He would have to tell Mill he couldn't carry on.

That night, however, he had a dream. His father and brother rose from the grave and begged him not to abandon the work. The next morning, Carlyle told Mill that he would take the money after all. He used it to buy paper, and started writing again.

(Legend has it that one day, Carlyle saw a mason building a wall, carefully laying one brick at a time. Carlyle took new courage. He could rewrite his book, the same way he wrote it the first time—one page at a time).[1]

Elder Allen D. Haynie wrote, "One day I walked into the cafeteria at Church headquarters to have some lunch. After getting a tray of food, I entered the dining area and noticed a table at which all three members of the First Presidency were seated, along with one empty chair. My insecurities caused me to make a quick detour away from that table, and then I heard the voice of our prophet, President Russell M. Nelson, saying, "Allen, there's an empty chair right here. Come and sit down with us." And so I did.

Near the end of the lunch, I was surprised to hear a loud crunching noise, and when I looked up, I saw that President Nelson had stood his plastic water bottle straight up and then flattened it and replaced the lid.

President Dallin H. Oaks then asked the question I wanted to ask, "President Nelson, why did you flatten your plastic water bottle?"

He replied, "It makes it easier for those who are handling recyclable materials because it doesn't take up as much space in the recycling container."

While pondering that response, I heard the same crunching sound again. I looked to my right, and President Oaks had flattened his plastic water bottle just like President Nelson. I then heard some noise to my left, and President

Henry B. Eyring was flattening his plastic water bottle, although he had adopted a different strategy by doing it while the bottle was horizontal, which took more effort than with the bottle straight up. Noticing this, President Nelson kindly showed him the bottle-straight-up technique to more easily flatten the bottle.[2]

Polyethylene terephthalate, also called PET, is the name of a type of clear, strong, lightweight and 100% recyclable plastic. The recycling rate of PET bottles and jars was 29.1 percent in 2018. The total amount of plastics combusted in municipal solid waste (MSW) in 2018 was 5.6 million tons. This was 16.3 percent of all MSW combusted with energy recovery in that year.

Thinking about what President Nelson said about how a light weight crushed water bottle "doesn't take up as much space in a recycling container," my thoughts imagined how much easier it would be for the entire plastic industry to handle the reduced volume of discarded water bottles. Even though municipal garbage dumps crush and flatten waste, I'll bet if everyone crushed their water bottle before throwing it away, there would be less volume of garbage filling our dumps. Little things can become big things if we all do our part.

First, Thomas Carlyle wrote volumes two and three of his history of the French Revolution. Then, he recreated volume one. Carlyle wrote the entire manuscript from memory, words that came "direct and flamingly from the heart".

The three-volume work — a heroic undertaking which charts the course of the French Revolution from 1789 to 1795 — was completed and published in 1837. It has never been out of print and is still in print nearly 200 years later.[1]

Like Thomas Carlyle's book, life is a monumental, long-term work. Just about everything good in life is built little by little, brick by brick—with patience and persistence. Success, happiness, contentment, and strong relationships don't happen overnight. They take time: time to make things right, time to mend and heal, time to learn and improve.

It's comforting to note that the great God of Heaven is a God of patience and longsuffering. If He can be patient with us, we would do well to be patient with ourselves.

So we stay with it, day after day, and do our best to carry on. Whether it's writing a book, planting a garden, overcoming a weakness, or building a friendship, we keep at it. Albert Einstein said, "It's not that I'm so smart, it's just that I stay with problems longer."

Persistence and patience will not make problems go away, but as we've all witnessed and experienced, they can give us the power and the hope to face our problems.[3]

Elder Allen D. Haynie goes on to say, "At that point, I leaned over to President Oaks and quietly asked, "Is flattening your plastic water bottle a new recycling requirement of the cafeteria?" President Oaks responded, with a smile on his face, "Well, Allen, you need to follow the prophet."

I'm confident that President Nelson was not declaring some new recycling-based doctrine in the cafeteria that day. But we can learn from the prompt response of President

Oaks and President Eyring to President Nelson's example and President Nelson's attentiveness to help teach those involved a better way.[2]

Perhaps we could all take a lesson from Thomas Carlyle; from the bricklayer, from President Nelson; from the plastic water bottle, from the French proverb; "little by little, the bird builds its nest", all these can accomplish great things "little by little."

Carlyle kept the charred leaves in his study for the rest of his life and one of his many quotes of encouragement states, *"Endurance is patience concentrated."*

1– *This entry was posted in Burned manuscripts and tagged French Revolution, John Stuart Mill, Thomas Carlyle on 30 January, 2011.*

2– *A Living Prophet for the Latter Days, by Elder Allen D. Haynie, of the Seventy April 2023.*

3– *Music & The Spoken Word, broadcast #4,598, 2017.*

26

CHANGE OF HEART

Simon Lovell was 31 and a professional con man who had spun the gambling tricks he'd learned from his grandfather into a lucrative if bloody-minded business fleecing strangers. Without hesitation or remorse, he left his marks broken in hotels all over the world.

Nothing suggested that this day in 1988 would be any different. Lovell, in Europe, had spotted his victim in a bar, plied him with drinks, and drawn him into a "cross"—a classic con game in which the victim is made to believe he's part of a foolproof get-rich scheme. The con went perfectly. "I took him for an extremely large amount of money," Lovell said later.

Lovell hustled the drunken man out of the hotel room and left him in the hallway for security to deal with. But then something unexpected happened. The mark went to pieces. "I'd never seen a man break down that badly, ever," Lovell recalled. "He was just sliding down the wall, weeping and wailing."

What followed was a moment Lovell would look back on as the hinge point of his life. "It was as if a light suddenly went on. I thought: This. Is. Really. Bad. For the first time, I actually felt sorry for someone."

Lovell's next move was hard even for him to believe. He returned the guy his money. Then he went back inside the hotel room, sat down, poured a drink, and declared himself done with this dodge. "There was an absolute epiphany that I just couldn't do it anymore." The next day he felt different. Lighter. "I had become," he said, "a real human being again." He never ran another con.

In the decades that followed, Lovell turned his gift for smooth patter and sleight-of-hand into a successful one-man show that ran off-Broadway for eight years. After he suffered a stroke, good wishes and cash donations for his care poured in from friends and fellow magicians. In his professional world and well beyond it, Lovell became respected, even beloved. His rehabilitation was complete.

But a central mystery remained. That moment in the hotel was Lovell's wake-up call. But what is a wake-up call? What could possibly explain an event so unexpected, forceful, and transformative that it cleaves a life in two: before and after?

Most of the time, ideas develop from the steady percolation and evaluation of thoughts and feelings. But every so often, if you're lucky, a blockbuster notion breaks through in a flash of insight that's as unexpected as it is blazingly clear.

So-called "aha moments" can be deeply personal and even existential, prompting the realization that you should quit your job, divorce your spouse, move to another city, mend a broken relationship, abandon an addictive behavior, or, like Lovell, redirect your moral compass. They can also be creative, generating the brilliant idea for a tech startup, the theme of a musical composition, the plot point of a novel, or the answer to an engineering quandary. In all cases, you apprehend something that you were blind to before.

The early-20th-century psychologist William James described such personal moments of clarity, in The Varieties of Religious Experience, as a snap-resolution of the "divided self." It's as if a whole lifetime's worth of growth is compressed into a single instant as dense as a collapsed star.

For his co-authored book, Quantum Change, William Miller, an emeritus professor of psychology and psychiatry at the University of New Mexico, interviewed 55 people who had experienced sudden realizations and life transformations. He found that by no means were all of the triggers, or even most of them, as Lovell's confrontation with his emotionally shattered victim. Many were downright banal. Among the things people were doing during or immediately preceding their moments of quantum change were walking to a nightclub, cleaning a toilet, watching TV, lying in bed, and preparing to shower.

There was a striking similarity, however, in how the moments felt, with many subjects reporting that it seemed more like a message revealed to them from outside than something their own minds had ginned up. It felt foreign, mystical even. Which may explain why so many historical accounts of this nature have been interpreted as communications from the Divine.

William Miller likes to recount psychologist David Premack's case study of a fiercely addicted smoker who pulled to the curb in front of a public library one day to pick up his kids. He rummaged in the glove compartment for his cigarettes without success. He looked under the seats, but could not find the damn smokes. It was starting to rain. The kids would be out in a second. But wait—there was a store not far away. He could zip over there and be back in just a few minutes. It wasn't raining hard. The kids wouldn't get too wet.

Then something shifted in this man. "He thought, Dear Heaven, I am the kind of father who would let his kids stand in the rain while he chased a drug." The insight was powerful enough to break through years of denial. "And that was it," Miller says. "He never smoked again."

Miller found that there was often a moral dimension to stories of quantum change—just like the moral dimension to Simon Lovell's U-turn from the ugliness of his life of crime. The same pro-social shift seemed to be happening, from selfishness to compassion, from an ethic of power to an ethic of care. "It's as though they got a fast-forward in self-actualization," Miller says, "and their values changed."

In almost half of his subjects, the big epiphany was preceded by intense psychological pressure. "They were at the end of their rope, and the rope broke," he says. Things simply could not continue as before; they couldn't not change. That would seem to make such epiphanies a different animal from simply cracking a word puzzle.

Yet researchers disagree about whether they really are. Miller believes they are different partly because of the force with which his subjects—almost universally—reported how different their aha moments felt from merely "coming to a conclusion or reasoning something through," he says. "The moment it happened, they knew they had gone through a one-way door—there was no going back." When Miller's co-author, Janet C'de Baca, followed up with them a decade later, not a single one had returned to the pre-epiphany life. Their aha moments really had changed them irrevocably.[1]

Charlie Bloom, coauthor of *Secrets of Great Marriages: Real Truths from Real Couples About Lasting Love*, wrote that it doesn't take long to have a life-changing experience. Sometimes a weekend workshop will do it. Sometimes a chance encounter is sufficient. Sometimes a moment can be enough time to create a permanent life change.

In 2006 I had one such experience. It occurred quite unexpectedly in India. I was on my way to Bangladesh on a two-month work assignment for the World Health Organization. I had a 13-hour layover on my itinerary between New Delhi and Dhaka, the capital of Bangladesh. Rather than spend the day in the airport, I decided to see the sights of the city, and I hired a driver to take me around town. The last stop that I asked him to make before returning to the airport was at one of the hospitals run by Mother Teresa's Order, the Sister's of Charity.

When we got there, the driver explained in Hindi to the sister who greeted us as we entered the building that I wanted to see the hospital. At least that is what I asked him to say. Something must have gotten lost (or found) in the translation, because the next thing I knew, I was being shown into a large, empty room and offered a bench to sit on. After about 15 minutes, Mother Teresa herself came into the room. She headed straight towards me, took my hands in hers, and with a smile as big as the sun said in English, "Hello! How are you? It's so good to see you!"

"Shocked" would be too mild a word to describe what I experienced as the tiny woman looked into my eyes in a way that made me feel like I was the most important person in the world to her. I was literally speechless. Mother Teresa sat down on the bench next to me and began asking me questions about myself, about what I was doing in India, and where I had come from. I eventually regained my ability to speak, and within a few minutes, I was feeling like I was with a friend I had known all of my life. Throughout the conversation, there was another background conversation going on simultaneously in my mind in which the words, "I can't believe that this is actually happening," kept getting repeated.

Towards the end of my visit, as if to provide me with concrete proof that what I had experienced was real and not an apparition, Mother Teresa gave me a small card. "My business card," she said. On the card was written these words:

> The fruit of silence is prayer.
> The fruit of prayer is faith.
> The fruit of faith is love.
> The fruit of love is service.
> The truth of service is peace.

Still somewhat stunned, but feeling blessed and blissed simultaneously, I left clutching the card which contained the life-changing words that would have a profound impact not only on my two months in Bangladesh, but on the rest of my life. It wouldn't be truthful to say that I have lived every moment of my life since that meeting being of service. I haven't. There have been lots of times when my ego took a higher place in my intentions than my commitment to serve. There have been times that I've put my self-interest ahead of my desire to contribute to others.

I'm still the same person that I was before I met Mother Teresa. What has changed is not who I am, but what I know and how that knowledge has informed my actions. What's different is that it's no longer possible for me to deny that my highest priority is to create peace within myself and to promote it through my relationships with others.

What's different is that it's no longer possible for me to deny that I have the power to influence the degree to which peace exists within my world. It's no longer possible to pretend that peace is someone else's responsibility. What's no longer possible is to believe that I am unworthy of being a peacemaker.

When I connected to Mother Teresa, I connected to the vision of me that she reflected back through her eyes. In her eyes, I saw the beauty, the strength, the love, and the power that she saw in me, and I simultaneously saw that it is in every one of us. Since that time, it has been impossible for me to continue to live the lie that who I am does not really matter in the great scheme of things. I know that it does.

For me, one of the things that being in service involves is the reflection back to others of the basic goodness that I know is in their heart, and the power that each of us has to touch others in a truly meaningful way. This is only one of an infinite variety of ways to be of service. Notice the words:

BE of service. That is, embodying a spirit of service, of caring, of contribution, simply by being genuinely who you are and touching others with that presence. In this moment of authentic presence, the war ends and peace begins. It begins with me. Always.[2]

The moment it happened, they knew they had gone through a one-way door—there was no going back. When followed up a decade later, not a single one had returned to the pre-epiphany life. Their aha moments really had changed them irrevocably.[1]

1– *Eureka!, Bruce Gierson, Psychology Today, 2015.*
2– *Life-Changing Moments, Tales from the East, Psychology Today, Linda & Charlie Bloom, 02/16/2018.*

27

TONY DUNGY, DAMAR HAMLIN, PRAYER

Tony Dungy, who coached the Indianapolis Colts to a victory in Super Bowl XLI in 2007 against the Chicago Bears, and is now a football analyst for NBC, spoke at the March for Life in Washington, D.C. on Friday and said that the march was more important than the ongoing NFL playoffs.

Dungy spent his entire adult life in football, but while he wasn't scheming up Indy's next big play, he could often be found giving back to the community and working with his local church.

In fact, it was through his local church that Dungy's life was changed forever, as he met his wife and the love of his life, Lauren Harris. Reportedly their meeting had been set up by their pastor. The Christian couple got married in 1982, and together are parents to a staggering 10 children, seven of whom were adopted. Sadly, their biological son James reportedly committed suicide when he was 18.

Dungy and his wife frequently give back to their community via the organization the Dungy Family

Foundation, which aims to "meet the physical, educational and spiritual needs of those in their community." Furthermore, Dungy acts as the spokesperson for the organization All Pro Dad. Together, the organization and Dungy partner with the Indiana Department of Child Services to recruit families across the state to join the foster care program.

Harris, a former elementary school teacher and Sunday school teacher, became a bestselling author via her and Tony's book, "Uncommon Marriage," which details their love story and the struggles they've encountered and overcome across 30 years of marriage. The couple also wrote a series of children's books. Additionally, Harris is also a women's bible study leader at the Central Tampa Baptist Church.[1]

During a Monday Night Football game on January 2, 2023 Damar Hamlin suffered cardiac arrest after making a tackle. Damar (born March 24, 1998) is an American football safety for the Buffalo Bills of the National Football League (NFL). He played college football at the University of Pittsburgh and was selected by the Bills in the sixth round of the 2021 NFL Draft. Hamlin spent most of his rookie season as a backup before becoming a starter in 2022.

Cardiopulmonary resuscitation (CPR) and automated external defibrillation (AED) were quickly administered before he was rushed to a local hospital in critical condition. After showing notable signs of improvement, Hamlin was transferred to a Buffalo hospital and later discharged nine days after the incident to rehabilitate from home.

In addition to his football career, Hamlin is a fashion entrepreneur, having started a fashion line, Chasing

Millions, while at the University of Pittsburgh. In 2020, Hamlin started organizing annual charity Christmas toy drives in his hometown of McKees Rocks, Pennsylvania. The GoFundMe campaign for his 2020 toy drive had set a goal of $2,500.

Following the collapse, numerous NFL players and teams quickly offered their support and prayers on social media. The following day, all 32 NFL teams changed their profile pictures on Twitter to a picture of Hamlin's jersey and text that reads "Pray For Damar." Tee Higgins offered his condolences to Hamlin's family, as did Cincinnati Bengals wide receiver Ja'Marr Chase. Buffalo Bills quarterback Josh Allen urged people "Please pray for our brother."

Fans began gathering outside the University of Cincinnati Academic Health Center following his collapse. Hours after the incident, the lights on Paycor Stadium, the location of the game, were lit blue in honor of Hamlin along with the lights on Fifth Third Bank's headquarters on Fountain Square.

Niagara Falls was illuminated in blue on the evening of January 3 in support of Hamlin. In the hours following his collapse, Hamlin's 2020 GoFundMe campaign for the Chasing M's Foundation toy drive received a massive influx of donations from fans and others. Many of the donations had messages of support for Hamlin. In the days that followed, dozens of NFL players, coaches, and executives donated to the campaign, which grew from its $2,500 goal amount to over $8.7 million as of January 12, 2023.

Chasing M's Foundation later updated their GoFundMe message saying the "fundraiser was initially established to support a toy drive for Damar's community," but was "hopeful about Damar's future involvement in disbursing the incredibly generous contributions." On January 12, The Buffalo News had a detailed story covering the enormous changes facing Chasing M's structure and operations in light of the large donations, including its tax-exempt status and governance.[2]

Seventeen days after the Buffalo Bill's safety, Damar Hamlin, was injured Tony Dungy addressed a March for Life rally:

"Hey, thank you so much. It is great to be here. Can't tell you how much excitement Lauren and I have to be here today--even though this march is taking place right at the biggest time of my profession, the NFL Playoffs-- this is way, way, way more important. It is amazing me that God actually used football to shine some light on the subject of life for all of us. Three weeks ago, during a game in Cincinnati, something happened that impacted our entire country. A young man named Damar Hamlin of the Buffalo Bills made a routine tackle and his heart stopped beating right on the field. It could have been tragic, but something miraculous happened. The team medical staff rushed out and they got Damar's heart started again. But you know what, that wasn't the miracle. The real miracle was the reaction to everyone to that. The announcers on the broadcast, what did they say? All we can do is pray. And all across the country, people started praying. Lauren and I, we were having dinner with friends of ours, and we stopped what we were doing and we prayed right there.

And usually, when that happens the cameras cut away from that because we don't like to see that. Back when I was coaching in the 1990s, a few Christian players got together and they said: We want to pray after the games. And we actually got a memo from the NFL office, said: Don't let your players do that. If you do, you'll be fined because that's not appropriate. Can you believe that? That's a true story. ... And then continued. The next week, at every stadium in the NFL, teams got together and prayed and it was amazing. Well, those prayers were answered. Damar's recovering now. He's home. He's been released from the hospital.

"But what's the lesson in that? You know, an unbelievable thing happened that night. A professional football game with millions of dollars of ticket money and advertising money on the line, that game was cancelled. Why? Because a life was at stake. And people wanted to see that life saved. Even people who aren't necessarily religious got together and called on God. Well, that should be encouraging to us because that is exactly why we are here today. Because every day in this country, innocent lives are at stake. The only difference is, they don't belong to a famous athlete and they are not seen on national TV. But those lives are still important to God and in God's eyes.

"Psalm 139 tells us that God is watching every one of these young bodies as they are growing in their mother's womb—because He placed them there.

"Now, we know there are a lot of people in this country that don't believe that. They don't see these babies as being important. They don't even see them as lives. So, what can we do about that? Well, I think we have to take a lesson from Damar's story. We have to pray. We need to pray with the same fervor that we prayed with during that week. Because

God answers prayer, and He will answer these prayers to save these precious unborn lives as we go forward.

"So, if we do our part, we'll save more and more of these lives."[3]

"Petitioning in prayer has taught me that the vault of heaven, with all its blessings, is to be opened only by a combination lock: one tumbler falls when there is faith, a second when there is personal righteousness, and the third and final tumbler falls only when what is sought is (in God's judgement, not ours) "right" for us. Sometimes we pound on the vault door for something we want very much, in faith, in reasonable righteousness, and wonder why the door does not open. We would be very spoiled children if that vault door opened any more easily than it does now. I can tell, looking back, that God truly loves me by the petitions that, in his perfect wisdom and love, he has refused to grant me. Our rejected petitions tell us not only much about ourselves, but also much about our flawless Father."[4]

1– *NFL Tony Dungy & His Wife Have 10 Kids Together, by Karl Rasmussen, 2022.*
2– *NFL Reactions, January 2023.*
3– *Coach Tony Dungy speaking at the March for Life, Jan. 20, 2023.*
4– *The Neal A. Maxwell Quote Book, pages 261-262, 1997.*

28

DIRTY HANDS AND FEET

The unaccounted years, also known as the 'Lost Years' of Jesus Christ, between the age of 12 and 30 is a biblical conundrum that has baffled scholars and Christians for years. There are no written records where Jesus may have been or travelled to during that period, leaving a religious vacuum that has been filled with theories largely inspired by religious belief, hearsay and folklore, depending on the sources.

Many attempts have been made to fill in the missing eighteen years when Jesus disappears from the scriptures. This has led to stories of him having travelled to far-flung places such as India to study with Eastern mystics, Persia and also tales of him having visited North America. Other stories, such as ones revolving around beliefs that Jesus made his way to Britain and even visited Cornwall, have generated colorful narratives linked to King Arthur and the legend of the search for the Holy Grail.

One theory about Jesus and his missing years is that he went on an epic 'walkabout' from his home in Nazareth. If this event occurred Jesus would have been little more than a boy of 12, so how emotionally equipped and knowledgeable would such a youth have to be to undertake a huge and possibly dangerous journey?

Most likely while living in Sepphoris the young Jesus may have gained his early knowledge of the world through both speaking the Aramaic language and learning to read. The one piece of written scripture suggesting this is found in the Gospel of Luke, which states that Jesus went into the synagogue and read from the scroll of the prophets.

Some scholars believe that Jesus' father Joseph died when he was about 12 and that this traumatic event could have been the catalyst for him, still as a young boy, to begin a personal quest to attain spiritual enlightenment. According to The New Testament, the principal locations for the ministry undertaken by Jesus were Galilee and Judea, with activities also taking place in surrounding areas such as Peres and Samaria. Christian texts refer to Jesus walking 3,125 miles during his ministry. Taking into account that a determined person, on a mission, could make the trip from Judea to Galilee (150 – 200 km) on foot in six days, it is possible that an experienced walker with knowledge of the terrain could venture far greater distances. Over Jesus' lifetime, a conservative estimate of the number of miles he may have walked is put at around 21,525 miles, almost the equivalent of walking around the entire world. The standard mode of transport was usually by foot with an estimated mileage of around 20 miles a day, but citizens also rode on oxen, donkeys and camels. Whether Jesus as a young man managed to reach the destinations claimed by some scholars and Christians is still a mystery.[1]

Caravaggio was a famous painter in the 16th century. His chiaroscuro paintings narrated high drama, acute realism, and minute detailing. Apparently aware of the difficulty of keeping hands and feet clean in the environment lived in during Christ's and his time - if you were look closely at his paintings, you will notice "dirty feet." The dirty feet got affixed to his art form, personality, and portrayed the catholic pauperism beliefs that were opposed by the Catholic Reformation. The baroque painter was born in Milan where he was baptized. His childhood and education were spent in catholic pauperism beliefs in the spirit of St. Charles Borromeo.

Caravaggio's naturalistic and unorthodox painting skills caught eyeballs of the Roman Catholic patrons during the counter-reformation in Rome. The "Boy Bitten by a Lizard" in the National Gallery London was painted by him during his beginnings in Rome. This painting revealed the authenticity and realism; he painted the model with dirty fingernails and gave surmountable importance to the detailing of the inanimate objects like the sprig of jasmine inside the glass vase.

In 1599, he was contracted by the Contarelli Chapel to decorate the Church with the paintings of the Evangelist Saint Matthew. His first version of Saint Matthew and the Angel was rejected by the Church patrons. The dirty feet of the Saint and impoverished nature did not match the idealization of their beloved Saint Matthew. The Church leaders found it really crude and could not see the image of a poor peasant depicting as their Evangelist. And so, he had to paint the second version The Inspiration of Saint Matthew depicting a more glorified and reverent image of the master that was accepted by the Church officials.

When Peter was crucified, he asked to be turned upside down to be the opposite of Jesus' crucifixion. This painting too depicted the dirty feet of the man pushing up the cross. The Counter-Reformation Popes in Rome opposed the ideology of pauperism. The Church patrons thought that all the poor; and especially the beggars, held no interest in the church reforms and were considered as 'ignorant of Christian truth'. According to them, the poor people were seen as sinners or criminals. Therefore, the Church outrightly rejected paintings with dirty feet by Caravaggio at first look and wanted to promote more glorified images of their Saints.

Caravaggio's school of thought was inspired by pauperism. And, so the naked and dirty feet of Caravaggio's saints were the feet of those who believed that Jesus, the son of God was "made man" and lived in poverty.

His compositions were being asked to alter by the Church to suit the desires of the patrons during that era. But Caravaggio's sense of authenticity, the rawness of human existence is still perfectly preserved in the Augustinian churches of Rome.[2]

All of this talk about dirty hands and feet leads us into one of the most powerful acts Jesus performed, and there was not one miracle to be found. John 13:1-17 is the story of Jesus washing the disciples' feet.

Imagine what the disciples must have been thinking when Jesus, the Messiah, takes off his outer clothes, wraps a towel around his waist and proceeds to reach for their rough, dirty and smelly feet. Feet stained with the dirt from the roads of Jerusalem Jesus and the disciples had recently walked as Jesus entered the city with cries of "Hosanna" and "Blessed is the king of Israel." Now this king, this Messiah is bowing before them and washing their feet. As Jesus scrubs and cleans the disciples' feet his hands are stained with the dirt and grime that have built up after the miles of walking. The "King of kings," "Lord of lords," humbling himself to take up the work of a common slave. The silence in the room must have been deafening, only broken by the splashing of water. Surely the disciples simply sat in awe of what they were experiencing and witnessing. Jesus, washing each of their feet, even the feet of the one who would commit the ultimate act of betrayal.

When Jesus finishes, he no doubt has the complete attention of the disciples, and he says, "Now that I, your Lord and Teacher, have washed your feet, you also should wash one another's feet. I have set you an example that you should do as I have done for you" (13:14-15). This last week of Jesus' life was not just about defeating sin and death. Jesus is showing the disciples and us what living a life in Christ is all about. Jesus is demonstrating the true nature what following him is all about; serving. We are called to serve God which means we serve others. Jesus does not simply talk about serving or give some spiritual, mystical definition of what serving means. Jesus physically serves through the washing of feet and ultimately through giving his body to be crucified. If this is the example the Savior of the world gives to use, what does that mean for us?[3]

A message posted on Facebook by Brennan Manning stated: "As I looked out over the shivering crowd, I suggested that perhaps Mary Magdalene thought the resurrected Christ was a gardener because Jesus still had the dirt from His own tomb under His nails. Of course, the depictions in churches of the risen Christ never show dirt under His nails; they make Him look more like a wingless angel than a gardener. It's as if He needed to be cleaned up for Easter visitors so He looked more impressive and so no one would be offended by the truth. But then what we all end up with is a perverted idea of what resurrection looks like. My experience, however, is that the God of Easter is a God with dirt under His nails.

Resurrection never feels like being made clean and nice and pious like in those Easter pictures. I would have never agreed to work for God if I had believed God was interested in trying to make me nice or even good. Instead, what I subconsciously knew, even back then, was that God was never about making me spiffy; God was about making me new.

New doesn't always look perfect. Like the Easter story itself, new is often messy. New looks like recovering alcoholics. New looks like reconciliation between family members who don't actually deserve it. New looks like every time I manage to admit I was wrong and every time I manage to not mention I was right. New looks like every fresh start and every act of forgiveness and every moment of letting go of what we thought we couldn't live without and then somehow living without it anyways. New is the thing we never saw coming – never even hoped for – but ends up being what we needed all along.

'It happens to all of us,' I concluded that Easter Sunday morning. 'God simply keeps reaching down into the dirt of humanity and resurrecting us from the graves we dig for ourselves through our violence, our lies, our selfishness, our arrogance, and our addictions. And God keeps loving us back to life over and over."[4]

When Mary Magdalene saw Christ at the empty tomb, she reached out her arms to embrace Him, uttering only the endearing and worshipful word, "Rabboni," meaning My beloved Master. Jesus restrained her impulsive manifestation of reverent love, saying, "Touch me not (hold me not) for I am not yet ascended to my Father," and adding, "but go to my brethren, and say unto them, I ascend unto my Father, and your Father; and to my God, and your God" John 20:17.

Why was it necessary for Him to return to God before he could not be touched by His loved ones? No one really knows. Was it a process his body still needed to go through for perfection of the resurrection process or was it necessary to return and report to God. Some bible scholars have offered explanations:

In loosening Mary's hold on Him, Jesus was, in effect, saying this: "I know you desire to keep Me here, always present with you. I know you want everything to be just the same as before I died. But our relationship is about to change. I'm going to heaven, and you will have the Comforter in My place. You need to start walking by faith, Mary, not by sight." *Got Questions, Your Biblical Answers.*

In the study of John, Pastor Armstrong states that the reason Jesus did not want Mary Magdalene to cling to Him was because He needed to be untouched before ascending to heaven to cleanse the temple. In the earthly tabernacle, the High Priest would enter once a year to cleanse it. On that day, no one was allowed to touch the High Priest until he had completed that work. So here Jesus tells Mary she is not permitted to touch Him – as He is our High Priest – because He had yet to ascend to the Father and complete His atoning work. *Why did Jesus not want Mary Magdalene to touch Him, Verse by Verse Ministry, 07/18/2018.*

Jesus needing to let us know that He was going to heaven and that we would be given a Comforter, that He needed to fulfill His responsibilities as a High Priest, He needed to return and report to God, His resurrected body needed to go through further perfection – no one knows for sure.

God simply keeps reaching down into the dirt of humanity and resurrecting us from the graves we dig for ourselves through our violence, our lies, our selfishness, our arrogance, and our addictions. And God keeps loving us back to life over and over.

I like the idea presented that Mary Magdalene thought the resurrected Christ was a gardener because Jesus still had the dirt from His own tomb under His nails and maybe on his feet.[4]

You have to go really dark and deep with yourself and get your hands (and feet) dirty and go into territories that you don't want to go into and feel things that you don't want to feel, but that's what ultimately pushes out the good and gives you some kind of a message that you can take and channel into something better. That energy's really powerful. *Diane Birch, singer-writer*

1– *Sky History, The Lost Years Of Jesus: The Mystery Of Christ's Missing 18 Years, Article written by Richard Bevan., history.co.uk.*
2– *Lessons from History, The Secret Behind Paintings With Dirty Feet, Kabir, 08/18/2020.*
3– *Journey Elgin, Getting Your Hands Dirty, 04/19/2016.*
4– *God with Dirty Fingernails, Brennan Manning, Ragamuffin Gospel, 10/06/2015.*

29

GUILT AND THE SPACE SHUTTLE CHALLENGER EXPLOSION

For 30 years after the space shuttle Challenger exploded, Robert Ebeling concealed a terrible secret: He felt personally responsible for the shuttle's destruction and the seven astronauts' death.

Although Ebeling and four of his colleagues had warned NASA that leaking jet fuel could cause the shuttle to blow up, the engineer thought he should have done more to stop the launch. Burdened by guilt and depression, he retired from NASA contractor Morton Thiokol soon after the 1986 disaster, and he has spent much of the past 25 years tending a bird refuge near his home in Brigham City, Utah.

Ebeling, 89, has won national awards for his volunteer work at the bird refuge and is a beloved member of his community, but few people knew the debilitating guilt he still suffered – until January, when an NPR report on the catastrophe, and Ebeling's desperate attempt to prevent it, opened a floodgate of love.

Now dying of cancer, the man who believed he was responsible for the disaster is hailed as an American hero, and the home he shares with his wife of 67 years is filled with letters and cards from people telling him how much they admire him. The magnitude of the response has brought much-needed absolution in the final stages of Ebeling's life, his daughter said. He's carried this burden for so long, and he's finally able to let it go. It's a godsend. It's a miracle. Things like this don't just happen after 30 years.

For Ebeling and his family, release from guilt was a long time coming. For many people, it never comes at all. One study published in the Archives of General Psychiatry in 2012 showed that feelings of guilt and remorse, visible through magnetic resonance imaging of the brain, can recur years after they were thought to be resolved.

Both science and religion regard guilt - and its corollary, shame - as appendages of conscience, useful in nudging human beings toward moral behavior. "Guilt can be a positive force. It's ideally there so we know we've done wrong, and we're motivated to do right," said Rabbi Harlan J. Wechsler.

But too much guilt for too long can devastate a body, both physically and emotionally. And modern culture has no shortage of things that cause Americans to feel guilty. Thirty-nine percent have told pollsters they feel guilty for wasting food; 21 percent said they feel guilty about their environmental footprint. In one survey of cruise-takers, 42 percent said they felt guilty for relaxing – while on vacation.

New York psychiatrist Peter Breggin argues that guilt, like shame and anxiety, have biologically outlived their usefulness to humans and are prehistoric "legacy emotions" that cause unnecessary suffering.

Many people of faith, however, view guilt as an inner compass that, when heeded, points to correct behavior and principles. All humans want to be good. It's a wonderful and basic part of the human condition. It's when people fall short that the trouble begins.

In the battle over who feels the guiltiest, Catholics often claim superiority, joking that while the Jewish people invented guilt, Catholics perfected it. "Catholic guilt" is a curious phenomenon, however, given that the Roman Catholic Church offers an institutionalized way to expunge it.

Through the sacrament of reconciliation, Catholics confess their sins to a priest, who acts on behalf of God to absolve it. The church teaches that the practice was given by Jesus to Peter when he told the apostle, "Whatever you shall bind on earth shall be bound in heaven, and whatever you loose on earth shall be loosed in heaven." Catholics are required to go to confession at least once a year.

The sacrament gives Catholics "clear assurance that they are forgiven," said the Rev. Father Raymond Studzinski. For most people, that's enough. Others are still troubled by conscience even after confessing.

There's the sin, and then there's the feelings one has about it. The sacrament deals with taking away the sin. It usually, but not always, helps with the feelings. But you can be freed of your guilt and still plagued by it. In cases like that - people should seek pastoral counseling and then, if recommended, psychotherapy.

"Guilt is a very real part of Jewish life," said Wechsler, author of *What's So Bad About Guilt?* The Bible presupposes that people do right or wrong; once you have a set-up like that, it's natural to feel guilty. We have at least 10 commandments, and the truth is, Jews have more than that – 613. Just as pain is an indication of something wrong physically, guilt is an indication of something wrong spiritually.

Wechsler teaches the "five Rs," stages of sins and forgiveness: remorse, recantation, renunciation, resolution (to do better) and reconciliation with both God and the people who have been wronged.

Yom Kippur is important in the process. Also known as the Day of Atonement, Yom Kippur is prescribed in the 23rd chapter of Leviticus, when God told Moses that he and his people should "afflict your souls" once a year to make amends for wrongdoing. During Yom Kippur, which lasts about 26 hours, observant Jews abstain from work, food, drink and all physical pleasures, and spend much of the day in prayer. It's nice to have a process to get rid of guilt. It's also really important that there's a beginning and an end. It has to be a limited process; otherwise, there's no end to it.

God did not create us to feel terrible. Even though there's an ultimate purpose for guilt, we shouldn't get too hung up on it.

Medical professionals and theologians differ on what comprises the subtle differences between guilt, remorse and shame. Giovanni Frazzetto, author of *Joy, Guilt, Anger, Love: What Neuroscience Can – And Can't – Tell Us About How We Feel*, puts it this way: "Basically, guilt happens in private, whereas shame has an audience." Others say we experience guilt because of something we did (or didn't do) but suffer shame about who we think we are.

Salman Akhtar, a psychiatrist and professor, said when most people talk of guilt, they mean remorse. Guilt is the feeling we have inside of us that we're bad, or did something bad, because we broke rules given by religion, by family, by our nation, by our state. Guilt is distinct from another feeling, remorse, in which we also feel bad, but the bad feeling has to do with hurting somebody you care about. People unfortunately use the word guilt for both, and sometimes the two can overlap, but actually they're separate.

Remorse is evident in children as early as age 2 or 3. Guilt comes later, typically around age 4 or 5, when children begin to understand rules of conduct. (For the record, despite all those Internet "pet-shaming" photos of animals looking guilty, most scientists believe animals don't feel guilt or shame – those long faces and hung heads are more likely an expression of fear.)

There are three bad things – and one good thing – that stem from the emotion, Akhtar said. The bad: A person suffering from unresolved remorse can become self-punishing, manifest in behavior such as excessive drinking or smoking, overeating, mismanagement of money, or physically harming oneself. Suicide is the ultimate expression, although self-destructiveness can result from factors other than guilt.

Secondly, a person can become abnormally afraid of authority. (Shakespeare wrote of this when he said, "Suspicion always haunts the guilty mind; the thief doth fear each bush an officer.")

Third, remorseful people constantly blame others, trying to direct the guilt away from themselves.

The solution to all this, however, is positive, and improves the outcome not only for yourself, but for others. For example: Akhtar and his wife have lived in the U.S. for 43 years, after he had earned his medical degree in his native India. For more than a decade, he said, he kept thinking "how tragic I am" because life was so difficult in a radically different country where he couldn't find the food of his homeland and he "had to repeat my name three times if I ordered pizza."

Then came a realization: "I woke up from this stupid dream and realized I felt horribly guilty. I felt I had abandoned my country, and I should have served in India."

While he chose not to move back to India, he realized he could do something about the remorse: do good for the people of India. Now he spends a week there every year, providing medical education at no cost. "Reparation is a good defense against remorse," he said.

When the Challenger exploded 73 seconds after lift-off on the morning of Jan. 28, 1986, Ebeling was consumed with grief and guilt, believing that, despite the desperate arguments he and his colleagues made to NASA on the eve of the shuttle launch, he should have done more. NASA documents made public during congressional hearings provide evidence of Ebeling's frantic efforts, including one urgent memo that said "Help!" When those failed, he thought about doing something more dramatic – storming into the office with his hunting shotgun – anything to force NASA to abort, Kathy Ebeling said.

In the aftermath of the explosion, vandals painted "Morton Thiokol Murderers" on an overpass leading to Ebeling's office. It would be years until the full story came out: how Ebeling and his colleagues knew the O-rings that kept rocket fuel from leaking would fail in the cold (it was 36 degrees at lift-off, 15 degrees colder than any previous shuttle launch) and how they argued for hours against proceeding on schedule but were overruled by their superiors at Morton Thiokol and, ultimately, NASA.

While Ebeling has finally been able to forgive himself with the help of strangers, his 30 years of remorse came at great cost. For years, he could not bring himself to say his name when talking to reporters, his daughter said, and he let go of an enviable career at age 59.

The guilt may also have taken a toll on his health. Now 89, Ebeling suffers from prostate and kidney cancer as well as intermittent dementia, and the family has summoned hospice care.

In his book *Guilt, Shame and Anxiety, Understanding and Overcoming Negative Emotions*, Breggin, says that, unlike shame and anxiety, which can cause physical changes such as blushing, tingling, rapid breathing and changes in blood pressure, guilt has no obvious physical manifestation.

However, people do experience guilt in their bodies in various uncomfortable ways, often involving gastrointestinal discomfort, headaches and exhaustion. Guilt commonly drives people into feelings of depression, which cause a wide variety of uncomfortable and even disabling physical symptoms.

Guilt's potential to disable, along with shame and anxiety are 'prehistoric legacy emotions' that people should work to banish from their lives. Guilt is the worst possible moral compass because what people feel guilty about has nothing to do with sound values.

He notes that many murderers feel no remorse for their crimes, while another person can be consumed with guilt if his dog steps off the curb while on a walk and gets hit by a car.

The differences in how people process guilt goes back to early childhood and formative experiences we probably don't remember. In ancient societies, guilt and other inhibitory emotions served a purpose by helping to temper humans 'violent impulses.' But Ebeling's experience is a good example of why it's no longer needed. Guilt paralyzes us; it does not give us good guidance.

In the years after the catastrophe, Ebeling tried antidepressants and prayed frequently. In 1989, he volunteered to work full-time for free at the Bear River Migratory Bird Refuge after it was devastated by the flood of the Great Salt Lake. Even after the refuge was restored, Ebeling continued to volunteer at its education center, and he won several awards for his decades of service, including Volunteer of the Year for the National Wildlife Refuge Association in 2013.

Through volunteer work, Ebeling was unconsciously following the path Akhtar recommends: seeking relief through helping others. But ultimately, it was others who helped him, by taking the time to reach out with their emails, cards and letters, and Ebeling's story makes clear that humans have a role to play in helping others escape from their self-guarded prisons of guilt and shame.

After NPR correspondent Howard Berkes told Ebeling's story on the 30th anniversary of the disaster, hundreds of emails, letters and cards came in, the writers assuring Ebeling that he is an honorable man who did all he could have been expected to do. The people who wrote included officials and former officials from both NASA and Morton Thiokol, chaplains and priests, and a 9-year-old who said he is inspired to become an engineer after hearing Ebeling's story.

"This has brought him some peace after all these years," Kathy Ebeling said. "I know God is going to welcome him with open arms. He did everything God wanted him to do."[1]

In my younger days it seemed that every time I was cock sure that I was right, I wasn't shy in letting others know. Not always being correct, I often lived to regret that I had ever opened my mouth and felt gilt and remorse.

I was especially good at this behavior when I had young children at home. Now that the rooster in me has become a fully castrated capon - I think twice, try to not rely just on my memory as to what is truth and keep my mouth shut. Aging has also changed my thinking. Now I tend to feel guilty and question if I somehow missed the truth.

In a general sports columnist's, Stephen A. Smith, recent book *Straight Shooter*, he discusses being fired after turning down a $1.7 million contract with ESPN. He writes, "I arrived at the Marriott lobby first. Five minutes later, the ESPN boss walked in. we shook hands and sat down at the table inside the mostly empty restaurant. It was just he and I and the waitstaff. He got straight to the point. 'We're not going to renew your contract, it was not a unilateral decision.'"…Sitting at that rest stop parking lot in the middle of Connecticut, fear and embarrassment started to mix with my rage, welling up inside me, suffocating me… "We'll be just fine without you." ESPN was the behemoth. No individual was bigger than that four-letter brand. Even worse: I knew they were right.

Whenever I got low – really low- I headed to my mother's house in Hollis…I didn't make or take any calls for those three days…My mother was there if I needed something to eat, but otherwise she pretty much left me alone…So I wasn't prepared for what she had in store when she came through the door on my third morning there with a tray piled with my usual breakfast. There was the bagel, eggs, and hot tea. This time however, she'd also placed a new item on the tray: a hand mirror…"what's this?" I asked, holding it up, a bit annoyed. "You know what it is," she snapped back. "I put it there because I'm wondering when you're going to start looking at yourself."…(she then summarized the comments she overheard him saying during negotiations with his agent and ESPN) and said, "Why should ESPN want somebody like that working for them? She asked, her accent rising and falling." "Who needs that headache? You don't like anyone questioning your decisions and you're not even a boss, so why should they like you doing it? I'm not saying they should've fired you, but how would you feel if you were them? you're not blameless here."

I'd forgotten the Golden rule: those who have the gold make the rules. Love it or hate it, that's the reality I'd come face-to-face with, because I had failed to recall – and follow – the golden rule on a number of occasions. The end result: I concluded that I was the one ultimately responsible.[2]

I remember doing some of what Stephen A. Smith did on a lesser scale when living at my home. If I was in trouble at school, done something stupid with friends (like throwing garbage cans out on the street on Halloween) or was not performing up to par – my parent's question was always what I had done to deserve being reprimanded and not what others had done to me.

Returning home from one Christmas vacation with my children we noticed all the lights on in our home and my youngest child's friends having a party inside. I came to find out that Jeremy's friends didn't expect us home because they knew he would not be coming home until a few days later. They didn't think that maybe the rest of Jeremy's family might be coming home at an earlier time. He had stayed in Utah to ski a few extra days.

Most the parents involved wanted me to throw the book at their children and "teach them a lesson." Others insisted that their children were not involved and completely innocent. My desire was to speak to the kids and let them know that our home was a sanctuary from the outside world and had been defiled by some of the activities they were doing. When I did, the ones present were apologetic and seemed remorseful.

I noticed most of the teenagers, my son and I kept in contact with, graduated from high school and moved on to good careers and happy family life. Some of the ones whose parents made a "not there – not guilty plea" didn't do as well.

Am I happy that I've felt unnecessary anxiety, feelings of quilt and stress over the years that helped contributed to the damage done to my physical body. Yes – I think it has helped me be a better person. However, many a time during anxiety, guilt trips and feelings of shame, I wished I were like the animal patients I care for – "despite all those Internet 'pet-shaming' photos of animals looking guilty, most scientists believe animals don't feel guilt or shame."

Does everyone feel guilt? Not necessarily. The degree to which people feel guilt varies, and those with certain personalities may experience relatively little (if any) guilt. A lack of guilt and remorse is one characteristic that experts have used to diagnose psychopathy.

Knowing this, I should be glad who I am and not wish to be like an animal that doesn't ever have guilt or shame.

1– *Advice for people suffering too long from a guilty conscience, by Jennifer Graham, Deseret News, 03/10/2016.*

2– *Straight Shooter, Stephen A. Smith, pages131-133, 136-138, 2023.*

30

THE DASH

May 14, 2019. Researchers from Wake Forest School of Medicine have reported that the Dietary Approaches to Stop Hypertension (DASH) diet reduces risk of heart failure by approximately 50%. Heart failure can lead to frequent hospitalizations and higher mortality rates. About 50% of people who develop heart failure will not survive longer than 5 years, with the risk being higher for men.

Why was the DASH diet ranked as the best diet, the healthiest diet, and the best diet for diabetes? The expert panel of physicians assembled chose DASH because it is proven to improve health, has a balance of healthy food groups, and it actually works. DASH has been proven to lower blood pressure and cholesterol, and is associated with lower risk of several types of cancer, heart disease, stroke, heart failure, kidney stones, reduced risk of developing diabetes, can slow the progression of kidney disease, and now is associated with reduced risk of depression.

Both the Mediterranean and DASH diets are plant-focused diets, rich in fruits and vegetables, nuts, with low-fat and non-fat dairy, lean meats, fish, and poultry, mostly whole grains, and heart healthy fats.

The Institute for Work & Health report on the Disabilities of the Arm, Shoulder and Hand (DASH) Outcome Measure test that first became available in 2003, discussed the self-report questionnaire to measure physical function and symptoms in patients with any or several musculoskeletal disorders of the upper limb. The questionnaire was designed to help describe the disability experienced by people with upper-limb disorders and also to monitor changes in symptoms and function over time. Testing has shown that the DASH performs well in both these roles. It gives clinicians and researchers the advantage of having a single, reliable instrument that can be used to assess any or all joints in the upper extremity.

The DASH Outcome Measure contains two optional, four-item modules intended to measure symptoms and function in athletes, performing artists and other workers whose jobs require a high degree of physical performance.

Dash pay-wallet recently became available that offers a platform technology stack for building decentralized applications on the Dash network. Dash provides digital cash that can be used anywhere. Dash gives you the freedom to move your money any way you want - anywhere, to anyone, instantly, for less than a cent.

Get on board with world social payments. Your identity on the blockchain is no longer restricted to cryptographic addresses. Register yourself on the network and start sharing your user-name with other Dash users.

DASH, the stock symbol for DoorDash, Inc. According to Wikipedia, it is an American company that operates an online food ordering and food delivery platform. The company is based in San Francisco, California that went public in December 2020. With a 56% market share, DoorDash is the largest food delivery company in the United States. It also has a 60% market share in the convenience delivery category. As of December 31, 2020, the platform was used by 450,000 merchants, 20,000,000 consumers, and one million deliverers.

DoorDash has been criticized and sued for withholding tips, reducing tip transparency, antitrust price manipulation, listing restaurants without permission, and allegedly misclassifying workers.

Dash can be used to describe an act of sudden activity of haste such as a dash for the door, an athlete running a 100-yard dash, a journey or period of time characterized by urgency and eager haste, a gust of rain being dashed against the bricks or a ship being dashed against the rocks.

Dash is used to describe a small quantity of a substance added to something else. A dash of salt, a drink with a dash of soda or a person with a small amount of a particular quality that adds a dash of sophistication or distinctiveness to something else.

A dash or horizontal stroke in writing or printing is used to mark a pause or break in sense or to represent omitted letters or words such as the Morse code or a short vertical mark placed above or beneath a note to indicate that it is to be performed in a very staccato manner.

Dash can be used to place impetuous or flamboyant vigor and confidence such as a young man showing his youthful energy, dash, and charisma.

Dashes are used to mark the beginning and end of a series, which might otherwise get confused, with the rest of the sentence. It can be used to separate a period of time between an event. According to wordonen.com there are 36 words that contain "dash" in them.

Bob Dole's (1923-2021) dash in public life began with his political career starting at 28 years of age serving in the Kansas state Legislature and eventually becoming a member of the U.S. House of Representatives, and a U.S. Senator. He also ran for vice president and president of the United States.

Dole's college career was interrupted by the United States' entry into World War II. He enlisted in the U.S. Army in 1942 and was summoned to active duty in early 1943. Dole was transferred to a post near the Po Valley, in northern Italy. That region still held a German machine gun nest, and, despite Dole's relatively small amount of combat experience, he was ordered to lead an assault against it.

The day of the assault was, as Dole put it, "the day that changed my life." During the attack, Dole was severely wounded. According to examinations by medics following the battle, Dole had sustained the following injuries: a shattered right shoulder, fractured vertebrae in his neck and spine, paralysis from the neck down, metal shrapnel throughout his body and a damaged kidney. The medics examining Dole thought him unlikely to survive.

After several surgeries and extensive rehabilitation, Dole not only lived but made a better recovery than had ever been expected. The only lingering physical limitations for Dole are his paralyzed right arm and hand, and during public appearances, he often kept a pen in his right hand to make it appear less unusual.

At Sen. Bob Dole's funeral service Chaplain of the United States Senate Barry Black stated, "Bob was a covert spiritual agent, he did not wear his religion on his sleeve. He resonated with the sentiment of Francis of Assisi. 'Preach the gospel wherever you go, when necessary, use words.'"

The senate chaplain said he had known both Dole and his wife, former Sen. Elizabeth Dole for many years and had had discussions on faith with them both. Citing Dole's love of brevity, he said the former senator understood that his time among the living was only temporary. During his 98 years of life, "He knew that there was brevity...It's temporary. He was not in that valley to stay," [1]

"When your eulogy is being read with your life's actions to rehash, would you be proud of the things they say about how you spent your life's dash?" Bob Dole died in his sleep on a Sunday morning at the age of 98. Sheila Burke, who served with Dole for 20 years, spoke at the funeral at Washington National Cathedral and said Dole often included a poem in speeches in later years. She stated, "I believe we will hear in these words a description of the man whose life, whose leadership, and whose legacy we celebrate today," Burke said before reciting the poem.

I read of a man who stood to speak at the funeral of a friend. He referred to the dates on the tombstone from the beginning to the end.

He noted first came the date of the birth and spoke the following date with tears. But he said what mattered most of all was the dash between the years.

For that dash represents all the time that they spent life on Earth. And now only those who loved them know what that little line is worth.

For it matters not how much we own, the cars, the house, the cash. What matters is how we live and love, and how we spend our dash.

So, think about this long and hard. Are there things you'd like to change? For you never know how much time is left that can still be rearranged.

If we could just slow down enough to consider what's true and real, and always try to understand the way other people feel.

Be less quick to anger and show appreciation more, and love the people in our lives like we've never loved before.

If we treat each other with respect and more often wear a smile, remembering that this special dash might only last a little while.

So, when your eulogy is being read with your life's actions to rehash, would you be proud of the things they say about how you spent your dash? *'The Dash' poem, by Linda Ellis.*

1– *Biography & Chaplain of US Senate says late Sen. Dole was a 'covert spiritual agent' December 10, 2021.*

31

I'M GETTING A LITTLE BETTER EVERY DAY

No matter the situation my mother seemed to always think about the good things rather than bad. During her later years she had the expected hearing difficulties, pre diabetes and arthritis that made it difficult for her to get around or raise her arms high enough to remove dishes from cupboards or brush her hair. Even with these difficulties her daily motto was "I'm getting a little better every day."

One day my sister Bobbie and her husband Mel went over to do their morning check up on her and found her in the bath tub. She had made a wrong turn or fell during the night going to the bathroom, ending up in the tub.

The family convinced her to not go downstairs in her home without assistance; they could not get her to always use her walker and she fell breaking a leg. Her doctor plaster casted it and she was placed in a convalescent area attached to the hospital. Taking everything in stride, she quickly socialized with a group of oldies and her cup seemed to be full to the brim. The last time I saw her we were showing her pictures on my computer and she asked me if I were about finished because she needed to go down for lunch with her friends. Hopefully not making mom feel impolite, I told her just about done and showed a couple of more photos. We walked her to the dinner table and the last thing I will always remember is her smile, shooing us down the hallway to the exit door with a wave goodbye.

It wasn't many days later that I received a call at work from Bobbie - mother had collapsed, was toxic with a high fever and unconscious. We discussed attempted care or whether it was best to "let her go." The answer came before we had the chance to express our feelings – she was gone.

When I got back to her home in Blackfoot, Idaho, the family met with the mortician and he showed the broken leg with a plastic bag placed over it. The bag was full of purulent debris. Mom's death resulted from septicemia caused by an undetected abscess forming under the cast.

The family was shocked and wondered how this could have happened with a hospital next door and who was monitoring her care. Jay, (a medical doctor and husband of Pat -my youngest sister) wisely advised us that no matter what we did our mother would not be with us again except in the hereafter. Also, could we know who was possibly at fault and whom might we accused that weren't? If there was fault, those involved knew it and would hopefully have the character inside them to learn from the experience.

As I have thought about my mother and her death I'm reminded of her philosophy about vengeance. "If you are offended let it go. If you let it fester it can destroy your life, but not the offender's." Even if we were in the right and took action against those caring for her, wasn't she telling us that it is best to let it go? Even if her care was mismanaged, we didn't know all the circumstances surrounding her health, and if there was neglect or mismanagement. Our family's relationship with each other along with challenging the character of the personnel and the reputation of the hospital and care center could have been damaged without reason. Thus, affecting all those involved in health care for the community.

A man's character is the reality of himself. – His reputation is the opinion others have formed of him. – Character is in him; - reputation is from other people – (character) is the substance, (reputation) is the shadow.[1]

In January 2014, I was approached by a web site business that an important part of its sale pitch was to "watch over the social media" and be sure that a company or its employees had not been misrepresented by an individual or entity bearing false witness. It made me sit back for a moment and think of the uncomfortable times over the last forty years when one challenged the character or reputation of my company, employees, family or religious pursuits. Fortunately, they have not been serious enough to fester into a painful ailment that absorbed all of my time and attention at least for very long. Guy de Maupassant has written an interesting chronicle that illustrates what can happen when one becomes obsessed after having his character and reputation challenged by others.

It concerns Master Hauchecome, who on market day went to town. He was afflicted with rheumatism, and as he stumbled along he noticed a piece of string on the ground in front of him. He picked it up and carefully put it in his pocket. He was seen doing so by his enemy, the harness maker.

At the same time, it was reported to the mayor that a pocketbook containing money had been lost. It was assumed that what Hauchecome had picked up was the pocketbook, and he was accused of taking it. He vehemently denied the charge. A search of his clothing disclosed only the piece of string, but the slander against him had so troubled him that he became obsessed with it. Wherever he went he bothered to tell people about it. He became such a nuisance that they cried out against him. It sickened him.

"His mind kept growing weaker and about the end of December he took to his bed. "He passed away early in January, and, in the ravings of [his] death agony, he protested his innocence, repeating:

"'A little [piece] of string—a little [piece] of string. See, here it is, (Mister Mayor.)'"[2]

Circumspect conduct on conspicuous occasions is not necessarily an indication of circumspect thought, or of goodness. It may be merely deference to conventions or appearances. And, the real test of civilization, the real measure of goodness it's not whether or not we can enforce the laws on the statute books, but whether or not we are fit company in our own solitude.

Outward immoral acts are an aggravated problem in any society, but only when, as a people, we can come to place emphasis on thoughts and motives and spiritual and inward purity, shall we approach a realization of the standards set by Him who said: "Blessed are the pure in heart, for they shall see God."

Strength and safety, peace and abiding happiness, lie in purity at the source, where thoughts are born and 'where deeds take shape—and not merely in concealing the outward evidence of an act that has already taken form within. In short, if a man can't think straight, there can be no assurance that he can live straight, "For as he thinketh in his heart, so is he." (Proverbs 23:7.)[3]

May we not bear false witness by testifying or passing along reports, insinuations, speculations, or rumors as if they were true, to the hurt of a fellow human being. Sometimes the practice stems from a lack of correct information – sometimes from lack of understanding – sometimes from misunderstandings – sometimes from a vicious disposition to distort and misrepresent…

"The words of a talebearer are as wounds, and they go down into the innermost parts of the belly". Proverbs 18:8

1– *Henry Ward Beecher, in Tryon Edwards, comp., The New Dictionary of Thoughts (1944), 67.*

2– *"The Piece of String," http://www.online-literature.com/Maupassant/270/.*

3– *Disciplined Hearts and Minds, Richard L. Evans, #754, 01/30/1944.*

32

YOU ARE WHAT YOU WEAR

Fashion shows are a great idea for groups trying to fundraise for a cause, organize community events, or to promote local fashion designers and businesses. The key ingredients to a good fashion show are a general theme, a well-coordinated team, and a well-designed program. It is important that you come up with a plan for your show: theme, location and date, music, lighting and decorations. To be successful they need to be organized by a team of people to run the show: designers, models, hair and makeup stylists, show coordinators, lighting and sound professionals. All of these people need to work together to make it succeed. Finally, you will need to come up with a detailed program of featured designers, order of models and styles, and music and lighting.

The ladies of our church organized a fun filled evening which was held in the cultural hall of the church and included everyone that was willing to participate. The placement of tables, chairs, linen, decorations, food, music, models, clothing, hair makeup and show coordinators were all provided by the women themselves. Some of the setup, take down, building cleanup and presence for security was provided by a few of their willing spouses. I don't know the theme, but the meal was eaten, the tables and food were cleared away, they modeled their clothing to music, sound "professionals" introduced the models and mentioned highlights about them as they showed off their clothing, walking forward and back aligning themselves on the half court line on the gym floor in the cultural hall.

I was asked by the program coordinator to be the photographer for the event. Being a "very" amateur photographer, I asked if my cell phone would do? With a yes, on the evening of the fashion show I dressed as I thought a real photographer would and had the opportunity to attend the event with my wife. During the fashion show I sat on one end of the half court line shooting photos and movies of the models showing off their clothing. It was quite an experience filming the youth, mothers and grandmothers of our church strutting their stuff and having a wonderful time.

After modeling everyone had the opportunity discussing why what they were wearing was of particular importance to them.

Observing the clothing worn, how they modeled it and described why they chose it for the occasion made me sit back and realize how what we wear does give off first impressions and also seems to have an effect on how one presents themselves. The wardrobe says a lot about you. What you wear can inform a passerby about your type of employment, as well as your ambitions, emotions and spending habits.

Clinical psychologist Dr. Jennifer Baumgartner wrote the book on this phenomenon, which she calls the "psychology of dress." In "You Are What You Wear: What Your Clothes Reveal About You," she explains not only how psychology determines our clothing choices, but how to overcome key psychological issues your wardrobe might be bringing to light in your everyday life, or even at work.

Shopping and spending behaviors often come from internal motivations such as emotions, experiences and culture. You look at shopping or storing behaviors, even putting together outfits, and people think of it as fluff. But any behavior is rooted in something deeper. I look at the deeper meaning of choices, just like I would in therapy.

Americans rely on clothing as an economic and social indicator because there aren't official marks of rank such as a caste system or aristocracy. When you don't have a specific system, people come up with their own. It's what helps you figure out where you fit in. Especially when you are having economic difficulties and feel that you are losing status in the community. Maintaining a sense of who we are becomes even more important. Our clothes help place us where we think we want to be.

Have you ever been told that you can judge a man by his shoes? Unfortunately, it's not that simple.

There's no one piece or style that makes a person look successful. Dr. Baumgartner recommends the basics when trying to project a positive image: the little black dress, the blazer, the pumps. With classics, history has done the work for you. It has lasted throughout time, so you already know it works. And what is it that makes a classic a classic? It has multiple functions, and it's appropriate for different age ranges and body types. It became a classic because it works no matter who you are.

A study from Northwestern University examined a concept called "enclothed cognition." Researchers define it in their report as "the systematic influence that clothes have on the wearer's psychological processes," meaning what your clothes are saying to you, not about you. And how they make you feel.

The researchers distributed standard white lab coats to participants, telling some that it was a doctor's coat and some that it was a painter's smock. All participants performed the same task, but those wearing the "doctor's coat" were more careful and attentive. Their actions were influenced by their clothing.

The same may be true of you. When your friend dragged you out of the house and told you, "Get dressed up! You'll feel better!" After your last breakup/failed interview/lousy day, she was onto something. When you dress in a certain way, it helps shift your internal self. We see that when we do makeovers, and even actors say that putting on a costume facilitates expression of character. That's just as true for everyday life.

Enclothed cognition gives scientific proof to the idea that you should dress not how you feel, but how you want to feel. Which clothes make you feel powerful? Sexy? In control? Wealthy? The clothes you choose are sending a message to those around you, but also to you, yourself.[1]

Without knowing it, the clothes I wore for the fashion show enclothed my cognition into wearing clothes that "made me feel powerful", sending the message to the ladies around me and myself that I was part of the fashion show and held the "important" title and responsibility of being their "chosen one" to be the photographer for such an event. I found myself fantasizing everyone watching me during the fashion show walking the black line in the center of the gym in the cultural hall in style, doing some cutesy moves and telling the world on film why each particle of clothing worn was important to me.

My chosen attire for the fashion show:

The battered dark pink plastic hat was taken from one of my grandsons whom I feared was in the process of destroying it after Halloween a few years ago.

The business card tucked under the hat band was procured from a memory pile of my wife Shauna's business cards. On the back side of it was written, "Photos Here" with a drawn smiling rabbit face to be sure everyone knew I was there not to just help in case of security issues but held the important function of "official photographer" for the evening.

The "beautiful light pink jacket" was found for Easter on a Kohl's discount rake. At the time I was on the phone with Shauna in Idaho listening to her discouraging remarks about such a foolish purchase. The pants were not used for the festive event. They were left on the hanger where they've been since the purchase. The pant leg length and hem have never been finished.

The pants worn were from my tux Shauna purchased for me many moons ago. They have been used two times to renew our wedding vows on cruise ships. The first time was September 5, 2007 on an around the islands cruise in Hawaii and the last September 3, 2022 with friends that celebrate their wedding the same month and day that we do. Each of them had been divorced, living together and according to her daughter, "were living in sin and it was not a good example for the grandchildren to watch such an affair." Ron, who I've known since grade school (he is a retired Army helicopter pilot and at the time was a truck driver), told me that during a night trip through Reno Nevada Dani and he decided to get married (for the children) at a stop by marriage chapel. "The wedding was a joke and judging by the smell - the "minister" was suspect of not having changed his Depends."

Five years ago, during a cruise to Alaska with Dani and Ron, Shauna and I surprised them on our anniversary date with a wedding on board the ship. There was a red carpet, flowers, the captain of the ship performed the event, Ron and Dani shared touching personal thoughts, and Shauna and me wearing the tux pants (worn at the fashion show) thoroughly enjoyed the affair.

I do not often wear a black shirt. The one I wore at the fashion show was purchased for a bit of a joke. Shauna's family's favorite color is pretty much black and when her son, Dustin, lived with me I purchased two black shirts to "join the family tradition."

Shauna's mother and father stayed with her mother's sister, Ethyl, for many weeks during her final days on earth in Iron Mountain Michigan. The clothing they brought with them was pretty much all black. One day Shauna's cousin asked her if Mormon's only wore black clothing. Her mother said, "No, I like black." Her cousin asking about Shauna's parents black clothing was triggered by her familiarity with the Amish people living in her area.

The rule of thumb for all Amish clothing is that it should be plain, to avoid calling attention to yourself or standing out from the crowd. The Amish believe this promotes modesty, and helps them live apart from the rest of society. Even buttons, neckties, zippers, and belt buckles are too flashy for most Amish, so you won't see men wearing them. Instead, they dress in dark trousers with suspenders, a dark vest or coat, and a straw or felt hat (depending on the season).

Their jackets don't feature collars or lapels, and use hook-and-eye fasteners instead of buttons. The Amish don't wear wedding rings, but you can spot a married Amish man by his beard. Boys stay clean shaven until they're married, then grow a beard - but not a mustache, which is too flashy and associated with the military by the pacifist Amish. Amish men take their beards seriously, and cutting one off can be considered a hate crime.

Most Amish women never cut their hair, and instead wear it in a braid or bun under a bonnet. The women only wear dresses, and must follow strict rules about sleeve and skirt length set by their community. Most Amish women are required to wear full sleeves and calf-length dresses, with plain fabrics made from one solid color. In fact, color plays an important part in an Amish woman's wardrobe. Young boys and girls usually wear lighter colors than adults, and begin wearing darker colors as they get older. Depending on their community, an Amish woman may swap a white bonnet for a black one after being married.

The most important quality for Amish dresses is that they're plain. They're designed to be easy to do chores in, and most women own very few dresses. An old saying says an Amish woman needs just "one for wash, one for wear, one for dress and one for spare."

Wearing jewelry is forbidden in most Amish communities, but there are some common accessories in an Amish woman's wardrobe. Aprons are a common part of an Amish woman's outfit, and as the weather gets cooler they'll put on capes and wool cloaks to stay warm.[2]

The Old Order Amish have many rules about how they live their lives to prevent worldliness. These rules govern transportation, clothing, power, education, and many other aspects of daily life. Some of their rules may seem complicated at times causing confusion among non-Amish people. The basic concept behind many of their rules is that they "try to be in the world but not of it." This means they reject many connections to the outside world in an attempt to remain unworldly.

For transportation, the Amish do not use cars. They may ride in them if they are driven by non-Amish. Instead, they drive horse drawn buggies. For shorter distances, they may use scooters, but bicycles are also banned. It is believed that cars and bicycles move too quickly over long distances, therefore connecting the Amish to the outside world.

Rules governing the use of power sources are may seem complex. If a power source is not artificial, but from God, the Amish can use it because it is not physically connected to the outside world. So, the Amish can use power sources such as solar, propane, and diesel. These rules allow many modern appliances to be used, such as refrigerators. In addition, generators or batteries are allowed by the Amish.

Phones are not permitted in the home but are commonly used for business purposes.

Rules regarding education exist to prevent worldly thinking. Amish children will only go to school to 8th grade before they begin working full time with their families. They do not attend high school or college. They also only celebrate and have off school for religious holidays such as Christmas and Easter, not federal holidays. This allows them to end school in early May after the legally required 180 days of school a year and help in the fields over the summer when there is more work to be done.[3]

In the beautiful hills of Pennsylvania are found a devout group of Amish Christian people living their simple life with restricted use of automobiles, electricity, or modern machinery. They work hard and live quiet, peaceful lives separate from the world. Most of their food comes from their own farms. The women sew and knit and weave their clothing, which is modest and plain.

In October 2006 a 32-year-old milk truck driver lived with his family in their Nickel Mines community. He was not Amish, but his pickup route took him to many Amish dairy farms, where he became known as the quiet milkman. He suddenly lost all reason and control. In his tormented mind he blamed God for the death of his first child and some unsubstantiated memories. He stormed into the Amish school without any provocation, released the boys and adults, and tied up the 10 girls. He shot the girls, killing five and wounding five. Then he took his own life.

This shocking violence caused great anguish among the Amish but no anger. There was hurt but no hate. Their forgiveness was immediate. Collectively they began to reach out to the milkman's suffering family. As the milkman's family gathered in his home the day after the shootings, an Amish neighbor came over, wrapped his arms around the father of the dead gunman, and said, "We will forgive you." Amish leaders visited the milkman's wife and children to extend their sympathy, their forgiveness, their help, and their love.

About half of the mourners at the milkman's funeral were Amish. In turn, the Amish invited the milkman's family to attend the funeral services of the girls who had been killed. A remarkable peace settled on the Amish as their faith sustained them during this crisis.

One local resident very eloquently summed up the aftermath of this tragedy when he said, "We were all speaking the same language, and not just English, but a language of caring, a language of community, [and] a language of service. And, yes, a language of forgiveness." It was an amazing outpouring of their complete faith in the Lord's teachings in the Sermon on the Mount: "Do good to them that hate you, and pray for them which despitefully use you."

The family of the milkman who killed the five girls released the following statement to the public:

"To our Amish friends, neighbors, and local community: Our family wants each of you to know that we are overwhelmed by the forgiveness, grace, and mercy that you've extended to us. Your love for our family has helped to provide the healing we so desperately need. The prayers, flowers, cards, and gifts you've given have touched our hearts in a way no words can describe. Your compassion has reached beyond our family, beyond our community, and is changing our world, and for this we sincerely thank you.

Please know that our hearts have been broken by all that has happened. We are filled with sorrow for all of our Amish neighbors whom we have loved and continue to love. We know that there are many hard days ahead for all the families who lost loved ones, and so we will continue to put our hope and trust in the God of all comfort, as we all seek to rebuild our lives."

How could the whole Amish group manifest such an expression of forgiveness? It was because of their faith in God and trust in His word, which is part of their inner beings. They see themselves as disciples of Christ and want to follow His example.

Hearing of this tragedy, many people sent money to the Amish to pay for the health care of the five surviving girls and for the burial expenses of the five who were killed. As a further demonstration of their discipleship, the Amish decided to share some of the money with the widow of the milkman and her three children because they too were victims of this terrible tragedy.

Forgiveness is not always instantaneous as it was with the Amish. When innocent children have been molested or killed, most of us do not think first about forgiveness. Our natural response is anger. We may even feel justified in wanting to "get even" with anyone who inflicts injury on us or our family.

Dr. Sidney Simon, a recognized authority on values realization, has provided an excellent definition of forgiveness as it applies to human relationships: "Forgiveness is freeing up and putting to better use the energy once consumed by holding grudges, harboring resentments, and nursing unhealed wounds. It is rediscovering the strengths we always had and relocating our limitless capacity to understand and accept other people and ourselves."

If we can find forgiveness in our hearts for those who have caused us hurt and injury, we will rise to a higher level of self-esteem and well-being. Some recent studies show that people who are taught to forgive become "less angry, more hopeful, less depressed, less anxious and less stressed," which leads to greater physical well-being. Another of these studies concludes "that forgiveness … is a liberating gift [that] people can give to themselves."[4]

The Northwestern University study called "enclothed cognition" concluded that when you dress in a certain way, it helps shift your internal self. Dr. Baumgartner recommends the basics when trying to project a positive image: the little black dress, the blazer, the pumps. With classics, history has done the work for you. It has lasted throughout time, so you already know it works.

The rule of thumb for all Amish clothing is that it should be plain, to avoid calling attention to yourself or standing out from the crowd. The Amish believe this promotes modesty, and helps them live apart from the rest of society.

Their response to the shocking violence and great anguish among the Amish was not anger. There was hurt but no hate. Their forgiveness was immediate. Collectively they began to reach out to the milkman's suffering family. As the milkman's family gathered in his home the day after the shootings, an Amish neighbor came over, wrapped his arms around the father of the dead gunman, and said, "We will forgive you." Amish leaders visited the milkman's wife and children to extend their sympathy, their forgiveness, their help, and their love.

Our clothes help place us where we think we want to be. I want to be more like the Amish - less worldly, not abusive with the demands placed on Mother Nature, be closer to loving others as the Good Book teaches and not standing out in the crowd trying to show my importance. However, I still plan on wearing my white lab coat at work even though the younger generation thinks I'm kind of an old fuddy duddy. If nothing else it hides my aging arms with patches caused by blood thinners and it keeps me warm.

1– *What Your Clothes Say About You, LearnVest, Forbes, 2012.*
2– *The Hidden Meaning Behind Amish Clothing Rules, By Zachary, Dec 19, 2017.*
3– *The Amish Farm & House, How Amish Rules Impact Their Lives, Lancaster PA.*
4– *The Healing Power of Forgiveness, President James E. Faust, April 2007.*

33

COULD YOU WOULD YOU IF YOU COULD - ROATAN FLOATING ROCK

While visiting the Isla Roatan, Honduras I purchased some rocks that can float on water and was told it was found floating in the ocean. I have it in my museum show at home (see photo). After I got home, I found that the common name for the rock is pumice. Pumice is a type of extrusive volcanic rock, produced when lava with a very high content of water and gases is discharged from a volcano. As the gas bubbles escape, the lava becomes frothy. When this lava cools and hardens, the result is a very light rock material filled with tiny bubbles of gas. The frothy material resembles the foam that forms when a soda is shaken. Commonly it is light-colored, indicating that it is a volcanic rock high in silica content and low in iron and magnesium, a type usually classed as rhyolite.

Pumice is mined through open pit and quarrying methods. Extraction and processing methods vary, depending on the end use. It can be cut into blocks or crushed. Pumice is used to make lightweight construction materials such as concrete block and concrete.

The remainder of the pumice mined is used in abrasives (for personal care, industrial cleaners, rubber erasers, stonewashing jeans, etc.) absorbents (potting soil, pet litter, etc.), and architecture (insulation, roofing, landscaping, etc.)

In August 13, 2019, NASA National Observatory commented on volcanoes. They have a lot of dramatic ways to announce their presence: thick plumes of ash and steam; rivers and lakes of molten lava; rockfalls and lahars; earthquakes; even the sudden rising of an island above the water line. One of the more subtle and rarely observed displays is the pumice raft.

Many of the world's volcanoes are shrouded by the waters of the oceans. When they erupt, they can discolor the ocean surface with gases and debris. They also can spew masses of lava that are lighter than water. Such pumice rocks are full of holes and cavities, and they easily float.

On August 13, 2019, the Operational Land Imager on Landsat 8 acquired natural-color imagery of a vast pumice raft floating in the tropical Pacific Ocean near Late Island in the Kingdom of Tonga. NASA's Terra satellite detected the mass of floating rock on August 9; the discolored water around the pumice suggests that the submarine volcano lies somewhere below. The Volcano Discovery web site reported that it received an email from a sailor on August 7, 2019, about clouds of smoke on the horizon in the direction of Fonualei volcano. According to a bulletin from the Smithsonian's Global Volcanism Program (GVP), sailors began reporting sightings of the pumice raft by August 9.

The crew of the catamaran Roam encountered the pumice and provided a detailed report on Facebook on. The sailors described a "rubble slick made up of rocks from marble to basketball size such that water was not visible," as well as a smell of sulfur.

Volcanologists at the Smithsonian believe the evidence points to an unnamed submarine volcano near Tonga. The last report of an eruption at the site occurred in 2001, and the summit of the seamount is believed to stand about 40 meters (130 feet) below the water line.

Volcanologist Erik Klemetti of Denison University wrote: "Pumice rafts can drift for weeks to years, slowly dispersing into the ocean currents. These chunks of pumice end up making excellent, drifting homes for sea organisms, helping them spread...The erupted pumice means this volcano erupts magma high in silica like rhyolite."

I was on a cruise with my brother and sister-in-law, Michael and Vonnie Retford, and their friend Sharon. On Thursday November 20, 2003 on the ship somewhere heading for Grand Cayman with several "floating rocks from Roatan" in hand I wrote a poem that I later gave it and one of the floating rocks to a friend of mine, Shauna, that on September 3, 2005 became my wife.

"Could You Would You If You Could
Roatan Floating Rock

When life's burdens over whelm you and you feel as if the weight will pull you into the deep abyss:

May you always have a friend (like this rock from Isla Roatan, Honduras) that will lift you into the light and help shine away despair and give you encouragement and confidence to go on.

COULD YOU WOULD YOU IF YOU COULD?

Could you would you be my friend: And travel the earth with me to the bitter end?

Could you would you sail the seas: And visit lots of places as we please?

Could you would you fly on a plane: And tolerate me when I'm having fun acting a little insane?

Could you would you ride on a catamaran, bike or moped: And not complain until after we get back and have been fed?

Could you would you tolerate biting, sucking and stinging bugs: To be with me and get some hugs?

Could you would you rub soothing creams on my red back: When earlier on an excursion sun block and screen I did lack?

Could you would you get muddy and wet: And not care about how you look, or feel or your forgotten hair net?

Could you would you eat and eat: And then
burn it off together by going for long travels
on our feet?

Could you would you get dressed up all
sharp and pretty: And go with me out to
eat and to a live theater in the city?

Could you would you take slow walks in
the light of the moon: And when we're done
walking feel that our time together ended
too soon?

Could you would you when we're old:
Remember our great times together and
the stories that could be told?

Could you would you be my friend: And
travel the earth with me to the bitter end?

Could you would you let us see: Because
here are some of the things that you would
have done if you had traveled with me!

Bike in a rainforest w/ mosquitoes, mud, water and
sweat; Mayan ruins; city tours, bus; catamaran sailing;
snorkeling; the town of Hell and Back; sea turtle farm and
hold one – they are heavy; boat ride to a stingray sandbar
stepping on, holding, feeding and playing with them; all day
ride around the island of Cozumel on mopeds; eat at least
three large meals a day; walking or any other exercise that

will keep the weight off; stage performances, auctions, bingo etcetera; getting sun burned; shopping….!!!!

Oh yes…the Mexican Train Game we played almost nightly and forgetting all the stuff that seems to be important – but too soon would be important again."

Visited: Belize City, Belize; Isla Roatan, Honduras; Grand Cayman; Cozumel, Mexico

There are islands in the ocean that don't show up on any map and that no one will also ever set foot on. Known as pumice rafts, these "islands" are made of volcanic rocks, and instead of being anchored to the seafloor they float wherever the currents take them. They can stay afloat for years (long enough to ferry small animals and seeds around the world), and scientists have long wondered about the secret of their longevity. New research is finally providing an answer.

Pumice rafts pop up after underwater volcanic eruptions. When the hot lava hits the water and cools quickly, gas bubbles are trapped in the rock, and chunks float to the surface. The pumice resists becoming waterlogged somehow, which keeps it afloat for a long time, and researchers have found that the rocks tend to sink at night and rise back to the surface during the day. Researchers at the University of California, Berkeley, used X-ray imaging to figure out just what is going on that makes the pumice behave so oddly. Their 3D images show that there are two forces at work.

First, water doesn't completely fill the pores of the rock, like it does in a sponge. Even though those pores are connected, some are so narrow that the surface tension of the water traps gas inside, which provides the enduring buoyancy. The pumice eventually sinks when this trapped gas diffuses out through the rock. And the bobbing? The trapped gas explains this, too, since it cools and contracts at night, which makes the rocks less buoyant. The warmth of the day then causes the gas to expand again, lifting the rocks back to the surface.

Understanding, tracking, and modeling pumice rafts can help scientists keep track of underwater eruptions in remote corners of the ocean. Further, pumice rafts can be a nightmare for ships—ashy, pulverized pumice isn't great for engines. Models can help ships steer clear, and a better understanding of when pumice rafts will sink only make those models more useful.[1]

Australia's Great Barrier Reef is in trouble, but the ocean itself might be sending some slow-moving relief. An enormous floating island of pumice is headed toward Australia, and it could deliver new marine life to the endangered reef, reports CNN. The odd development is the result of an underwater volcano that erupted near Tonga in the Pacific Ocean in the first week of August, explains NASA. The volcano sent pumice rocks to the surface, some of them as small as marble, others as big as a basketball, according to the first-person account from the crew of a catamaran that sailed through the resulting field. The rocks are pocked with holes, allowing them to float, and they're currently bunched up in a mass the size of Manhattan.

"At the moment there are more than a trillion pieces of pumice all floating together, but over time it will break up and disperse across the area," says Scott Bryan of Queensland University of Technology. Still, a bulk of the natural raft could reach Australia in perhaps seven months, bringing with it all kinds of microorganisms and larger marine life. "This is a potential mechanism for restocking the Great Barrier Reef," Bryan tells the BBC. The floating pumice field isn't unheard of, with marine experts saying the phenomenon is spotted every five years or so (Another possibility of helping the reef involves the clouds).[2]

Imagine a vast "raft" of volcanic pumice rocks, in 2019, stretching as much as over 150 sq km (58 sq miles) drifting through the Pacific Ocean and I have in my possession some of these type of rocks from my cruise in 2003.

Imagine that Shauna and I commuted back and forth by airplane from Boise Idaho to San Jose California from the fall of 2005 until May of 2021. That's when the moving truck brought all her temporal things to our current home. It took so long because she was a bank manager and needed to take care of her young children, her father had health issues and used a walker or wheel chair from the time I first met him, and her mother later needed assistance until she passed.

I felt somewhat like Jacob of the Old Testament. Soon after his arrival in Harran, Jacob fell in love with the beautiful and lovely Rachel, daughter of his cousin Laban (Genesis 29:17). Laban warmly welcomed him to his family, but asked a steep price for Rachel's hand in marriage: Jacob would first have to work as a shepherd for seven years, tending Laban's flocks. The annual wage for a shepherd in the Bronze Age was about 10 shekels; hence, seven years of labor was a stiff demand. But Jacob, a fugitive from Esau, was in no position to bargain.

And Jacob served seven years for Rachel; and they seemed unto him but a few days, for the love he had for her (Genesis 29:20). When the seven years were fulfilled at last, Jacob spent his wedding night only to discover at dawn that it wasn't Rachel, but her elder sister Leah whom Laban had delivered to Jacob's tent. Laban explained that according to tribal custom, the oldest daughter should be married first (Genesis 29:26). If Jacob wanted to marry Rachel as well, he would owe Laban another seven years of labor.

It took Jacob 14 years and a lot of work to marry Rachel and ended up with another wife unexpectedly. Shauna and I commuted for 16 ½ years and I ended up having her son Dustin living with or near me in San Jose unexpectedly for 11 years starting before we were married (the summer of 2005 until September of 2016). I was able to become part of Shauna's great family, got a bunch of her worldly possessions added to mine and I didn't have to work for her dad. My investment was time, a good expense account and some great experiences.

Jacob lived 147 years. Being realistic, I'd like a couple of 10 more good years with my lady. Like pumice is used to make lightweight construction materials such as concrete block and concrete - our pieces of floating rocks from the Isle of Roatan, Honduras are placed in my home museum to remind us that our relationship is strong as a block of concrete and when we feel like we're in the deep abyss we can triumphantly float to the surface of happiness and wellbeing like pumice floating on the wide, wide seas.

When life's burdens over whelm us and we feel as if the weight will pull us into the deep abyss: May we always be friends (like this rock from Isla Roatan, Honduras) and lift up each other into the light and help shine away despair and give encouragement and confidence to go on.

1– *Scientists Have Figured Out How Floating Islands Work, Spongy rocks don't exactly act like sponges, by Kelsey Kennedy, May 2017.*

2– *Huge Raft of Pumice Is Floating in the Ocean, it rose up from a volcano, and might end up helping the Great Barrier Reef, by John Hohnson, Newser Staff, Aug 31, 2019.*

34

MAN'S EXPERIENCE
WITH FAITH

Sterling Memorial Library at Yale was intentionally designed to look like a European Cathedral, but not for the glory of God. It was built with the funds set aside for a spectacular new chapel, but by 1924 mandatory chapel had fallen out of fashion at Yale. In one area of the library there is featured four bas relief sculptures on corbels. Three portray students at their desks, but none are studying. One listens to his radio, another ogles a pinup, and another is asleep next to a mug of beer.

The fourth of these carved images, however, is of a student who is indeed studying, and who ever since he came into being under the carver's chisel in the late 1920s has been earnestly looking at the pages of a stone book. On the left page are carved the letters U, R, and A, and on the right page the letters J and O, and below them the letters K and E. the japery here committed to stone – "You Are a Joke" – may be read two ways. On one hand it is perfectly puerile – ha, ha - as if it might instead have read "Ain't You Dumb? Hub-Yaw." But on another level, it is rather dark, It seems to say that if you study well enough you will discover something unpleasant that your less studious brethren have missed. You will discover that there is no meaning to life, nor any meaning at all in the universe – so that you yourself and your own life have no meaning but are rather merely a cosmic joke.

So, since you who have been studying at least seem to have wished to know, you may now know. You are the product of a random and meaningless evolutionary process that oddly enough has produced a creature who longs for meaning in a world without meaning. You will find that at the end of all your labors, if you keep searching for meaning you will at last come upon the grim notion that your study – and all you do henceforth in your life – you do in vain.

You will discover that you are not the beloved creation of a loving God, but are the random sputtering of a blind, deaf, and dumb cosmos, and that whatever noble ideas your young head holds about knowledge, wisdom, or love are specters, phantasms created by a blind process whose purposeless purpose is a perpetuation of your species. So, you yourself are actually nothing. Messrs, Darwin and Freud and some others have made this quite plain. While we will not advertise this dark theme to those parents whose children may one day attend this institution, we will at least here make a winking nod to it, here where you are standing now.[1]

Depressing stuff comes forth from the halls of Sterling Memorial Library at Yale. Stephen Hawking, a famous theoretical physicist and scientist, doesn't help me feel any better with his statement, "It is my view that the simplest explanation is there is no God. No one created the universe and no one directs our fate. This leads me to a profound realization. There is probably no heaven, and no afterlife either. We have this one life to appreciate the grand design of the universe, and for that, I am extremely grateful."

As far as we know, God created Adam and Eve not just with the ability to speak but with ability to speak meaningfully in some kind of a language. Created as adults, Adam and Eve were created with the ability to communicate with one another and with God. The speech they had learned was taught to their children and their children after them. This was the first form of human communication. This was an oral culture in which words were not written but, rather, memorized and recited. What they did not remember or choose to record in their memories was lost forever.

Consider a world in which there existed no copy of the Words of God outside the memories of a small number of people. Many people would know snippets of these words, but only a small elite would know exhaustive words, exhaustive scriptures. When God told Adam and Eve not to eat of the tree of the Knowledge of Good and Evil, when he told them of the judgment that would fall upon them for their disobedience, these words were recorded only in the memories of those first humans. It was up to them to pass those words, faithfully and carefully, to their children.

Within such a culture, a culture with no access to writing, virtuous living was based less around an abstract set of values than it was based on interpersonal interaction. At this time, right living and wrong living was often defined by heroes and villains, and epic tales encouraged people to live like their heroes had lived. According to the Eerdmans Dictionary of the Bible, "Moral norms, trade skills, history, and every aspect of communal life were passed on in oral history."

Within these cultures, a class of oral expert arose, a class of oral poets who would commit to memory vast histories and genealogies. Words were passed from one expert to the next with careful and deliberate memorization.

Though Adam and Eve could speak and remember, as far as we know they could not write. Known recorded writing developed approximately 4,000 years before Christ. First came pictures, often depicting simple human activities such as hunting. Soon after that came pictures used to record historical events. Drawn on the walls of caves, for example, pictures began to take the place of oral transmission. Then came pictograms, pictorial representations for letters or sounds.

As scribes communicated with one another, these markings became standardized across a culture. First an advance in economics, writing allowed records to be kept of land, harvests and loans. Pressed into soft clay and hardened in a kiln, marks would represent a commodity or a transaction. Syllabic writing soon developed, allowing each symbol to represent not a concept but a sound. The alphabet was not far behind, with evidence indicating some cultures may have turned to it as early as 2000 BC. Now each letter equaled a sound and words were composed of a string of letters put together, harmonizing reading and pronunciation.

By the third millennium (3000 to 2001 BC) the Egyptians had discovered that they could make a paper-like medium from papyrus plants and from the skins of animals. Paper was introduced from Asia to Egypt about 1000 years before Christ.

Many of Jesus' words were recorded in memory and maintained there for years or decades before being written down by the chroniclers of his life, the writers of the gospels. The gospels were written down from oral and written sources 30 to 70 years after Jesus died. They tell of many incidents in the life of Jesus.

There is no scholarly consensus on the date of composition of the latest New Testament texts. Bible scholars have dated all the books of the New Testament from 70 AD, 115 AD to the mid to late second century. The New Oxford Annotated Bible states, "Scholars generally agree that the Gospels were written forty to sixty years after the death of Jesus.

They thus do not present eyewitness or contemporary accounts of Jesus's life and teaching." Early Modern English Bible translations are of between about 1500s and 1800s, the period of Early Modern English. This was the first major period of Bible translation into the English language.

This period began with the introduction of the Tyndale Bible. The first complete edition of his New Testament was in 1526. William Tyndale used the Greek and Hebrew texts of the New Testament and Old Testament in addition to Jerome's Latin translation. He was the first translator to use the printing press – this enabled the distribution of several thousand copies of his New Testament translation throughout England. Tyndale did not complete his Old Testament translation.

Uplifting and enlightening thoughts have come from the most read book in the world for hundreds of years. In the past 50 years, the Bible has sold over 3.9 Billion copies. It is the most recognizable and famous book that has ever been published. With all the years of history passed down from memory and Christ's Gospel teachings written forty to sixty years after his death there must have been influences of light and knowledge to preserve the truthfulness of the scriptures.

Elder Keith K. Hilbig most likely sheds light on how this may have been accomplished. "When we invite the Holy Ghost to fill our minds with light and knowledge, He 'quickens' us, that is to say, enlightens and enlivens the inner man or woman. As a result, we notice a measurable different in our soul. We feel strengthened, filled with peace and joy. We possess spiritual energy and enthusiasm, both of which enhance our natural abilities. We can accomplish more than we otherwise could do on our own. we yearn to become a holier person."

Thomas Stuart Ferguson lay in his hammock, certain that he had found the promised land. It had been raining for 5 hours in his camp in tropical Mexico on this late January evening in 1948, and his three campmates had long since drifted off to sleep. But Ferguson was vibrating with excitement. Eager to tell someone what he had seen, he dashed through the downpour to retrieve paper from his supply bag. Ensconced in his hammock's cocoon of mosquito netting, he clicked on his flashlight and began to write a letter home.

"We have discovered a very great city here in the heart of 'Bountiful' land," Ferguson wrote. According to the Book of Mormon, Bountiful was one of the first areas settled by the Nephites, ancient people who supposedly sailed from Israel to the Americas around 600 B.C.E. Centuries later, according to the scripture, Jesus appeared to the Nephites in the same region after his resurrection. Mormons like Ferguson were certain that these events had happened in the ancient Americas, but debates raged over exactly how their sacred lands mapped onto real-world geography. The Book of Mormon gave only scattered clues, speaking of a narrow isthmus, a river called Sidon, and lands to the north and south occupied by the Nephites and their enemies, the Lamanites.

After years of studying maps, Mormon scripture, and Spanish chronicles, Ferguson had concluded that the Book of Mormon took place around the Isthmus of Tehuantepec, the narrowest part of Mexico. He had come to the jungles of Campeche, northeast of the isthmus, to find proof.

As the group's local guide hacked a path through the undergrowth with his machete, that proof seemed to materialize before Ferguson's eyes. "We have explored four days and have found eight pyramids and many lesser structures and there are more at every turn," he wrote of the ruins he and his companions found on the western shore of Laguna de Términos. "Hundreds and possibly several thousand people must have lived here anciently. This site has never been explored before."

Ferguson, a lawyer by training, did go on to open an important new window on Mesoamerica's past. His quest eventually spurred expeditions that transformed Mesoamerican archaeology by unearthing traces of the region's earliest complex societies and exploring an unstudied area that turned out to be a crucial cultural crossroads. Even today, the institute he founded hums with research. But proof of Mormon beliefs eluded him. His mission led him further and further from his faith, eventually sapping him of religious conviction entirely. Ferguson placed his faith in the hands of science, not realizing they were the lion's jaws.

The Church of Jesus Christ of Latter-day Saints (LDS) doesn't take an official position on where the events in the Book of Mormon occurred. But the faithful have been trying to figure it out practically since 1830, when church founder Joseph Smith published what he said was a divinely inspired account of the ancient Americas. Smith said an angel had led him to buried ancient golden plates, which he dug up and translated into the Book of Mormon. Smith's account of buried wonders was one of many in the United States at the time. As white settlers moved west, they encountered mounds filled with skeletons and artifacts, including beautiful pottery and ornaments. Newspapers, including those in Smith's hometown of Palmyra, New York, buzzed with speculation about who the "mound builders" were and how they came by their refined culture. Many settlers, blinded by racism, concluded that the mound builders— now known to be indigenous farming societies—were a lost people who had been exterminated by the violent ancestors of Native Americans. The Book of Mormon, with its saga of righteous, white Nephites and wicked, dark-skinned Lamanites, echoed these ideas.

The Book of Mormon also spoke of sprawling ancient cities, none of which had been identified in the United States. So, in the 1840s, Mormons, including Smith himself, took notice of a U.S. explorer's best-selling accounts of visits to the ruins of Mayan cities in Mexico and Guatemala. In 1842, as editor of a Mormon newspaper, Smith published excerpts from a book about the ruins of the Mayan city of Palenque in Mexico, with the commentary: "Even the most credulous cannot doubt ... these wonderful ruins of Palenque are among the mighty works of the Nephites— and the mystery is solved." But non-Mormons continued to doubt, and church authorities gradually retreated from explicit statements about Book of Mormon locations. By the 1930s, when Ferguson learned about Mesoamerican civilizations as an undergraduate at the University of California (UC), Berkeley, the matter had been largely ceded to amateurs who pored over maps and the Book of Mormon looking for correspondences.

Ferguson wasn't impressed by their efforts. "The interested and inquiring mind of the modern investigator is not satisfied with explanations which are vague, unsound, and illogical," he wrote in an article in a church magazine in 1941. By then he was a law student at UC Berkeley and intrigued by the idea of scientifically testing Smith's revelation. In a later letter, he wrote, "It is the only Church on the face of the earth which can be subjected to this kind of investigation and checking." And in another, to the LDS leadership, he declared, "The Book of Mormon is either fake or fact. If fake, the [ancient] cities described in it are non-existent. If fact—as we know it to be—the cities will be there."

Ferguson never received a formal education in archaeology. He practiced law to support his growing family—he eventually had five children—as well as his research. But in 1951, he recruited leading archaeologists to explore the origin of Mesoamerican civilization as part of a new institution, the New World Archaeological Foundation (NWAF).

In 1954, LDS authorities granted NWAF $250,000 for 5 years of work. Intensive excavations at Chiapa de Corzo uncovered stone pyramids and tombs, and a wealth of pre- Classic pottery. This pottery at the time was not very common anywhere, and the region was entirely new offering scientific contribution.

The NWAF grew in scientific stature, and was finally assured continued existence when BYU took it over in 1961. Ferguson was quietly becoming frustrated. When an ancient manuscript discovery did come, however, it was from a different quarter of the world. In the summer of 1835, Joseph Smith had received a curious visitor in Kirtland, Ohio, then the headquarters of his burgeoning LDS church: a traveling showman, with four Egyptian mummies and some hieroglyphic texts in tow. The church bought the mummies and texts, and Smith said he translated the hieroglyphics, resulting in the Book of Abraham, which lays out Smith's cosmic vision of the afterlife. (Although Egyptian hieroglyphics had been deciphered in France in 1822 with the help of the Rosetta Stone, the news had barely reached U.S. shores.) As Smith and his followers moved around the Midwest, often fleeing angry mobs, they carried the mummies and papyri with them. After Smith's death at the hands of one of those mobs in Nauvoo, Illinois, they were sold by his family.

The fate of the mummies remained a mystery. But in 1966, a University of Utah professor examining artifacts at the Metropolitan Museum of Art in New York City came across 11 Egyptian papyri with an 1856 certificate of sale signed by Smith's widow, Emma. The professor realized he was looking at the Book of Abraham papyri, and the documents were returned to the Mormon church.

Ferguson learned the news from a frontpage article in the newspaper Deseret News on 27 November 1967. Within days, he wrote to a friend in the church leadership, begging to know whether the papyri would be studied. Hearing that no studies were planned, Ferguson, took matters into his own hands. He received photos of the documents from the church and hired Egyptologists at UC Berkeley to translate them. He told the scholars nothing about the religious significance of the papyri. He was conducting a clearly blind test.

The results started coming in 6 weeks later. "I believe that all of these are spells from the Egyptian Book of the Dead," UC Berkeley Egyptologist Leonard Lesko wrote to Ferguson. Three other scholars independently gave Ferguson the same result: The texts were authentic ancient Egyptian, but represented one of the most common documents in that culture.

After decades of stressing the importance of the scientific method and using it to shore up his own faith, Ferguson now found himself at its mercy. "I must conclude that Joseph Smith had not the remotest skill in things Egyptian-hieroglyphics," he wrote to a fellow doubting Mormon in 1971. What's more, he wrote to another, "Right now I am inclined to think that all of those who claim to be 'prophets', including Moses, were without a means of communication with deity."[2]

Thomas Stuart Ferguson seems to have placed too much effort trying to prove himself right through science and not adjusting when his hypothesis about the America's was not proving true. Who knows where the peoples of the Book of Mormon resided, where the golden plates were kept until Joseph Smith was led to them or whether the Egyptian Papyri Book of the Dead message was what he was given during his translation. He received many passages in the Doctrine and Covenants from directly asking questions and receiving revelation from God. Who knows, he may have seen the papyri, asked questions and prayed about it, and if he were a true prophet, seer and revelator received revelation containing the book of Abraham - which is much more valuable.

Truths found through faith in the Lord Jesus Christ and obedience to His commandments and truths found through the diligent study of His scientific processes here on earth can combine into a beautiful blessing of knowledge that can enhance our lives, save our children, bless our earth, and help us return to our heavenly home with the blessings of exaltation.

Let me first start with definitions. All too often we find ourselves in a battle of semantics fueled by a misunderstanding of basic terminology. So, let's define these two symbiotic ways of knowing:

1. Knowing through scientific explanation is a process through which we gather evidence from the natural world to find explanations for natural phenomena.

2. Knowing through religious faith is a process through which we gather spiritual evidence through study and revelation to find explanations for spiritual truths.

I will begin with the first. As a scientist, I find comfort and friendly familiarity in the walls of a scientific laboratory. I find joy and wonder in the beauty of logic and evidence and all things analytical. I find comfort and safety in the defendable explanations provided by science.

Science is a process through which we describe the natural world and find explanations for natural phenomena. In a beautiful editorial written by Dr. Bruce Alberts, a biochemist and then the editor in chief of the journal Science, Dr. Alberts explained the difference between "little-s science" and "big-S Science." Little-s science is the process of experimentation through which big-S Science is eventually born. Little-s science is exciting, dynamic, collaborative, and wonderful. But it is tentative, amendable, and still under investigation. "[Big-S] Science emerges from [little-s] science" as "collective, public knowledge; . . . universal and free of contradiction," but only after repeated confirmation by independent, robust investigations. Often, we get caught up in the little-s science and impatiently reject a scientific idea simply because it is in its infancy and may seemingly contradict what we think we know from a religious standpoint. Other times we foolishly reject big-S Science because we don't fully understand how it plays in harmony with our religious beliefs. Both are errors born of impatience. President Gordon B. Hinckley in praising the benefits of science to mankind stated, (The twentieth century) has been the best of all centuries. . . . The life expectancy of man has been extended by more than 25 years. . . . The fruits of science have been manifest everywhere. . . . This has been an age of enlightenment.

Now let's talk about the nature or seeking of religious truths. It is an entirely different epistemology, but it is not entirely different in the process. The main difference is in the evidence...When I was seventeen, I decided to find out for myself if God was real. Since then, I have been convinced again and again, by evidence, that God does, in fact, exist. Unfortunately, the type of evidence I have to offer is mine, and mine alone. It is not the type of evidence that I can share with anyone else because it is based on intense, undeniable feelings as well as personal experiences that wouldn't mean the same thing if I explained them to someone else. However, I have performed tests.

Let's take a simple example in the Book of Mormon. At the end of the book, Moroni offered us a test. He said: Behold, I would exhort you that when ye shall read these things, if it be wisdom in God that ye should read them, . . . that ye would ask God, the Eternal Father, in the name of Christ, if these things are not true; and if ye shall ask with a sincere heart, with real intent, having faith in Christ, he will manifest the truth of it unto you, by the power of the Holy Ghost. And by the power of the Holy Ghost ye may know the truth of all things. (Moroni 10:3–5)

So here is a clear test with a clear prediction: Test: Ask God. Prediction: If this record is true (my proposed hypothesis) and I ask God (my experiment is to pray about it), then I will be given confirmation by the Holy Ghost (the evidence).

Here is where the processes differ: the evidence here is different. It is not tangible, measurable evidence by a scientific definition, but it is real evidence nonetheless. However, this test assumes that you know how to recognize the Holy Ghost and the evidence—in other words, that you have the necessary tools to detect the evidence. These spiritual tools take practice to develop, but they do exist and you can develop them. In terms of science, there is nowhere that this type of hypothesis testing fits in. However, this is not to say that this "spiritual" hypothesis testing is in any way less valid. It is just a different way of approaching truth.

In a well-done study at Arizona State University, my colleagues surveyed more than 1,000 college students and found that 48 percent of them believed that in order to accept evolution, you have to reject God. They also found a direct negative correlation between this atheistic viewpoint and acceptance of science.

This misconception is harmful and counterproductive to science and religion, as it drives an unnecessary wedge between these two ways of knowing. Science is no more atheistic than it is theistic. There is no scientific evidence for or against the existence of God. As we have already discussed, the evidence of God's existence does not even belong within the epistemology of science; it is a different epistemology altogether. Science is agnostic.

Francis S. Collins, director of the National Institutes of Health, was recently awarded the Templeton Prize for his work in reconciling science and religion. In his acceptance address, he described his previous attempt to prove atheism. He said: I began a journey to try to understand why intellectually sophisticated people could actually believe in God—and, to my dismay, I found that atheism turned out to be the least rational of all the choices! To quote Chesterton, "Atheism is . . . the most daring of all dogmas, . . . for it is the assertion of a universal negative." Scientists aren't supposed to do that, (he remarked with a chuckle).

This brings me to another important principle I would like to discuss that, if understood correctly, can help to save your faith. This principle is to avoid a "God of the gaps." What is a God of the gaps? It is when an individual inserts God as an explanation for anything that science cannot currently explain... It is dangerous to believe in God because His existence resolves uncertainty or His existence explains things that you cannot explain. (For example, how can lifeforms be so complex? They must have been created in their present form by God.) What happens when science comes up with a reasonable and even testable explanation for this "gap" in our understanding? (For example, evolution has led to the great diversity of life we see.) Does your faith disappear just because something you attributed to God can be explained by science? It shouldn't and it won't if your belief is not based in gaps.[3]

"There isn't anything to worry about between science and religion, because the contradictions are just in your own mind. Of course, they are there, but they are not in the Lord's mind because He made the whole thing, so there is a way, if we are smart enough, to understand them so that we will not have any contradictions." Henry Eyring, Chemist

1– *Is Atheism Dead? Eric Metaxas, p 389-90, 2021.*
2– *How Thomas Ferguson a Mormon lawyer transformed archaeology in Mexico—and ended up losing his faith, Science, By Lizzie Wade, 2018.*
3– *Faith and Science: Symbiotic Pathways to Truth, Jamie L. Jensen, Ass Professor of Biology, BYU, 2020.*

35

PEACE BE STILL

If we were to allow ourselves to be frightened by the daily impact of all we see and all we hear and by all the disappointing circumstances of life, we should soon be so upset that we would lose sight of ultimate objectives. If we should leave our thoughts and our lives open to all of the actual and potential disturbances of each day, we could easily become utterly ineffective— paralyzed with the fearful awareness of impending doom and with the constant awareness of threatened calamity. If we should tremble before all the troubles and tragedies that could or might happen, and fret about them as though they already had happened, life could surely become a fearful ordeal. If every crosscurrent, if every flurry, if every breaker were permitted to capsize us, we would be daily drenched and drowning.

When we live in this world, the storms come, sometimes frequently, sometimes occasionally, and sometimes it seems almost constantly, but a firm faith in the Lord God and in ultimate objectives make the storms worth weathering, no matter how furious or how frequent. The ground swells, the quick squalls, and the deep and elemental disturbances are inevitable in life. And they must not be permitted to upset us to the point where we lose our bearings or swim in circles.

The temporary setbacks, the heartaches, the passing disappointments, the deep and bitter sorrows—some of which all of us pass through—must not be permitted to confuse our course. No [person] ever had freedom from trouble, or from the prospects of trouble, but many have lived above it and have found peace and quiet accomplishment in spite of the disturbance and confusion of the day.

In life we must learn this lesson: There is no smooth surface from shore to shore, from season to season, for anyone. When we're on the ocean, the storms come. Of course, life will upset us if we let it. But we can keep from capsizing if we don't lose sight of our ultimate objectives. We can keep on our course if we keep planning and working and pursuing useful purposes in the present—and keep faith in the future.[1]

Dr. Daniel K. Judd a counselor in psychology shared a poem, *In the Wilderness*, written by a depressed patient and colleague who made a "miraculous recovery:"

> *Lost in a maze of confusion*
> *I wonder –*
> *not knowing what to think,*
> *who to believe.*
>
> *Afloat in a sea of discouragement,*
> *I am tossed –*
> *riddled with self-doubt:*
> *Who am I? am I of worth?*

From a dark mist of despair
I cry for help,
for strength.
Then I feel the arms of a loving Father
and hear His voice, saying,
"My child, my daughter, I am here always. These
things are for you to learn, to grow, to become.
Talk, I will listen. Ask, I will help. Cry, I will
comfort always."
Suddenly, out of the wilderness I emerge
into a shining pathway of hope.[2]

Once there was a king who offered to give a prize to an artist who could best paint a depiction of peace. Many artists decided to participate and sent the king their masterpieces.

Among the various masterpieces, one picture was of a calm lake closely resembling peacefully towering snow-capped mountains where a blue sky with fluffy clouds was overheard. The picture was exemplary. Most of those who viewed the paintings of peace from different artists thought that this painting was the best among all others.

But the king had another winner in mind. To the crowd's surprise, the picture that won was of a mountain too but was more plain and rugged than the other piece. The sky was shady and looked angry because there was lightning, threatening storm clouds and their appeared to be no place to find shelter. It was exactly the opposite of what peace should look like. The others thought that maybe the artist submitted a wrong painting showing storm rather than peace.

What others didn't notice was that if you look closely at the painting, there is a tiny bush growing in the cracks of a rock. In the bush, there is a nest built by a mother bird and in the midst of the stormy weather, the bird sits sheltered from the storm, peacefully on her nest.

In that specific portrait, it was depicted that in the presence of all the turmoil, we can have the presence of the still small voice comforting and calming us as we weather the storms in our lives.[3]

"I am here always…Talk, I will listen. Ask, I will help. Cry, I will comfort always."[2]

Master, the tempest is raging! The billows are tossing high! The sky is o'ershadowed with blackness. No shelter or help is nigh. How canst thou lie asleep when each moment so madly is threat'ing a grave in the angry deep? …Whether the wrath of the storm-tossed sea or demons or men or whatever it be, no waters can swallow the ship where lies the Master of ocean and earth and skies. They all shall sweetly obey thy will: Peace, be still; Peace be still.[4]

Silence of the heart is necessary so you can hear God everywhere, in the closing of the door, in the person who needs you, in the birds that sing, in the flowers, in the animals. *Mother Teresa*

1– *Fearful Voyager, Richard L. Evans, first delivered in the midst of World War II, Music & The Spoken Word, 2003.*

2– *RELIGION AND MENTAL HEALTH, Daniel K. Judd, page 97, 2021.*

3– *Author unknown.*

4– *Master, the tempest is raging, Mary Ann Baker, 1831–1921.*

36

THE JAPANESE MADE THREE MISTAKES ATTACKING PEARL HARBOR

Near Christmas Eve 1941, the pilots of the Empire of Japan pulled off a surprise sneak attack on America's 7th Fleet anchored at Pearl Harbor, Hawaii. These pilots had practiced their attack to perfection, or so they thought. Considering the damage, one would think the attack devastating.

Of the eight battleships, all were damaged, including four sunk. Eleven other ships were destroyed or damaged. Ninety-two naval aircraft were destroyed and 31 damaged. The Army Air Corps lost 77 aircraft with 128 damaged. The human cost was staggering: 2,403 killed and 1,178 wounded, including civilians.

The Japanese launched 353 aircraft from four of their largest aircraft carriers for their early Sunday morning raid. They lost 29 planes and five midget submarines. Included in their massive battle fleet were two large battleships, two heavy cruisers, two light cruisers, 11 destroyers, nine oilers, and 35 submarines. Ironically, only one of the Japanese warships that participated in the Pearl Harbor attack survived the war, the destroyer Ushio, although she was heavily damaged.

As smoke billowed above Pearl Harbor and Navy ships capsized, as hospital corridors filled to capacity with the injured and dying, as sailors' bodies floated on the oily surface, and as the horrible news hit the airwaves to paralyze the entire nation, doom and gloom spread like a wildfire. The West Coast was in panic mode, believing with some validity that they were vulnerable to attack. The Hawaiian beaches were soon pitted with foxholes and laced with barbed wire as soldiers, sailors, Marines and airmen braced for an expected invasion. Defeat, misery and dread were the order of the day, as if the Japanese had already won the war.

Meanwhile, back in Washington, D.C., Admiral Chester Nimitz was attending a concert on Dec. 7, 1941 when he was paged and told a phone call awaited him. President Franklin Roosevelt was on the line and informed the admiral that he was now the commander of the Pacific Fleet. Nimitz's plane touched down at Pearl Harbor on Christmas Eve, 1941. The next day, Christmas, Nimitz took a boat tour of Pearl Harbor to assess the damage.[1]

When Nimitz arrived at Pearl Harbor, he observed frustration. The Pacific Fleet's officers hungered for an opportunity to strike back at the Japanese. Tension between those who stressed caution and those who wanted to attack risked tearing the fleet apart. When he assumed command on 31 December, Nimitz departed from tradition and, rather than bringing on his own staff, retained the entire team in place. This was quite unexpected. Nimitz implicitly—by retaining those officers—and explicitly—in personal conversations with them—expressed his faith in their skills and abilities. It was an essential first step in rebuilding morale.

Assigning responsibility required some staff to give up sea commands and for the fleet, it meant taking the offensive. An aggressive plan had been formulating a series of estimates for counter attacking ever since the Japanese attack. On Christmas Day, a plan had been devised to strike the Japanese-held islands and protect Hawaii.

Nimitz now had to win the confidence of his superiors who were anxious for results. Franklin D. Roosevelt's Secretary of the Navy, had his doubts about his plans. Nimitz repeatedly adjusted his command and staff structure, regardless of its specific configuration, he maintained his ability to seize opportunities and couple tactical success to strategic outcomes. Nimitz demonstrated this ability repeatedly throughout the war. It was Nimitz's determination to maintain that ability that allowed him to deliver on the promise of the "vast and efficient organism" envisioned by Rear Admiral Bradley A. Fiske three decades before.[2]

Nimitz, born in 1885 in Fredericksburg, Texas, was blessed with an abundance of common sense and optimism. His biological father died six months before his birth, so Nimitz's childhood was strongly influenced by his German-born grandfather, a former sailor in the German Merchant Marine, Charles Henry Nimitz. Charles had also served as a Texas Ranger and held the rank of captain in the Confederate Army's Gillespie Rifles Company.

Chester Nimitz first applied to West Point, but no appointments were available. Only one appointment was available for the Naval Academy to the most qualified candidate. Nimitz studied hard and won the appointment. He graduated with distinction in January of 1905, seventh in a class of 114.

He served aboard battleships, cruisers, destroyers, and the ill-fated gunboat Panay. The Panay was a river patrol boat assigned to the Yangtze River in China. Years after Nimitz served aboard the Panay, she was attacked and sunk by 12 Japanese aircraft on Dec. 12, 1937; four years before America entered the war. Several of our sailors died or were wounded. Even though the pilots had been advised of an American gunboat presence on the Yangtze, they claimed it was impossible to distinguish a Chinese flag from an American flag. Several big American flags were posted on the Panay, including one painted atop the cabin, in other words, the Japanese pilots were full of shshi. Japanese leaders admitted responsibility but claimed the attack was an accident. They, too, were full of shshi. America received an indemnity of $2 million, a sizable sum in the late 1930s, then the incident was swept under the diplomatic rug.

Nimitz had his own problems early in his career. On July 7, 1908, the destroyer Decatur ran aground on a mud bank in the Philippines. The man in command, Ensign Chester Nimitz, was court-martialed for negligence of duty, found guilty, and issued a letter of reprimand. Nevertheless, Nimitz returned to the states for a variety of assignments in the First Submarine Flotilla.

Fluent in German, Nimitz studied engines at the diesel engine plants in Nuremberg, Germany, and Ghent,

Belgium, in 1913. He served in WWI as chief engineer aboard the refueling ship, the Maumee, and under his supervision conducted the first-ever at sea and underway refueling. Later in his career, Nimitz lost part of one finger in a diesel engine accident. The rest of his finger, and most likely his entire hand, avoided amputation when the engine jammed against his Annapolis ring.

Experienced with command responsibilities and familiar with just about every ship in the United States Navy, including his masterful knowledge of submarines, one Japanese failure at Pearl Harbor, and most likely the most noteworthy, escaped Nimitz's initial comments: the untouched and disregarded American submarines.

Four American submarines were tied up at Pearl Harbor when the attack began at 0755 on Dec. 7, 1941. One of these, the USS Tautog, would come to haunt the Japanese Navy. Even without attacking the submarines, a well-placed bomb or strafing run would have ignited 4.5 million gallons of fuel and virtually blown away the sub base and all four docked submarines. The Japanese Armada had 35 submarines at its disposal for reconnaissance, to launch their midget subs, and to stay submerged outside of the entrance to Pearl Harbor to bushwhack any American warship attempting to escape the carnage.

In short, the Japanese were well-aware of the importance of their own stealthy submarines, yet they failed to see the future potential of the American submarines based at Pearl Harbor, plus failed to realize the sub base would be a pivotal station for the Americans as they entered the war seeking revenge.

During the Pearl Harbor attack, the crewmen aboard the four American submarines manned their anti-aircraft weapons and are considered the first Americans to swing into action against the attackers. The Narwhal's gunners hit two Japanese planes and downed another. The Tautog's crew knocked down one torpedo bomber that crashed 150 feet from the stern of their ship. The Dolphin shot down one aircraft that exploded near the Cachalot. Considering all the firepower from ground anti-aircraft fire and dozens of American warships, it's interesting to note that three of the 29 Japanese planes shot down are credited to American submarines, plus two more damaged.

The Tautog was destined to become a thorn in the side of the Japanese Navy. By war's end, she was the second highest by number of ships sunk and 11th by tonnage. She was nicknamed "The Terrible T" and credited with sinking 26 Japanese vessels for a total of 72,606 tons. She damaged many more. Tautog returned stateside in April of 1945, one of the most highly decorated submarines of WWII. In due course she became a reserve training ship and was not placed out of service until September of 1959.

> "When I assumed command of the Pacific Fleet in 31 December, 1941; our submarines were already operating against the enemy, the only units of the fleet that could come to grips with the Japanese for months to come. It was to the Submarine Force that I looked to carry the load until our great industrial activity could produce the weapons we so sorely needed to carry the war to the enemy.

It is to the everlasting honor and glory of
our submarine personnel that they never
failed us in our days of peril."
                              - Admiral Chester Nimitz -

According to the book, *Reflections on Pearl Harbor*,
by William H. Ewing: At the end of Nimitz's boat tour
on Christmas 1941, a young helmsman asked him what
he thought of the destruction. The admiral replied, "The
Japanese made three of the biggest mistakes an attack force
could ever make, or maybe God was taking care of America.
Which do you think it was?"

The helmsman was stunned by Nimitz's statement as
would be any American after surveying the almost complete
destruction of an entire fleet in the oily harbor. The key
word in that last sentence is "almost." Nimitz was spot on.
Here are the three Japanese mistakes, according to Admiral
Nimitz.

One: The Japanese chose a Sunday morning believing
most of the fleet would be asleep, caught off guard, on shore
leave, and certainly not at battle readiness. They were right,
but Nimitz believed their decision to strike on a Sunday
saved countless American lives. Nine out of 10 crewmen were
still ashore that Sunday morning, and most of them were
most likely in no shape to engage in meaningful combat.
Had the crewmen not been ashore on a typical hell-raising
Saturday night, plus had the 7th Fleet been enticed out to
sea and sunk, 38,000 men would have perished instead of
3,000, and in deep water the sunken warships could not
have been recovered.

Two: Although the dry docks and repair facilities were targeted by the Japanese, the young pilots became so enthralled sinking the big battleships and other easy targets that the maintenance shops and docks and cranes and repair facilities were mostly ignored and suffered only light damage. The ships sunk and seriously damaged were in the shallow waters of the harbor, therefore, the vessels could be salvaged, repaired at intact facilities, and back in action in the time it would take to tow them to the states for refurbishing.

Three: Five miles from the central harbor, or as Nimitz stated, "Just over that hill," a tank farm housed 4.5 million gallons of fuel, every drop of petroleum for the Pacific. One well-placed bomb dropped by a Japanese dive bomber or if a Zero fighter had strafed the above-ground fuel tanks, the Pacific Fleet would have been instantly out of fuel and out of service. Too, the resulting explosions and massive fires would have resulted in untold casualties, extensive damage, and virtually blown away the sub base and all four docked submarines.

President Roosevelt had chosen the right man for the right job. We desperately needed a leader that could see silver linings in the midst of the clouds of dejection, despair and defeat. There is a reason that our national motto is, "IN GOD WE TRUST". Why have we forgotten? PRAY FOR OUR COUNTRY!!

Is God taking care of America? Is America a promised land? There are lands that the Lord promises as an inheritance to His faithful followers, and often also to their descendants. There are many promised lands. Often in the Book of Mormon, the promised land spoken of is the Americas.

Unto thy seed will I give this land, *Gen. 12:7 (Abr. 2:19).*

I will give unto thee and to thy seed the land of Canaan, *Gen. 17:8 (Gen. 28:13).*

Moses specified the borders of the land for Israel in Canaan, *Num. 34:1–12 (Num. 27:12).*

Ye shall be led to a land of promise, *1 Ne. 2:20 (1 Ne. 5:5.*

The Lord leadeth away the righteous into precious lands, *1 Ne. 17:38*

If Lehi's descendants keep God's commandments, they will prosper in the land of promise, *2 Ne. 1:5–9.*

Israel shall return to their lands of promise, *2 Ne. 24:1–2 (Isa. 14:1–2).*

Whatsoever nation shall possess this promised land should serve God, or they should be swept off, *Ether 2:9–12.*

This is the land of promise, and the place for the city of Zion, *D&C 57:2.*

Judah may begin to return to the lands of Abraham, *D&C 109:64.*

The New Jerusalem will be built upon the American continent, *A of F 1:10.*

1– *A Veteran's Story: The Japanese failed miserably, by Pete Mecca, Special to the Citizen, 12/07/2018.*
2– *"A vast and efficient organism"–Admiral Chester W. Nimitz and the art of command, Trent Hone, published by De Gruyter Open Access, 09/07/2022.*

Nimitz: Reflections on Pearl Harbor by William H. Ewing (out of print & I could not find a copy)

37

PEACEMAKERS NEEDED

President Russell M. Nelson stated, "During my surgical internship many years ago, I assisted a surgeon who was amputating a leg filled with highly infectious gangrene. The operation was difficult. Then, to add to the tension, one of the team performed a task poorly, and the surgeon erupted in anger. In the middle of his tantrum, he threw his scalpel loaded with germs. It landed in my forearm!

Everyone in the operating room—except the out-of-control surgeon—was horrified by this dangerous breach of surgical practice. Gratefully, I did not become infected. But this experience left a lasting impression on me. In that very hour, I promised myself that whatever happened in my operating room, I would never lose control of my emotions. I also vowed that day never to throw anything in anger—whether it be scalpels or words.

Even now, decades later, I find myself wondering if the contaminated scalpel that landed in my arm was any more toxic than the venomous contention that infects our civic dialogue and too many personal relationships today. Civility and decency seem to have disappeared during this era of polarization and passionate disagreements."[1]

We all know what anger is, and we've all felt it: whether as a fleeting annoyance or as full-fledged rage. Anger is a completely normal, usually healthy, human emotion. But when it gets out of control and turns destructive, it can lead to problems—problems at work, in your personal relationships, and in the overall quality of your life. Anger can make you feel as though you're at the mercy of an unpredictable and powerful emotion.

Anger is "an emotional state that varies in intensity from mild irritation to intense fury and rage," according to Charles Spielberger, PhD, a psychologist who specializes in the study of anger. Like other emotions, it is accompanied by physiological and biological changes; when you get angry, your heart rate and blood pressure go up, as do the levels of your energy hormones, adrenaline, and noradrenaline.

Anger can be caused by both external and internal events. You could be angry at a specific person (such as a coworker or supervisor) or event (a traffic jam, a canceled flight), or your anger could be caused by worrying or brooding about your personal problems. Memories of traumatic or enraging events can also trigger angry feelings.

The instinctive, natural way to express anger is to respond aggressively. Anger is a natural, adaptive response to threats; it inspires powerful, often aggressive, feelings and behaviors, which allow us to fight and to defend ourselves when we are attacked. A certain amount of anger, therefore, is necessary to our survival.

On the other hand, we can't physically lash out at every person or object that irritates or annoys us; laws, social norms, and common-sense place limits on how far our anger can take us. People use a variety of both conscious and unconscious processes to deal with their angry feelings. The three main approaches are expressing, suppressing, and calming.

Expressing your angry feelings in an assertive—not aggressive—manner is the healthiest way to express anger. To do this, you have to learn how to make clear what your needs are, and how to get them met, without hurting others. Being assertive doesn't mean being pushy or demanding; it means being respectful of yourself and others.

Anger can be suppressed, and then converted or redirected. This happens when you hold in your anger, stop thinking about it, and focus on something positive. The aim is to inhibit or suppress your anger and convert it into more constructive behavior. The danger in this type of response is that if it isn't allowed outward expression, your anger can turn inward—on yourself. Anger turned inward may cause hypertension, high blood pressure, or depression.

Unexpressed anger can create other problems. It can lead to pathological expressions of anger, such as passive-aggressive behavior (getting back at people indirectly, without telling them why, rather than confronting them head-on) or a personality that seems perpetually cynical and hostile. People who are constantly putting others down, criticizing everything, and making cynical comments haven't learned how to constructively express their anger. Not surprisingly, they aren't likely to have many successful relationships.

Finally, you can calm down inside. This means not just controlling your outward behavior, but also controlling your internal responses, taking steps to lower your heart rate, calm yourself down, and let the feelings subside.

Dr. Spielberger notes, "when none of these three techniques work, that's when someone—or something—is going to get hurt." Under these circumstances it is encouraged to seek help through anger management. The goal of anger management is to reduce both your emotional feelings and the physiological arousal that anger causes. You can't get rid of, or avoid, the things or the people that enrage you, nor can you change them, but you can learn to control your reactions.[2]

President Nelson continues, "Vulgarity, faultfinding, and evil speaking of others are all too common. Too many pundits, politicians, entertainers, and other influencers throw insults constantly. I am greatly concerned that so many people seem to believe that it is completely acceptable to condemn, malign, and vilify anyone who does not agree with them. Many seem eager to damage another's reputation with pathetic and pithy barbs!

Anger never persuades. Hostility builds no one. Contention never leads to inspired solutions. Regrettably, we sometimes see contentious behavior even within our own ranks. We hear of those who belittle their spouses and children, of those who use angry outbursts to control others, and of those who punish family members with the 'silent treatment.' We hear of youth and children who bully and of employees who defame their colleagues.

My dear brothers and sisters, how we treat each other really matters! How we speak to and about others at home, at church, at work, and online really matters. Today, I am asking us to interact with others in a higher, holier way. Please listen carefully. 'If there is anything virtuous, lovely, or of good report or praiseworthy' that we can say about another person—whether to his face or behind her back—that should be our standard of communication.

...we can literally change the world—one person and one interaction at a time. How? By modeling how to manage honest differences of opinion with mutual respect and dignified dialogue. Differences of opinion are part of life. I work every day with dedicated servants of the Lord who do not always see an issue the same way. They know I want to hear their ideas and honest feelings about everything we discuss—especially sensitive issues...

Charity is the antidote to contention. Charity is the spiritual gift that helps us to cast off the natural man, who is selfish, defensive, prideful, and jealous. Charity is the principal characteristic of a true follower of Jesus Christ. Charity defines a peacemaker. When we humble ourselves before God and pray with all the energy of our hearts, God will grant us charity.

Those blessed with this supernal gift are long-suffering and kind. They do not envy others and are not caught up in their own importance. They are not easily provoked and do not think evil of others.

Brothers and sisters, the pure love of Christ is the answer to the contention that ails us today. Charity propels us "to bear one another's burdens" rather than heap burdens upon each other. The pure love of Christ allows us "to stand as witnesses of God at all times and in all things"—especially in tense situations. Charity allows us to demonstrate how men and women of Christ speak and act - especially when under fire.[1]

To be peacemaker, you must know the peace giver. *Billy Graham*

1– *Peacemakers Needed, Russell M. Nelson, President of The Church of Jesus Christ of Latter-day Saints, April 2023.*
2– *Control anger before it controls you, American Psychological Ass, Home/Psychology, updated 2022.*

38

MY DREAM (2004)

Research shows that romantic love is just one component of a successful marriage. Our society sells romance and Valentine's Day and we don't see the reality. After they are married, most couples are really disillusioned when the romance begins to simmer down and they start to deal with everyday issues.

Couples who have been married for 50 years or more say it wasn't the romance that kept them together over time, but rather what they describe as a deep, caring friendship and the ability to enjoy each other's company. Happily married people enjoy doing things together, have similar interests, they're good friends. Romantic love is important because it brings the couple together and establishes a level of intimacy, over-romanticized expectations about married life can be difficult for new couples to reconcile with reality.

Research shows that most couples go through several predictable phases in their relationship, including a post-honeymoon period characterized by "disillusionment" and "distraction."

Over time, not only do we expect more of each other, but we fail to understand that our love for each other is going to change too, from a romantic love to a more mature companionate love.

Fueled by a myth that romance is the key to sustaining the relationship, many couples will never successfully navigate the transition phase. National statistics show that half of all divorces occur in the first seven years of marriage, many within the first two years. Daily challenges take a toll on us physically and emotionally and the vitality of our relationship suffers. These transitions are not inherently bad-they are an unavoidable part of life-but they are often more difficult than we thought they would be.

Just like a car needs regular tune ups, a marriage checkup will evaluate the health of three general factors that determine marital satisfaction: 1) individual traits (mental health, social skills); 2) couple traits (including communication and conflict resolution skills); and 3) contexts (backgrounds, relationships outside the marriage).

It's not uncommon for couples to get "in a rut" after a few years of marriage. When love has waned, couples can revive the marriage by: 1) thinking about a time in the past when you felt love and resuming the behaviors, attitudes and rituals that worked before; 2) giving love to get love, regardless of where your spouse is along the way; and 3) setting goals to improve the love in your marriage by increasing nourishing behaviors and avoiding destructive behaviors.

Nourishing behaviors include sharing feelings regularly, thoughtfulness (gestures, unexpected gifts), compliments, shared activities that you both enjoy, sacrificing for each other, service to each other, kind words, empathy, prioritizing your marriage, accepting your partner's faults, looking your best and showing respect.

You have to change the way you do things, develop new ideas, interests, or activities. It involves prioritizing your marriage more, learning how to connect more with each other, and finding out what makes your spouse feel valued, unique, and important.[1]

Shauna and I commuted 17 years back and forth from her home in Idaho and mine in California. Two of those years were before we got married. Her concerns were her two children that still lived at home and parents that had health issues. Mine was a veterinary practice with clients that were "like family" to me; many I had known since I started practicing there in 1976 and having been raised in Idaho – I preferred California weather.

Shauna told me that if she could fulfill her family's needs and I found a way for us to see each other on a regular basis – she was "interested." I thought about the story of Jacob in the Bible and how he stayed under the power of his father-in-law for many years earning the right to marry his daughter. It ended up that he stayed many unexpected years and was tricked into marrying two of his daughters. Why couldn't this work out for us? After all, we had cell phones on a daily basis and visited each other on most weekends.

Jacob had a family disagreement after buying Esau's birthright and needed to quickly leave his home. He ended up at the family farm of Laban, his mother's brother. Jacob worked for Laban for twenty-one frustrating years, during which Laban broke a string of promises to him. Despite this,

Jacob succeeded in marrying two of Laban's daughters and starting a family. Jacob wanted to return home, but Laban convinced him to stay on and work for him with the promise that he could "name (his own) wages" (Gen. 30:28). Clearly Jacob had been a good worker, and Laban had been blessed through his association with Jacob.

During this time Jacob had learned the trade of breeding animals, and he used this skill to get back at Laban. Through his breeding techniques, he was able to gain a great deal of wealth at Laban's expense. It got to the point that Laban's sons were complaining that "Jacob has taken all that was our father's; he has gained all this wealth from what belonged to our father" (Gen. 31:1-2).

Jacob noticed that Laban's attitude toward him was not what it had been. Yet Jacob claimed the gain as a gift from God, saying, "If the God of my father, the God of Abraham and the Fear of Isaac, had not been on my side, surely now you would have sent me away empty-handed" (Gen. 31:42).

Nearly 1½ years before our marriage I wrote down the following experience:

It had been a bad couple of weeks. Not work or home or family – just me: My inner self was being torn as to who and where and what I was becoming and wanting to be.

Some would call it depression which in the normal person it comes and it goes: But this had lasted for two weeks and more and it affected my mind and soul and even me physically from my head to my toes.

Then early this morning I awoke from an interesting and perplexing dream: You and I were there looking over one large perfectly formed seed that looked to me like it was a lima bean.

I remember we were aware but seemed not to care about anything here or there or all around about: Except our full attention was placed on that lima bean which was submerged in what looked like water and it was starting to sprout.

We seemed totally united in self, mind and spirit and our communication was only by thought and our lips not a word had to say: The environment around us seemed warm, bright, loving, sweet, beautiful and kind. It was to me how one would describe a most perfect day.

It felt good you and me together looking at that seed: Just being with you seemed to fill my every need.

And as we looked at that lima bean – roots, stalk and leaves appeared as it started to sprout: It seemed that in some way the seed represented you and me and what our lives were about.

Then the seed sprouted from within the ground and placed deep roots for nutrition and stability thus helping it face the challenges it would encounter during its life: It also pushed a stalk up through the ground towards the light of the sun and then experienced life, filled all measures of its creation, and overcame all Earth's challenges and strife.

And as we watched that lima bean live out its life and adjust the best it could to both the good and the bad: It produced a bountiful harvest with more beautiful fruit than any other plant could have had.

After awakening this morning and pondering this very vivid dream: I realized that your life and mine together was beginning to sprout as that lima bean.

Our life together seems so right and appears to fill every need: And I know more than ever if we continue along this path we are taking, the fruit of our life will yield much more than that one perfect seed.[2] Early morning of April 8, 2004…Married Sept 3, 2005

Couples who have been married for 50 years or more say it wasn't the romance that kept them together over time, but rather what they describe as a deep, caring friendship and the ability to enjoy each other's company. Happily married people enjoy doing things together, have similar interests, they're good friends. Money, fame, and social status come and go; they make for a shaky foundation for life. Instead, build your life on loving relationships, and they will be the bedrock of lasting happiness.[1]

Other than a yearly anniversary cruise, our contact time together was mostly by phone or weekend visits. Now living 24/7 together we have not had a serious disagreement or felt our marriage was in a rut. It seems to me that we formed healthy habits by spending our short times together "on our best behavior" and we have remained the best of friends. A French proverb says that "little by little, the bird builds its nest." We are still progressively building ours.

1– *Strong Marriages Need…, Jeffry Larson, Professor/ therapist, BYU Research, 01/30/2003.*

2– *My Dream, Walter R. Hoge, 04/08/2004.*

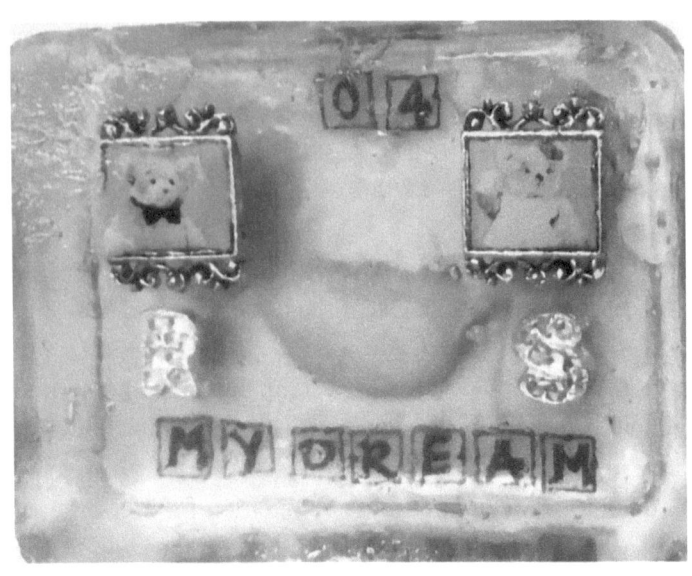

One of two epoxy paper weights I
made from MY DREAM...
April 8, 2004

39

DRESS THE PART IT MEANS A LOT

There's a phenomenon scientists have dubbed "enclothed cognition." This is simply the scientific term for the idea that clothing impacts how we think. The theory says the clothing we wear (or that others are wearing) actually changes our thought patterns.

And this isn't anything new. Humans have been wearing clothing almost since the dawn of our existence. Although it began out of necessity and practicality, it quickly morphed into an art form and means of communication. For centuries, dress was the number one status symbol. It told people where you ranked in society, how much you could afford, and what your profession was.

What you wear is a message to others and to yourself about who you are. The "psychology of clothing" tells us that there's more than meets the eye when it comes to the clothes you choose. Wearing a pilot uniform shows that you're a pilot. Putting on athletic clothes implies that you're sporty and fit. Rocking a bright red dress tells us that you're daring and adventurous!

But the association between clothes and perception runs even deeper than that. What you wear directly influences your thoughts and behaviors. It also impacts how others perceive your personality and actions. The social and psychological aspects of clothing are more intertwined with outfit choice than you think.[1]

For many years I voluntarily worked with youth between the ages of 12 and 18 in my church congregation. One evening I was chaperoning a darkened Halloween dance and a witch appeared on the dance floor. She slowly walked around the room and randomly tapped young men on the shoulder and silently danced for a few moments with each of them. Then she walked out the door and no one knew who she was.

Dressing up for Halloween and Christmas has helped make these my most loved holidays. The mystery witch event really excited my imagination about how cool it would if I could participate in an event, make an impression and leave without anyone knowing who I was or why I was there. Kind of like a masquerade ball with no one knowing who was there.

In 1995 my receptionist, Pat LaPointe, had arranged to have one of her son's wedding receptions at a local park near Camden Pet Hospital on a Saturday afternoon. She knew that I worked that day and asked me to come but not make a big deal about dressing for the occasion. After work that day I finished work and parked in the park as close as possible to the event.

I changed clothes into a homeless beggar's attire with a wig and hat on, crumpled up a brown paper bag and started working my way toward the reception as I was going through garbage cans and picking out empty cans and bottles. When I arrived at their tables I started placing empty containers from their reception into my bag. I made my way slowly up to the center table where Pat sat and couldn't help but notice the veins about to burst on the neck of the groom's brother who was giving me a cold stare. My flight or fight response kicked in but I kept my cool thinking it was a good thing that I had told my employee Dana to have her husband John jump in if things got out of control.

When I got to where Pat was sitting it was obvious she did not recognize me and she would not make eye contact. I could hear her say, "give him food or money -anything he wants. Just don't let him spoil my son's reception." I asked for help in short broken sentences, it wasn't long before she figured out who I was, we had a good laugh and I have a memorable photo.

For our churches Halloween party in 2006 Shauna and I dressed like convicts. We wore wigs, striped black and white pajamas that had Alcatraz written on the front, we had makeup on our faces and signs that had written on them our prison ID, picture and an arrow pointing to Shauna or me. Above the arrow was written "SHE DONE IT" or "HE DONE IT." We quietly sat on chairs in the cultural hall and no one approached us and we did not attempt to strike up a conversation.

Meanwhile, Shauna's son Dustin (whom no one knew) walked into the church wearing a policeman's uniform with my Labrador Retriever Maui on leash and started searching through the church building. Steve Hayden, the bishop of the congregation, found Dustin "looking for drugs?" in the building without saying a word. The bishop followed the "cop" saying he knew everyone here, there were no drugs, we all were obeying the law and no damage to the building had occurred! After the inspection, Dustin and Maui without a word or bark vacated the building and left the premises. What a great high and Halloween memory that I'll never forget.

I traveled to Blackfoot Idaho a couple of days before Halloween weekend 2010. My sister's niece, Tiffany, had sent me a wedding announcement and if I went it would conflict with my beloved Halloween where I could dress and act out another dream for a day.

Not being discouraged about the upcoming events; I grew a Van Dyke beard, dressed like a cowboy, put on a wig, Stetson on my head and walked into Tiffany's wedding reception. Her sister's husband, Shaun, had been a bull rider and performed at the Cow Palace in San Francisco. I alerted him to mention that I was a friend from his rodeo days as I walked into the cultural hall. After all my effort I did not want to be thrown out of the event.

I sauntered around the tables and made small talk with the folks. Several asked me if I had some good stories about Shaun when he was riding on the rodeo circuit. I grunted out short statements about how we must talk later.

I walked to the reception line and shook hands with everyone in the line – including my sister and her husband and then went over and visited with my two aunts, a cousin and other relatives for several minutes and left. My heart was pounding and it was great. To the guests I was just another out of town stranger and no one recognized me.

I then placed my wife Shauna's arm in mine and we briskly entered the cultural hall towards the reception line. What a surprise, we had a good laugh, a wonderful time, some great photos and I excused myself to change into more proper attire.

The night after the reception Shauna and I stayed at my sister's home. The next morning there was a knock at their door. The groom's mother and father entered the room. His wife just wanted to take a moment to get a good look at me. She said she knew when a person entered the wedding reception that looked like me it couldn't have been part of their family.

Everybody knows the secular holiday of Halloween. But not everybody knows it derives from a holy day, All Saints' Day on Nov. 1, which is followed by All Souls' day on Nov. 2. The root word of Halloween - "hallow" - means "holy." The suffix "een" is an abbreviation of "evening." It refers to the Eve of All Hallows, the night before the Christian holy day that honors saintly people of the past.

According to Rev. Richard Donohoe, vicar of Catholic Charities for the Diocese of Birmingham: All Souls' Day is a traditional day to pray for all souls. Among Catholics, prayers are offered for those in purgatory, waiting to get into heaven. Catholic churches have a Book of the Dead that is placed near the alter where parishioners have an opportunity through November to write the names of relatives to be remembered.

Most Episcopal churches will observe All Saints' Day on Sunday, Nov. 3. Churches often read the names of those who have died in the last year.

More than a thousand years ago in Ireland and Britain, a common custom of Christians was to come together on the eve of the feast of All Hallows Day to ask for God's blessing and protection from evil in the world. Often, they would dress in costumes of saints or evil spirits and act out the battle between good and evil around bonfires. That's the source of the modern observance of Halloween.

All Saints' Day and All Souls' Day are related, but they are two separate celebrations. On All Saints' Day there's a call to live as saints, to remind us how we're supposed to live. On All Souls' Day, we're talking about all souls and asking God's mercy for them. We're talking about those people who have died before us, and their process of getting to heaven, through Christ. All Saints' Day emanates from early Christian celebrations of martyrs in the Eastern Church. It has its roots all the way back to the fourth century.[2]

The tradition of dressing up for Halloween most likely comes from the Medieval practices of "mumming" and "going a-souling," which historically took place on All Saints Day and All Souls Day. Mumming meant dressing up in costumes, singing, dancing, play-acting and making other general mischief. Souling meant going door to door offering prayers for the dead in exchange for treats. Current Halloween customs are an amalgamation of traditions from Celtic, various pagan and Roman traditions.

The tradition of trick or treating as it is known in America today was likely started by Irish immigrants to the country in the 1800s. By then the traditions of mumming and souling were more or less forgotten and unobserved back in Britain and Ireland. Trick or treating and general costuming were barely mentioned in American culture until after the 1930s. More than likely, the traditions of mumming and souling were somehow merged together in various festivities surrounding Halloween in America. Because the most common association with Halloween is that of honoring the dead, supernatural festivities became associated with the holiday. This eventually morphed into costume parties with partygoers dressing as various supernatural creatures. Halloween has long been a source of consternation for religious organizations, with many decrying it as a Satanic or evil holiday despite its partially Catholic roots.[3]

Rumors of tainted, poisoned or otherwise murderous Halloween candy handed out to unsuspecting youngsters are as much a part of the Halloween tradition as costumes and sing-song pleas for sweets. The myth goes like this—no kid is safe on October 31 because psychotic murderers may hand out tainted treats to trick-or-treating children.

But is poisoned Halloween candy a terrifying threat or an urban legend? "Many, if not most, reports of Halloween sadism are of questionable authenticity," write sociologists and criminal justice experts Joel Best and Gerald T. Horiuchi.

When they conducted an extensive study on so-called "Halloween sadism," or crimes specifically committed using Halloween treats or customs, they concluded that the threat is greatly exaggerated. Though both parents and kids are taught to be on the alert for tampered-with sweets, most of the cases the researchers analyzed were either overstated or could not be linked to Halloween itself.

Best and Horiuchi suggest that fears of Halloween sadism rise during fearful times. For example, paranoia about tainted candy spiked in the early 1980s after a rash of Tylenol poisonings in which cyanide-laced acetaminophen was placed on store shelves and sold. The high-profile crime led to the introduction of childproof containers and tough federal laws aimed at punishing those who tamper with drugs. After the Tylenol murders, which are still unsolved, warnings about adulterated Halloween candy increased.

Despite the fact that rumors of randomly distributed poison candy or threats like apples that contain razor blades are nothing more than urban legends. If you're looking for something to fear on All Hallows' Eve, you might want to look away from the treat bag and toward the nearest car. Halloween night can be deadly due to DUIs and pedestrian accidents. According to the National Highway Traffic Safety Administration, 45 percent of all Halloween fatalities between 2011 and 2015 involved a drunk driver, and in 2020, 56 people were killed on Halloween night in drunk driving crashes.[4]

Both actors and psychologists devote enormous amounts of time to understanding how people think, act, and respond even if for completely different reasons. While there are psychological studies that look at the way clothing influences attraction, aggression, and attitude, none of it looks critically at theatrical performance.

Costuming is a vital part of the theatrical process that has yet to be studied empirically. As such, my study is an inter-disciplinary endeavor dedicated to developing an understanding of exactly how and whether costuming affects an actor's personality perception as a way to contribute to the field of psychology, future theatrical performances, and general knowledge. I achieved this through an interview process utilizing both graduate and undergraduate student-actors at The University of Southern Mississippi who had been cast in the Spring 2018 show *You Can't Take It With You.*

I closely observed and detailed the change of an actor's sense of self, from identifying as their own personality to identifying as their character's personality after putting on their costume for a theatrical production as a unique phenomenon.

The main data I reviewed and used as evidence was the participants' usage of first-person pronouns; because, when a person internalizes an experience or feeling they use the first person. Upon review of the data and a thorough analysis, I concluded that there is a noticeable relationship between a shift in sense of self and the participants' degree of costuming.

The summarized results of my phenomenology study in correlation with each Research question I posed earlier are as follows:

1: Actors connect to their character during the transformation process in a variety of ways, including understanding time period of the show, socioeconomic status of the character, and specific personality traits unique to one of the fictional characters.

2: 3 out of 4 participants considered costumes and makeup as a luxury rather than a necessity. However, despite this attitude, all participants reported a direct relationship between the way they shaped their characters' style of movement and their characters' costume.

3: Actors use "pink" pronouns (first-person pronouns related to the fictional character's experiences rather than the participant's) to describe their character both while in full costume and while talking about their character's look.

4: Actors' sense of self changes primarily in their relationship to their character's costume during their overall transformation into their fictitious character. When asked to answer, "who are you?" half answered as their personal identity and half as their characters' identity. When asked "what are you wearing?" all participants answered as their characters' identity.

The conclusions I have drawn from this data should not be considered as absolute and indisputable facts. Instead, they should be regarded as a confirmation of the relationship between a theatrical costume and self-perception and a stepping stone towards further research and better understanding.[5]

David Musselman, a Bishop for the Church of Jesus Christ of Latter-day Saints in Taylorsville near Salt Lake city, disguised himself as a homeless man during the Thanksgiving season to teach his congregation a lesson about compassion. To make his appearance more convincing, he contacted a Salt Lake City makeup artist to transform his familiar face to that of a stranger not even his family recognized.

During Sacrament meeting Musselman's congregation encountered someone they thought was a homeless person at church on Sunday. The main thing he was trying to get across was we don't need to be so quick to judge.

He received varied reactions to his appearance at church: "Many actually went out of their way to purposefully ignore him, and they wouldn't even make eye contact. I'd approach them and say, 'Happy Thanksgiving.' I wouldn't ask for any food or any kind of money, and their inability to even acknowledge me being there was very surprising." At least five people asked him to leave the church property, some gave him money but most were indifferent.

The reaction that touched Musselman the most was from children. "I was impressed by the children. I could see in their eyes they wanted to do more."

Musselman, who had told only his second counselor that he would be disguised as a homeless man, walked to the pulpit during the service. He finally revealed his true identity and took off his wig, fake beard and glasses. He said, "It had a shock value that I did not anticipate. I really did not have any idea that the members of my ward would gasp as big as they did." One ward member mentioned that she started feeling ashamed because "I didn't say hello to this man ... He was dirty. He was crippled. He was old. He was mumbling to himself."

Musselman said his takeaway from this experience is not one about human faults, but about the desire of people to improve themselves. "I learned that more people want to be better than I had originally thought, "I learned that we don't know what happened to an individual, and so we can't and never should try to judge."

It wasn't Musselman's goal to embarrass ward members or make them feel ashamed, he said. Instead, he wanted to remind them to be kind to people from all walks of life not just at the holidays, but all year long. "To be Christ-like, just acknowledge them."[6]

The association between clothes and perception runs even deeper than that. What you wear directly influences your thoughts and behaviors. It also impacts how others perceive your personality and actions. The social and psychological aspects of clothing are more intertwined with outfit choice than you think.[1]

There is a noticeable relationship between a shift in sense of self and the participants' degree of costuming. Actors' sense of self changes primarily in their relationship to their character's costume during their overall transformation into their fictitious character.[5]

Bishop Musselman was dirty. He was crippled. He was old. He was mumbling to himself.[6]

She did not recognize me and she would not make eye contact. I could hear her say, "give him food or money -anything he wants. Just don't let him spoil my son's reception."... The bishop followed the "cop" saying he knew everyone here, there were no drugs, we all were obeying the law and no damage to the building had occurred! ...I walked to the reception line and shook hands with everyone in the line – including my sister and her husband and then went over and visited with my two aunts, a cousin and other relatives for several minutes and left. My heart was pounding and it was great. To the guests I was just another out of town stranger and no one recognized me.

I have continued to dress for work in clothing that is acceptable attire for church (without the suit coat and tie). I find that when I'm dressed in my "actor's attire": it is easier to obtain a good history about the pet's condition, receive permission to perform diagnostics and obtain recommended treatment compliance by the owner.

I've noticed that when in public areas, wearing a surgery smock, people are more polite and courteous. Things like moving out of my way, offering me to go ahead of them in line, trying to help me get things off a grocery shelf etcetera. I've noticed this behavior occurring on a more regular basis. I don't think it's all respect for the smock. I'm quite sure it's my aging costume of skinny age marked arms when not covered by a long-sleeved shirt, my physical movements, white hair and an aging face. What you wear and your actions are a message to others and to yourself about who you are.

When asked questions about veterinary medicine away from work I often not find myself commenting, "wait a second while I put my thinking cap on." I find myself slipping into the "actor's sense of self changes primarily in my relationship to my character's costume" by replying: "give me a second to put on my white coat."

What you wear is a message to others and to yourself about who you are. The "psychology of clothing" tells us that there's more than meets the eye when it comes to the clothes you choose.[1]

1– *Look Good, Feel Great: The Psychology of Clothing,*
    Carmen Lopez, Current Boutique, 2023.
2– *Days of the Dead: What's the difference between All*
    Saints' and All Souls?, Greg Garrison, 2013.
3– *Why Do People Dress up for Halloween?, History staff*
    writer, 2020.
4– *How Americans Became Convinced Their Halloween*
    Candy was Poisoned…, Erin Blakemore, 10/31/2022.

5– *The Art of the Dress: How Getting Into Costume Affects an Actor's Self-Perception, Ella Embry, U of Southern Mississippi Fellow, May 2018.*

6– *Mormon bishop disguises himself as homeless man to teach congregation about compassion, by Abby Stevens, Nov 27, 2013.*

40

MY THOUGHTS ON BUILDING SUCCESS

MY
THOUGHTS ON BUILDING SUCCESSFUL
RELATIONSHIPS WHILE WORKING
WITH OTHERS
IN THE BUSINESS WORLD…
February 8, 2006

Prepare yourself for success – it's your decision whether to do something with your life or nothing (each is a choice):

– Write down what success means to you. Is it riches and power, respect of your family and friends, contributing your efforts to help mankind live or feel better, gaining an understanding of who you are – why you are here – and where you are going after leaving this earth, maintaining a healthy body and living to the age of ninety-six or a combination of the above.

- Remember one accomplishes by self-directing their desires, not by ignoring them.
- To me it is all about who you are inside and how much you really want it. Success is goal oriented and one must be willing to go the extra mile to live their dreams. A rule of thumb is to give 110% in every task you attempt.
- In general 20% of the population provides for the remaining 80%. Who do you want to be?
- Gain experiences and an education in areas where others find it difficult to penetrate. For example there are only so many individuals granted licenses to practice law, accounting, medicine, mortgage banking etc or given the responsibility of teaching, fighting fires or policing the land in which we live.
- Never get yourself in a situation where you may be denied a career in which you seek. For example if you have been convicted of a felony there are many vocations in which your community will not want you to be entrusted.
- Always be honest with yourself and those around you. A liar or a cheat is soon found out and others will not trust or work with them.

Success requires working with others. No one ever becomes successful without others helping them along the way. It all began with a loving father and mother caring for your every need, the teacher, the scout master, the uncle or aunt, grandparents, acquaintances and friends as well as just good people thinking a little bit about you from time to time instead of just their needs.

Much about you was determined at the time of the union of an egg and sperm. But, who you really are has been mostly determined by the influences of others around you. How successful you are in the future will also be determined largely by the company you keep.

The individuals that will have the most influence on your life will be who you choose to be your wife and the children you share. In other words, "Everybody has to be somebody to somebody to be anybody", Malcolm S. Forbes. Below are some thoughts to consider when dealing with others:

- You have at least two families. One family resides at home and the other one resides at work. Both must be functioning well if you are going to be a success.
- The relationships you leave behind are often your road to success in the future (I believe this is called networking).
- In life to be successful it's not all about me. It's all about us!
- There should always be a fair shake for everyone in a business transaction.
- Greed never leads to true success. We all have wants and desires but they must be kept bridled enough to not allow them to be our only purpose in life.
- It's always a good idea to scratch another's back when they scratch yours.
- Remember what goes around – comes around. And I'm not only talking about the seasons of the year or the rotation of the earth.

- Don't kill the goose that lays the golden egg. Even the provider needs to eat, sleep and be let known once in a while they are appreciated.
- In all negotiations maintain a win- win situation. You may win one and they lose; however, there is a good chance that this win will be the last because they will never play again.
- In all relationships I feel a good philosophy is to have the attitude of you take care of me and I'll take care of you.

Use your successes to help build security for the future. The only thing constant in this world is change. It's a guarantee that you will have many challenging ups and downs as you go through your life. Anticipate them and prepare the best you can. "When you know that you're capable of dealing with whatever comes, you have the only security the world has to offer." Harry Browne.

- Put away 10% of the money you earn before counting what you have to spend on your personal needs. Serious money demands seem to crop up at the most inconvenient times. As savings grow there will be the opportunity to invest for the future.
- Make arrangements to care for your and your family's needs if you can't provide for them. Knowledge concerning life and disability insurance, food and clothing storage, trusts and agreements with family, professional groups or friends to provide needed care etc may very well help get you through the tough times.

- If possible sink roots in the area in which you wish to live. In my book stability is synonymous with security. If you own your home, stay healthy and are able to work full time you can't help but have a secure future.

Share your success with the less fortunate. Franklin Delano Roosevelt said, "Our true destiny is not to be ministered unto but to minister to ourselves and to our fellow men". I know that one does not have a truly fulfilling life without serving others, preferably without their knowledge.

- Consider setting aside 10% of earnings to help care for those who have temporal needs. Throughout our lives others have shared with us and it should be our duty to follow their example. Choose charities that spend little on administration and most on "those in need" of care. I donate to my universities, fraternities (the one I lived in at the University of Idaho plus honors fraternities in my field of studies) and to cancer research funds that are of interest to me. I have found the Salvation Army, USO and Second Harvest Food Bank good choices in our area and regularly donate to them. I also give private donations to my church. They have tithing to help build and maintain facilities for worship, fast offerings to care for those in our local area with special needs, a perpetual education fund where money is loaned interest free to those in need for education etc and later returned to the church when they are back on their feet, and a disaster relief fund to help those in need after earth quakes, floods or other disasters.

– Volunteer of your time. Soup kitchens, toy drives, scouting, visiting the sick etc will help bring happiness to your life experience. Support your local business associations and other service groups in your community. And, make time to give a helping hand to those in your chosen profession as they are learning how to be successful.

To me being truly successful requires that you keep in perspective why you are earning money. It's not just keeping score of who has the biggest pile or dies with the most toys (no one really cares but you). You came naked and penniless into this world and so far everyone leaving has left naked and penniless. The purpose of earning a living is for the aid and support of you and those in your private life.

Such statements as nothing compensates for failure in the home and behind every successful man is a caring and loving spouse are eternal principles. As you go through your life there will be conflicts within your family as to what is important. The mother of your children's agenda will be providing food, clothing and shelter for your children as well as training and educating them to become productive physically and mentally happy citizens. Your agenda will more than likely be to provide for your family and become the richest most productive individual in your chosen profession.

The take, take, take to provide for your family may result in resentment and conflict because you will feel frustrated that your goals aren't being met because of the economic and time demands being placed on you by your family. Be thankful that you have others that need you. The best investment you will ever make will be on a loving caring spouse and providing the resources needed to properly care for your children. Within three years after your death there will be few that will speak of you and your great accomplishments in the business world. However, within your children there will be a legacy of who you are that will be passed down from generation to generation.

February 8, 2006

41

AGENCY - LOVE

Thoughts expressed to my family (Hoge's & Isaacson's 04/13/2015)

AGENCY:

- there is opposition in all things
- we are free to choose and act for ourselves
- if others or things control your thoughts or actions it's because you have let them do it
- freedom of choice is given to all living on this earth. According to scripture 1/3 of our brothers and sisters were cast out of Heaven with Satan in the pre-existence because Satan's plan was to save us all by force (no agency) and Christ's plan was for us to obtain personal salvation through exercising our own agency. The struggle between these two principles continues today:

  Life on this earth is all about choices and
  where these choices will lead you…

LOVE:

1– Love one another, as I have loved you (John 15:12, see also verse 17)

– God through Jesus Christ created everything from the smallest sub atomic particle to the vastness of the universe including us and all living things found on this planet.

– He loves Hitler, Mother Teresa, kings, paupers and all of us the same.

– according to God, man is that he might find joy (happiness).

2– Love thy neighbor as yourself (Matthew 22:39)

Why would He ask us to love our neighbors? He knows that if we don't love our neighbors we risk falling into the trap of the Seven Deadly Sins: wrath, greed, sloth, pride, lust, envy, and gluttony. Each of which is a form of IDOLATRY-OF-SELF:

3– If we don't show love to our neighbor, we may find ourselves: talking and belittling others behind their backs about their short comings, the things they wear, poor grooming habits, way they spend their money, the company they keep, how they raise their children etc. Unfortunately, this behavior often leads one to stress over how others are judging them.

4– not trying to understand or show compassion for other's challenges and putting them down if they don't perform the way we think they should.

5– finding ourselves getting offended by others actions and taking the position that we will never talk to or want to be around that person, organization etcetera ever again. We might pick our enemies, never forget what they have done to us and willing to miss special future relationships - meanwhile, the offender probably is clueless why you have abandoned them and gone on with their lives.

6– taking advantage of others that happen to be less fortunate than we are.

7– using our power or authority over another who are responsible to us.

Judging and putting down our neighbors may make us feel important or special for the moment but often leads to poor self-esteem and the feeling that others are judging us when we are around our friends, in front of a group or in unfamiliar circumstances.

Judging others in the presence of our friends often makes them question what we may say about them when they aren't present. This damages trust and closeness with others.

Consider the 13th Article of Faith when dealing with family or friends…We believe in being honest, true, chaste, benevolent, virtuous, and in doing good to all men; indeed, we may say that we follow the admonition of Paul-We believe all things, we hope all things, we have endured many things, and hope to be able to endure all things. If there is anything virtuous, lovely, or of good report or praiseworthy, we seek after these things.

Love your enemies (Mathew 5:44): Christ stated, "For verily, verily I say unto you, he that hath the spirit of contention is not of me, but is of the devil, who is the father of contention, and he stirreth up the hearts of men to contend with anger, one with another. "Behold, this is … my doctrine, that such things should be done away" (3 Nephi 11:28–30; emphasis added).

Similarly, the Bible teaches that "wise men turn away wrath" (Proverbs 29:8). The early Apostles taught that we should "follow after the things [that] make for peace" (Romans 14:19) and "[speak] the truth in love" (Ephesians 4:15), "for the wrath of man worketh not the righteousness of God" (James 1:20).

Corrie ten Boom was a Dutch watchmaker (first woman to receive a license) who became a heroine of the resistance, and a survivor of Hitler's concentration camps. In World II she and her family risked their lives to help Jews and underground workers escape from the Nazis, and for their work they were placed in the Nazi death camps. Corrie began serving her sentence at the age of 52 in solitary confinement, later being transferred to the death camps. She managed to conceal a small hand written Bible suspended on a chain and daily taught the scriptures to her cell mates. Of her entire family only she survived and witnessed the death of her sister. A mix up in orders saved her from the gas chamber. She passed on her 91st birthday after spending her life traveling the world doing missionary work and helping support organizations that cared for those in need.

Note page 247-248 in her book, *The Hiding Place,* when Corrie meets an S.S. man that guarded the showers. Corrie ten Boom, a devout Dutch Christian woman, found such healing despite having been interned in concentration camps during World War II. She suffered greatly, but unlike her beloved sister Betsie, who perished in one of the camps, Corrie survived. After the war she often spoke publicly of her experiences and of healing and forgiveness. On one occasion a former Nazi guard who had been part of Corrie's own grievous confinement in Ravensbrück, Germany, approached her, rejoicing at her message of Christ's forgiveness and love.

"'How grateful I am for your message, Fraulein,' he said. 'To think that, as you say, He has washed my sins away!' His hand was thrust out to shake mine. And I, who had preached so often ... the need to forgive, kept my hand at my side.

Even as the angry, vengeful thoughts boiled through me, I saw the sin of them. ... Lord Jesus, I prayed, forgive me and help me to forgive him.

I tried to smile, [and] I struggled to raise my hand. I could not. I felt nothing, not the slightest spark of warmth or charity. And so again I breathed a silent prayer. Jesus, I cannot forgive him. Give me Your forgiveness.

As I took his hand the most incredible thing happened. From my shoulder along my arm and through my hand a current seemed to pass from me to him, while into my heart sprang a love for this stranger that almost overwhelmed me.

And so, I discovered that it is not on our forgiveness any more than on our goodness that the world's healing hinges, but on His. When He tells us to love our enemies, He gives, along with the command, the love itself." Corrie Ten Boom was made whole.[1]

FAMILY:

- life begins and ends with family and family relationships can last forever…
- when the planes are falling out of the sky, one is drowning or dying one's thoughts are not about their great accomplishments in life – they are about their family.
- wouldn't it be great if we treated each other in our home with the same courtesies we do in the work place. In the work place we are trying to keep a job – in our homes we are trying to preserve a family relationship.
- Prior to Tim's death, his last thoughts were 1-questions about a grandpa he loved growing up and 2-asking to please try to keep the family together.
- Tim's parents (Olivia and Nate) have been given council by their bishop that if they were to get over their grief they must forgive (repent) and forget (notice that they must forgive first before they can get over their grief).
- I invite you to read Jeffrey Holland's article "Like a Broken Vessel". He has lived a very successful life personally, financially and as a councilor living with MDD ("major depressive disorder"). Depression is very real and often slips into a family grieving for a lost one.

LIFE BEGINS AND ENDS WITH FAMILY…FAMILY RELATIONSHIPS CAN LAST FOREVER…

42

ARMOR OF GOD

IN ORDER TO KEEP MY ARMOR SHINY AND CAPABLE OF PROTECTING MY ENTIRE BODY THROUGHOUT MY LIFE:

> I WILL CONSTANTLY SEEK THE COMPANIONSHIP OF THE HOLY GHOST AND STUDY THE SCRIPTURES SO THAT I CAN INCREASE MY KNOWLEDGE AND FAITH AND TESTIMONY REGARDING THE GOSPEL.

> I WILL KEEP THE COMMANDMENTS. I WILL BE HONEST AND TRUTHFUL IN MY DEALINGS. I WILL KEEP THE SABBATH DAY HOLY. I WILL OBSERVE THE WORD OF WISDOM. I WILL PAY AN HONEST TITHING. I WILL ATTEND MY MEETINGS AND RESPOND TO THE CALLS MADE BY THOSE IN AUTHORITY. I WILL BE VIRTUOUS AND CLEAN AND PURE IN HEART AND MIND AND DEED.

I WILL ALWAYS ASK MYSELF IF I AM CONSTANTLY FIGHTING AGAINST THE EVILS AROUND ME – PORNOGRAPHY, ABORTION, TOBACCO, ALCOHOL, AND DRUGS. I WILL HAVE THE COURAGE TO STAND UP FOR MY CONVICTIONS. I WILL TRULY BE ABLE TO SAY I AM NOT ASHAMED OF THE GOSPEL OF CHRIST. I WILL LIVE PEACEABLY WITH MY NEIGHBORS AND AVOID GOSSSIP AND BACKBITING AND SPREADING UNFOUNDED RUMORS. I WILL TRULY LOVE MY NEIGHBORS AS MYSELF.

I KNOW IF I CAN DO THESE THINGS THAT I WILL HAVE ON THE WHOLE ARMOR OF GOD AND I WILL BE PROTECTED FROM HARM AND BE PRESERVED FROM MY ENEMIES. MY GOAL IS TO HAVE MY LOINS GIRT ABOUT WITH TRUTH, MY CHEST PROTECTED WITH THE BREASTPLATE OF RIGHTEOUSNESS, MY FEET SHOD WITH THE PREPARATION OF THE GOSPEL OF PEACE, MY ARM HOLDING THE SHIELD OF FAITH TO PROTECT ME FROM THE FIERY DARTS OF THE WICKED, MY HEAD PROTECTED WITH THE HELMET OF SALVATION, AND MY HAND HOLDING THE SWORD OF THE SPIRIT (PRAYING ALWAYS IN SUPPLICATION WITH THE SPIRIT).

I WILL OFTEN EXAMINE MY ARMOR. IF THERE ARE UNGUARDED OR UNPROTECTED PLACES I WILL ADD WHATEVER PART IS MISSING. NO MATTER HOW ANTIQUATED OR LACKING IN PARTS MY ARMOR MAY BECOME, I WILL ALWAYS REMEMBER THAT IT IS WITHIN MY POWER TO MAKE THE NECESSARY ADJUSTMENTS TO COMPLETE MY ARMOR.

February 18, 1994
ALMADEN FIRST WARD YOUTH CONFERENCE

(Adopted from Conference Report, Apr. 1979, p. 65; or Ensign, May 1979 p. 46 President N. Eldon Tanner's comments on Ephesians 6:13-18.)

43

RON REIMEERS

My friend Ron Reimers lived across the street from my house in the American Legion Home (AL). His parents helped care for the building and organizational activities. Ron's mother treated me with kindness and respect, and we had some fun times in the home.

The AL is located on 436 North Fisher Street in Blackfoot Idaho within three blocks of the railroad tracks and Main Street. I was told and Google confirms Main Street is the widest street in the country. That is because there are two Main Streets in Blackfoot. A North West and a North East Main Street. They parallel each other with one-on-one side of the train tracts and one on the other side of the train tracts. For a town of a few thousand I thought that was pretty cool.

The AL is the nation's largest wartime veterans service organization, committed to mentoring youth and sponsorship of wholesome programs in their communities, advocating patriotism and honor, promoting strong national security, and continued devotion to fellow servicemembers and veterans.

The AL Home in Blackfoot had a large room on the main floor where meetings and dinners were held. One floor up was a balcony that encircled the large room below. There were pictures on the walls around the balcony. In the basement was a collection of old military rifles, swords and other military items. We often took out the guns and played war games in the building.

The American Legion Family brought National Poppy Day to the United States by asking Congress to designate the Friday before Memorial Day, as National Poppy Day. On the Friday before Memorial Day, citizens are encouraged to wear a red poppy in honor of the fallen and support the living who have worn our nations uniform. Ron and I helped pass out artificial red poppies attached to a wire before Memorial Day, asked folks to wear them on their clothing and donate money to help take care of our veterans.

There were narrow steps leading down into a dark basement in the AL that was lite by one light with an off/on cord hanging from its base. Ron's parents let us target practice with our BB guns in this area of the home. One of our favorite targets was the off/on light cord. There were times when the BB guns missed the target and hit the light bulb. Total darkness was the result along with an uncomfortable moment of not getting cut from the glass, finding another light bulb and cleaning up the broken glass without letting his parents know.

During a Blackfoot High School class of 1964 reunion we visited this basement and looked up original, cataloged and stored, original printed articles from the local paper about our high school days. (*The Morning News (Blackfoot, Idaho* - Articles published since 1983 to current are now found in the Library of Congress.gov. I'm not sure if the articles are still in the AL Home).

An incident (I'm sure I remember being there) Ron Reimers and I have discussed, sums up to my who Ron is inside. He told me: "Preparing for a breakfast at the AL Home there were tables scattered over the large room on the first floor. I had picked a chip of paint off one of one of the picture frames hung on the walls around the second floor balcony. I carefully aimed and dropped the chip towards a pitcher full of orange juice and unfortunately it hit dead center and sank into the orange juice." I asked him what he did about it. Ron told me, "I told my mother what had happened and she took care of the problem." I've watched Ron face several events in his life where it would be easier for him to take the easy way out – but he has faced the music. He is of good character, a true friend and one who can be trusted.

Ron and his mother would occasionally crack heads and not speak to each other. Ron mentioned one time when he was prevented from going to a dance resulting in the silent treatment. I remember being the go between – telling Ron's mom this and her telling me that back and forth. This behavior seemed to last forever and I was glad when the cold relationship warmed with time.

In high school we attended dances and participated in other activities (many were at Linda Hadley's home and other double dates). Ron mentioned he often parked in front of Linda's after a date. They "visited" until the front lights started to flicker on and off.

One of our favorite dancing songs was Moon River by Andy Williams. It gave us a chance to get a little hugging even under adult chaperone or parental supervision. Driving Ron and his date home always occurred after I dropped off my future wife, Sheryl Gardner. She lived in Rose and it gave Ron a little more time to be with his date in the back seat of my car during these drives back to town. In my head as I tried to stay on the darkened road and glancing in my rear view mirror to take a peek at Ron's "progress," - I would imagine myself being Paul Evans singing in my mind his 1959 hit *Seven Little Girls Sitting in the Back Seat* substituting with my own words at the appropriate parts of the song:

(*I can remember two beautiful girls*) sittin' in the backseat
Huggin' and a kissin' with (*Ron*)
I said, "Why don't you come up and sit beside me?"
And this is what (*she*) said
All together now, one, two, three
Keep your mind on your driving
Keep your hands on the wheel
Keep your snoopy eyes on the road ahead
We're having fun, sittin' in the backseat
Kissin' and a huggin' with (*Ron*).
Drove through the town
Drove through the country
Showed 'em how a motor (*From my 1957 Mercury Monterey could go*)
I said, "How do you like my (*made for old folks*) (*single*) carburetor?"
And one of them whispered low

SING CHORUS…

(*young girls*)
Smooching in the backseat
Everyone in love with (*Ron*).
I said, "You don't need me, I'll get off at my house"
And this is what the (*girl*) said
SING CHORUS…
All of them in love with (*Ron*).
(Dee doodee doom doom)
Kissin' and a huggin' with (*Ron*).
(Dee doodee doom doom)
Wish that I could be like Fred (*Ron - doom*)…

I had a crush on Sheryl Gardner and so did Ray Blake. In fact Ray called me out to a "fight" for a winner take all after school. I was 120#s in body weight and kept alive by running away from trouble and became a good enough runner to be on the high school track team (Blackfoot's mile 440 yard relay team took third in state finals our senior year at a Boise track meet – Reid Morrell, Mark May, Terry Hopkins and me).

Ron told me not to fret – he'd take care of Ray Blake if he had the guts to try working me over. I never heard another thing about it.

We stayed good friends right on through high school and during our senior year applied for the Air Force Academy together. After written exams we went to Hill Airforce Base in Utah for physicals. Each of us were not offered enrollment at the academy but I'll always remember that trip. While I was in a dental chair word filtered through the building that

John F. Kennedy had been assassinated and I was amazed how quickly the mood change on that base.

During our physical exams the doctor had us all get in a circle, bend over, pull down our shorts and spread our cheeks. They were looking for abnormalities of the anal area. I looked over at Ron and he was pulling open the cheeks in his mouth. Wonder why he didn't get in.

After a year of Ron playing football at BYU and a photo of him sitting on a pony keg of beer with the campus in the background - Ron and I ended up together at the University of Idaho. I always knew that he did not like the church I attended but never discussed religion with him.

One Sunday while attending the U of I, I was going to meet my fiancée at church. Ron mentioned that he was going to go with me and let the members of my church know exactly what he thought about them. He walked across campus with me towards the Institute of Religion where we held services. I was getting concerned that he really meant it and didn't have any idea what he might have to say. As we started up the steps into the building Ron turned away and headed to his apartment.

Many years later I asked him why he had such strong feelings about my church. He said that he had an uncle that was a member with a supposed high-ranking authority that chastised his family for not having interest in the Gospel. Also, when Ron was Cub Scout age a vacancy came up in the church's troop. His mom volunteered for the job and was refused because she "was not a member." Ron joined the Baptist Cub Scouts and had a great time. Also, he agreed that some of those experiences may have helped influence him to make the military his career.

Ron graduated in the Army ROTC (Reserve Officer Training Corps) at the University of Idaho majoring in education. He did student teaching in Twin Falls Idaho and decided he never wanted to teach school. He became an Army Ranger. The training was in three phases. Running & swimming five miles, mountain training and survival training in the Florida swamps suffering sleep deprivation for up to 48 hours.

He mentioned they set up a practice ambush during the night during his mountain training. A lady with a lantern and a small child came along the ambushed trail looking for brass on the ground left from spent rounds of blank bullets. Ron's group unloaded their rifles filled with blanks - the lady dropped and broke her lantern and they scared her and her child near to death. At the time, this was a highlight to his training.

Ron eventually flew helicopters in Vietnam for the Army and for a short time after retirement he continued to fly to and from oil rigs in the Gulf of Mexico. Later he flew helicopters for transporting patients between hospitals, including recovery from isolated areas for emergency care.

Sheryl and I got married in the summer of 1967. The day after our marriage, we drove to Ron and Jean's wedding where I was his best man. He gave me an envelope and told me to give it to the Paster but not until his car was out of site. Of course, the envelope contained money and little enough to be embarrassing for Ron to give in person for the wedding. Not knowing how much money was in the envelope, I didn't know how much embarrassed I should be. During our 2023 cruise I asked Ron about the event. I'm not going to divulge the amount, but he should have been very embarrassed (even though there was no charge for those performing my wedding). At the time, my concern attending Ron's wedding was dealing with my first past marriage conflict with Sheryl. She was not happy having to wait an extra day before traveling to California on our honeymoon.

Ron and Jean had a son named Dan. The nature of Ron's work required him being away from home for fairly long periods of time. He mentioned one bonding experience he remembers with Dan (about 3 years of age) on Washington beach, WA. He had just purchased a new Volvo and was driving it on the beach. There was a long stretch on the beach where the surface was solid enough to allow vehicles to drive on the area. Ron with Dan sitting on his lap and their hands on the steering wheel, were having a great time until the new car got stuck in sand. Ron freaked out because he knew that the tide was coming in and if he didn't move the car soon it would be under salt water and ruined.

He put Dan up on his shoulders and started running down the beach looking for someone who could help pull the car out of the sand. Ron finally found help from an owner of a four-wheel drive outfit who saved the day.

Ron and Jean's relationship was drifting apart and when their son Dan married it was the catalyst that eventually resulted in their divorce.

I had little contact with Ron until we met with our wives at our 50th high school class reunion. Ron and I hooked up and had a fairly long visit. It was finally mentioned that we had best look for our wives because they knew none of our class mates and must be getting tired of waiting for us. We found them in heavy conversation with smiles on their faces and they seemed a little irritated that we broke into their social intercourse.

It wasn't long before we all were having such a good time that Shauna and I mentioned an Alaskan cruise we were going on in a couple of weeks. Talk went into action and it wasn't but about an hour before we had reserved plane tickets and the cruise for them to join us all accomplished in our car in the parking lot. They came to stay at our home for a few days before and after the cruise and we've been close ever since.

Reconnecting with Ron felt like it was just yesterday since we had seen each other and it has led to several more cruises together, stays in San Jose with Shauna and me, and a relighting of a glow that has always been between Ron and me.

Ron is quite artistic. He paints, draws, makes flutes and other hand crafted items. I have a pencil drawing he made of Shauna and me while sitting by a fire vacationing with us in Denali National Park and a buffalo he mounted on piece of granite I had at my home.

When Ron and Dani married it was basically to satisfy Dani's daughter so that her children didn't have a grandmother that was "living in sin." They stopped off at an all-night drive-in marriage chapel in Nevada. It was mentioned by Ron that the experience was terrible and they were married by a man in the middle of the night that smelled like he hadn't changed his Depends in a while. So, one of the cruises Shauna and I arranged to have the captain of our cruise ship marry them. There was a red carpet laid out, flowers, music, Ron played a native American love song on his flute, and they each renewed their marriage vowels. The day was on September 3rd - the same month and day Shauna and I were married. We now share our wedding anniversaries on the same month and day of the year and try to do it together.

In preparation for another shared wedding anniversary cruise to Hawaii 09/02-09/2023, Ron, Dani, Shauna and I met at our house in San Jose for a few days. Our baggage has now become loaded with vials of medication, walkers, canes, arrangements for assists at the airport and ship – the list goes on.

On our flight to Honolulu activities were mostly sleep, eating our snack and waiting for the restroom. The highlight was when Dani spilled her soda and snack on the floor, herself and Shauna, and Ron falling asleep and spilling his drink on himself. The flight attendant was a real "hoot" and helped turn the event into a positive experience. Since this is all about Ron, I won't bring up Shauna or my embarrassing moments. The little embarrassing moments on our flight, good natured flight attendant and us in his presence helped create another great memory to share.

Our work on this earth may nearly be done! We're old enough, lame enough, senile enough and ugly enough - but we still get our thrills. They're just not on Blue Berry Hill…

Informing me that May 24th was Brothers Day, several years ago my dear friend Ron Reimers texted me this quote from Mark Linton that summarizes parts of our relationship and who Ron is: A real man is the kind of man that when your feet hit the floor each morning the devil says "Oh …(darn)! He's up!

Brother, life is too short to wake up with regrets. So, love the people who treat you right. Forgive the ones who don't just because you can. Believe everything happens for a reason. If you get a second chance, grab it with both hands. If it changes your life, let it. Take a few minutes to think before you act when you're mad. Forgive quickly. God never said life would be easy. He just promised it would be worth it.

Today is Brother's Day, send this to all your Brothers, Fathers, Sons. Happy Brothers Day!

I LOVE YA RON – CAUSE YOU'RE MY BROTHER!!!

"In Reverence of Life and Love: A Gold Seal Review of 'Thoughts on my Thoughts III: The TALES that Wagged this Veterinarian' by Dr. Walter R. Hoge"

"Thoughts on my Thoughts III: The <u>TALES</u> that Wagged this Veterinarian" by Dr. Walter R. Hoge, is a heartwarming and thought-provoking masterpiece that takes readers on an extraordinary journey through the lens of a veterinarian who has not only cared for animals but also discovered profound lessons about life, love, and the human spirit.

Dr. Hoge's storytelling is nothing short of captivating. With each tale, he weaves a rich tapestry of experiences that range from poignant to downright hilarious. His ability to blend humor, wisdom, and a deep sense of empathy is truly commendable. As I delved into the pages of this book, I found myself laughing out loud at one moment and wiping away tears the next.

What sets this book apart is its universal appeal. Whether you're an animal lover, a seeker of life's truths, or simply someone looking for a heartwarming read, Dr. Hoge's tales will resonate with you. He effortlessly translates the intricate bond between humans and animals into lessons that are both relatable and inspiring. His musings on love, family, and the importance of forgiveness are profound and resonate deeply.

One of the remarkable aspects of this book is Dr. Hoge's ability to infuse each story with genuine emotion. His compassion for the creatures he treats, his dedication to his family, and his unwavering commitment to his principles shine through brilliantly. His reflections on family, particularly his emphasis on the enduring nature of family relationships, are both heartening and deeply moving.

As an author, Dr. Hoge's writing style is incredibly engaging. He possesses a unique talent for drawing readers into his world, making you feel like a close friend sharing stories over a cup of coffee. His words have a way of touching your heart and leaving a lasting impact.

"Thoughts on My Thoughts III" is not just a book; it's a testament to the power of love, compassion, and the resilience of the human spirit. Dr. Hoge's stories will stay with you long after you've turned the last page, reminding you of the beauty in the world around us and the boundless capacity of the heart to love.

In closing, "Thoughts on my Thoughts III: The Tales that Wagged this Veterinarian" stands as a shining example of the power of storytelling. Dr. Walter Hoge, DMV, has masterfully crafted a collection of stories that resonate with the essence of life, love, and resilience. His dedication to his craft is evident on every page, and as a reader, you will undoubtedly find yourself deeply moved and inspired. This book is a testament to the enduring beauty of the human-animal bond and the profound wisdom that can be gleaned from it. It is with utmost sincerity and respect that I bestow upon this book the esteemed Gold Seal.

Thoughts on My Thoughts Book III:
The TALES That Wagged this Veterinarian

by Dr. Walter R. Hoge
MainSpring Books
book review by Mihir Shah

"If you are offended let it go. If you let it fester it can destroy your life, but not the offender's."

True to the spirit of the title, the author undoubtedly runs the gamut of topics, yet each one, from the prism of the fictional McEaster Valley to the stories he told his children, speaks to the overall human experience and our responsibility to understand nature. The text appears to point to a better understanding of ourselves when we understand nature, which then can lead to understanding those with whom we interact. The inspiration, or rather catalyst, for the author envisioning McEaster Valley derives from tragedy—the loss of the mother of his children.

Right from the onset, Hoge's discussion of out-of-body experiences assures readers that this isn't a typical exploration of one's thoughts. On the contrary, it is deeply researched with examples that probe deeper than what is at the surface level. Perhaps what makes the narrative so intriguing is Hoge's ability to add descriptions for the layman to understand. There are rarely complex scientific terms but rather well-placed examples of imagery, such as "a feeling of floating outside your body, an altered perception of the world," to create instant relatability with the audience. Of course, the most narrated out-of-body experience is in the operating room, where life and death hang in the balance, and the patient nearly always reports seeing a bright light among their other details.

As the work progresses, Hoge makes the reader at home with a soothing, conversational tone as he journeys into discussions of parallel universes—even attempting to explain them from a theoretical physics standpoint—and origin stories. His fearlessness in tackling notoriously polarizing topics with tact and knowledge is commendable. Interestingly, the work is far from barbershop fodder. Rather, it references renowned, influential figures like psychiatrist Raymond Moody Jr., author of Life after Life, works such as Viktor Frank's Man's Search for Meaning, and the Bible itself to add evidentiary support to his claims. Further, contemporary figures that made national headlines, like Damar Hamlin and his public health scare, keep youth audiences engaged and connected as well.

From the travails of Wilford Woodruff and Phoebe Whittemore Carter to the chaos surrounding four neurosurgery residents whose lives are nearly cut short yet intricately tied to near-death experiences, every new revelation, new story, and discussion is illuminating. In the case of Michael McLean, the direct commentary dives into faith and sexual orientation, one's own identity, and the notion that praying harder would "correct" McLean's son. The anecdote is even further magnified because of McLean's deeply entrenched role within the church as a filmmaker and songwriter. In short, the author's narratives impel the audience to react and discuss, to probe within themselves, and to challenge the status quo. Yet, each one takes the author back to McEaster Valley, where seemingly his innocence, peace, and nostalgia reside and where his fears are put to rest. Unsurprisingly, Hoge has a knack for connecting unrelated ideas, but the green light being emitted from the valley leads to a conversation on radioactivity, and how nuclear energy is likely the pathway into the next frontier for the world.

Aside from Hoge's dissection of world issues, his reflections on McEaster Valley present a biblical utopia where the law of love resonates with all beings in this valley in as authentic a manner as humanly possible. Regardless, the communal nature of ants is given the same shine as the use of lasers and the discovery of the Yeti in the Himalayas. Truly, nothing is off limits for Hoge and his infinite reservoir of thoughts and commentaries on what makes our world tick. Including, but not limited to, talks on peer pressure, kindness, grief, ambition, and commitment, this text is filled with emotions that bridge birth and death.

www.ingramcontent.com/pod-product-compliance
Lightning Source LLC
Chambersburg PA
CBHW020429130626
46549CB00001B/59